ALSO BY PETER S. ONUF

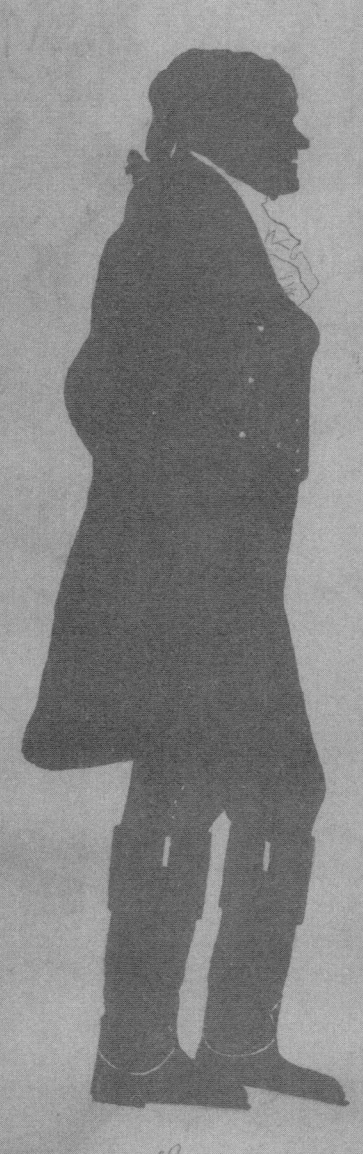

THOMAS JEFFERSON SURVIVES

American Independence in His Time and Ours

PETER S. ONUF

and

FRANCIS D. COGLIANO

Liveright Publishing Corporation

A Division of W. W. Norton & Company
Independent Publishers Since 1923

For information about permission to reproduce selections from this book,
write to Permissions, Liveright Publishing Corporation, a division of
W. W. Norton & Company, Inc., 500 Fifth Avenue, New York, NY 10110

For information about special discounts for bulk purchases, please contact
W. W. Norton Special Sales at specialsales@wwnorton.com or 800-233-4830

Manufacturing by Lakeside Book Company
Book design by Daniel Lagin
Production manager: Louise Mattarelliano

Frontispiece: Portrait of Thomas Jefferson by John Marshal /
Library of Congress Prints and Photographs Division

ISBN 978-1-324-09807-2

Liveright Publishing Corporation, 500 Fifth Avenue, New York, NY 10110
www.wwnorton.com

W. W. Norton & Company Ltd., 15 Carlisle Street, London W1D 3BS

Authorized EU representative: EAS, Mustamäe tee 50, 10621 Tallinn, Estonia

10 9 8 7 6 5 4 3 2 1

TO THE FUTURE GENERATION:

Edward Cogliano, Sofia Cogliano, Rob Lim, Thomas Roscoe Lim, Robert Söderström O'Gorman, Rachel Onuf, Zee Onuf, Emmi Tallqvist, and Ben Tiefenthaler

CONTENTS

FOREWORD

By Annette Gordon-Reed

e approach the 250th anniversary of the American Declaration of Independence—a document tradition-ally thought of as bringing the United States of America into being—at a difficult moment in the country's history. Indeed, there is great concern about the health and long-term viability of the republic created in 1776. Can it last another 250 years?

History tells us that republics are fragile, always in danger of fail-ing if citizens do not work diligently to maintain them. Americans are now learning that very hard and sobering lesson. Many of the core tenets that have guided the country seem to have lost their salience for much of the populace. A surprising number of Americans today either actively embrace or are nonchalant about the rise of authori-tarianism as a feature of American politics and governance. Members of the "Founding Generation" conceived of their rebellion against and ultimate rejection of a king and the system of monarchy that sup-ported him as their proudest achievement, an act that defined the American character as innately hostile to tyranny. In Thomas Paine's famous formulation—"in America, law is King"—"law" means rules of governance that were put in place by representatives of the people rather than the will and words of one individual. Maintaining an exemplary democracy requires electing honorable leaders, dealing with other nations fairly, and treating people within the country's borders with dignity. Abandoning those requirements and accepting authoritarianism portends the end of the American republic as it was and aspired to be.

This indifference to the spread of authoritarianism is matched by a rise in cynicism about the country's special place in the community of nations. The ideology of American exceptionalism certainly has its faults and has suffered under the weight of its own contradictions— not least of which is that a nation born to promote liberty was also a race-based slave society that has struggled with racial problems ever since. The concept of exceptionalism at least had the virtue of sug-gesting that the country wanted to be perceived as a beacon of light to the world. That self-image, warranted or not, was often used to justify efforts to move beyond the legacies of the country's founding contradictions and other problems that kept America from fulfilling the ideals stated in the preamble to the Declaration of Independence. This was known as "progress," and many Americans believed in it. The danger of American exceptionalism, however, is that it can lull people into a sense of complacency about the state of the nation, even when it is obviously in peril. Democratic norms are eroded, and liberties are curtailed, but because people assume that such things simply cannot happen in America, they will not accept the evidence of degeneration. This is where we are today.

In our current fraught circumstances it makes sense to go back to first principles and examine where we are now in relationship to where we began. It is more than fitting to do this by consider-ing the life and thoughts of the chief author of the Declaration of Independence and the third president of the United States, a man who embodied the strengths and weaknesses of the country he helped found and who has been called the "Architect of American

Democracy": Thomas Jefferson. There are no historians better suited to this task than Francis D. Cogliano and Peter S. Onuf. Cogliano has written extensively about Jefferson, expertly tracking the vicissitudes of the Sage of Monticello's legacy from his death in 1826 up until the present day. Onuf was for many years the Thomas Jefferson Foundation Professor at the University of Virginia. To date, no one has written as much or more perceptively about Jefferson's intellectual life and philosophy than Onuf. The combination of Cogliano and Onuf is precisely what we need to explain the utility of engaging with Jefferson's thoughts about the nature of and possibilities inherent in democratic republicanism.

This might seem a tough sell for many Americans. There is currently widespread and understandable ambivalence about the members of the Founding Generation. Many aspects of their values are anathema to present-day mores. All of the southerners, Jefferson included, enslaved people. Some of them were involved to varying degrees with the displacement, sometimes violent, of Indigenous people. Jefferson stands out among this group because the contradictions between his words and actions are especially chasmic. We know this because he left a paper trail. He wrote more about slavery and race than any other member of the Founding Generation, and much of what he had to say is confusing and deeply troubling to many modern Americans. There is the Jefferson of the Declaration, who averred that "all men are created equal" and whose original draft of the document criticized the slave trade for its violation of the rights of "MEN" who were denied their "sacred right to liberty." Then there is the Jefferson of *Notes on the State of Virginia*, musing about the possibility that Black people were mentally inferior to whites; expressing negative views about racial mixing, despite his own family situation; and arguing that the enslaved should be freed *and* required to leave the United States because Blacks and whites would not likely ever live together without conflict. What could a person who expressed these views say to us today?

The answer is that for as much as Jefferson reflected the often-benighted times in which he lived, he rose above them in ways that have a great deal to tell us about the political straits in which we find ourselves and how we can go about moving beyond them. Jefferson, who fervently believed in progress, had faith—perhaps too much—in future generations. He was convinced that they would be better and "wiser" than his generation, just as he believed that his generational cohort had learned critical lessons that allowed them to meet the challenges they faced during the imperial crisis.

Crucially, Jefferson understood that progress is never guaranteed. He knew that his optimistic vision of future advancement would come to fruition only with the expenditure of real and perpetual effort. Each generation would have to do the work of ensuring that the democratic republican spirit remains alive, and each would be responsible for figuring out exactly how to do that in a way that suited its particular moment in history. The American Revolution, and the war that made it, unfolded in the midst of a larger battle between two great powers—Great Britain and France. It was a global event, a fact that helped Jefferson and his revolutionary cohort determine what was needed for the effective functioning of the new republic during the time of their stewardship. Jefferson had the advantage of being more than the armchair "philosopher," supposedly out of touch with reality, of his Federalist adversaries' taunt. He was, in fact, a working politician, the most effective one of his age, who knew what to do to preserve the democratic values that were the promise of the American Revolution.

Similarly, the current discontents of the American polity—the embrace by a large number of people of authoritarianism in a country that put rejecting a king at the core of its identity—are part of a worldwide phenomenon of skepticism about democracy as a form of governance. The current generation must face this challenge and determine what to do about it. All the lessons we have learned between Jefferson's time and our own—and there have been very many—must inform how we work to both maintain and extend democratic values.

In three cogent and accessible essays, "Generations," "My Country," and "The People," Cogliano and Onuf show how Jefferson tried, sometimes successfully and sometimes not, to rise to the occasion that he and his fellow revolutionaries faced when they challenged what they saw as overreaching British authority and decided to create a republic. One does not have to embrace or accept all of this tremendously flawed and talented person to benefit from the insights to be gleaned from his work as a nation-builder. In short, Jefferson matters because the United States of America matters.

THOMAS JEFFERSON SURVIVES

INTRODUCTION

THE EARTH BELONGS
TO THE LIVING

"Jefferson Survives"

"Jefferson survives." Purportedly these were John Adams's final words as he lay dying in Quincy, Massachusetts, on July 4, 1826. Strictly speaking, Adams was incorrect. Thomas Jefferson had died at his home, Monticello, on the outskirts of Charlottesville, Virginia, mere hours before Adams's death. That the two great revolutionary leaders died on the same day and that that day was the fiftieth anniversary of the Declaration of Independence, which both men had helped to craft, seemed to be a sign, albeit a somber one, of providential blessing for many in the early American republic.[1]

While Adams may have been incorrect about the state of Jefferson's earthly body as he faced his own mortality, he was correct in a larger sense. Thomas Jefferson has continued to survive in the memories of the American people in the two centuries since his death. Indeed, as biographer James Parton claimed in 1874, Americans tend to identify Jefferson *with* America, abstracting him from his own time and place and exaggerating his historical significance. "If

Jefferson was wrong," wrote Parton, "America is wrong. If America is right, Jefferson was right."[2] Across generations, Americans have reinvented and reimagined Jefferson according to their contemporary needs and concerns, effectively taking him out of history and making him *their* contemporary.[3]

From immediately after Jefferson's death until the Civil War, supporters and opponents of slavery sought to deploy him in support of their causes. Slavery's defenders looked to his defense of states' rights in the Kentucky Resolutions (1798) to secure the "peculiar institution." They invoked Jefferson's idea of state nullification of federal law and the implicit threat of secession from the union. Abolitionists, on the other hand, drew on Jefferson's antislavery writings and the egalitarian premise of the Declaration of Independence to claim that opposition to slavery was integral to the establishment of the United States. In so doing, opponents of slavery fashioned the Declaration and its author as antislavery.

After the Civil War, Jefferson's reputation went into a long period of decline. Tainted by his (posthumous) association with secession and disunion, the spokesman for agrarian democracy seemed out of place in a nation that was rapidly becoming more urban and industrial. Then, beginning in the 1920s, Jefferson's reputation began to recover. Incorporated in New York in 1923, the Thomas Jefferson Memorial Foundation purchased Monticello, which it opened to the public as a museum dedicated to Jefferson's ideals: equality, consent, and religious freedom. During the Great Depression of the 1930s, President Franklin Roosevelt, an ardent admirer of Jefferson, cast him as a universal advocate of global liberty. On July 4, 1936, Roosevelt spoke at Monticello, declaring that Jefferson's "passion for liberty led him . . . to better the lot of mankind." Seven years later Roosevelt expanded on this theme at the dedication of the Jefferson Memorial in Washington, DC. Speaking to a crowd of five thousand and millions more on the radio, Roosevelt dubbed Jefferson the "Apostle of Freedom." "Today in the midst of a great war for freedom," Roosevelt intoned, "we dedicate this shrine to freedom." Jefferson was no longer the author of secession but rather the embodiment of the values for which the United States and its allies were fighting during World War II.[4]

The image of Jefferson as Apostle of Freedom persisted through World War II and the early years of the Cold War and still resonated in 1976 during the bicentennial of the Declaration of Independence.[5] However, against the backdrop of the civil rights movement, the war in Vietnam, and the Watergate scandal, historians and many Americans began to take a more critical view of the United States, of both its leaders and its institutions. Beginning in the 1960s and continuing through 2000, when the Thomas Jefferson Foundation formally acknowledged that Jefferson had had a sexual relationship with Sally Hemings, a woman he enslaved, the Declaration's author was subject to increasingly intense criticism. Not coincidentally, scholarship on Jefferson and his time has flourished since then, depicting him as a complex—and controversial—figure. We are indebted to that scholarship. It informs our own thinking about Jefferson and his time.

In recent years the American political left has largely jettisoned Jefferson. For his critics, Jefferson is no longer seen as the man who articulated the "American creed" but rather as a plantation patriarch and enslaver who epitomizes the hypocrisy of the founders of the American republic.[6] As early as 2007 the Utah Democratic Party changed the name of its annual Jefferson–Jackson Dinner, meant to celebrate the founders of the party, because of their complicity in slavery and Indigenous removal. After the mass shooting of Black worshippers in Charleston, South Carolina, in 2015, other state parties including those of Iowa, Georgia, Connecticut, Missouri, and in 2018 Jefferson's own state, Virginia, followed suit. The New York City Council voted to remove a statue of Jefferson from its chamber in City Hall in October 2021.[7]

As Jefferson's stock declined on the left, he was taken up by the right—and embraced and repurposed as an avatar of white nationalism. In the aftermath of the white supremacist rioting in Charlottesville, Virginia, in 2017, President Donald J. Trump invoked Jefferson and Washington to oppose the Charlottesville City Council's decision to remove a statue of Robert E. Lee, the pretext for the disorder. Washington and Jefferson were both slave-holders, observed Trump. "I wonder, is it George Washington next week?" Trump said. "And is it Thomas Jefferson the week after?"[8] Protecting (certain) American icons, like Jefferson, was a recurring theme throughout Trump's first term as president. In an address that he delivered on July 4, 2020, at Mount Rushmore in South Dakota, Trump lauded Jefferson: "He was an architect, an inventor, a diplo-mat, a scholar, the founder of one of the world's great universities, and an ardent defender of liberty. Americans will forever admire the author of American freedom, Thomas Jefferson." On July 2, 2025, Florida's Republican governor, Ron DeSantis, dedicated a statue of Jefferson. According to a press release issued by the governor's office, "Governor DeSantis underscored Thomas Jefferson's legacy as the 'Father of the Declaration of Independence,' whose words provided moral clarity and philosophical weight to America's pur-suit of liberty. The Governor also emphasized Jefferson's commit-ment to religious freedom, civic virtue, and education—principles that continue to shape Florida's approach to civic instruction."[9] Trump's and DeSantis's celebrations of Jefferson were reminiscent of Roosevelt's in 1936. Indeed, their positive views of Jefferson sit nicely within the Apostle of Freedom version of Jefferson that was a mainstream view in the middle of the twentieth century. But unlike Roosevelt, Trump ascribed Jefferson's beliefs to *his* supporters, not to *all* Americans, excoriating those who disagreed with his version of American history. "Our nation is witnessing a merciless campaign to wipe out our history, defame our heroes, erase our values, and indoctrinate our children," Trump asserted. "Angry mobs are trying to tear down statues of our Founders, deface our most sacred memo-rials, and unleash a wave of violent crime in our cities."

According to Trump, those who sought to topple "the heroes of 1776" were enemies of true Americans. Trump thus called on his supporters to defend the founders, including Jefferson. "We will never let them rip America's heroes from our monuments, or from our hearts," Trump proclaimed. "By tearing down Washington and Jefferson, these radicals would tear down the very heritage for which men gave their lives."[10] For Trump and many of his followers, Jefferson is no longer a synecdoche for America or a spokesman for universal liberty. Jefferson is instead seen through the narrow, sectarian lens of reactionary populism. He has been reduced to a partisan talisman.

Rejected by the left as an enslaver whose legacy is forever marred by his moral failings and enlisted by the right to determine who is a true American, whither Jefferson as we approach the 250th anniversary of his greatest achievement? Against such a backdrop Jefferson, once a unifying figure for Americans because he articulated the creed that bound them together as a people, seems to have lost his relevance. The best way forward, anxious citizens might understandably conclude, is to exorcise Jefferson from the national narrative. After all, it was the American *people* who declared independence, *not* Jefferson, and the ideals that animated them were—as they thought, and many Americans still think—timeless and universal.[11] But such an exorcism would be a grave mistake. As a historical figure situated in his own time and place, Jefferson has important things to say to us in our own radically uncertain and equally epochal historical moment.

"Dreams of the Future"

Jefferson's contemporary critics and admirers are engaging in a zero-sum game. For them he is either a villain, responsible for America's lamentable history of slavery, racism, and Indigenous displacement, or a hero to be defended at all costs. This stale and pointless exercise achieves little: Both sides are fixed in their positions, talking (or more

often shouting) past each other. Neither side in the contemporaneous culture war listens to the other. Both sides fail to hear what the
historical Jefferson had to say and therefore to understand why he
still matters.

The Declaration of Independence, beginning with its assertion of equality, was premised on the aspiration of patriotic British
Americans to become a new people, distinct from their British forebears. This is why Jefferson, to justify American independence
from the British Empire, chronicled the history of King George III's
alleged crimes against his American subjects in the Declaration.[12]
Determined to make their own history, American patriots became a
people by mobilizing in defense of the rights and liberties they had
historically claimed and enjoyed in their continental homeland and
by seeking recognition and support from other nations in the ongoing war George III had declared against *them*. Americans pledged
to uphold the universal and timeless principles of equality, liberty,
and self-government that Jefferson expressed so eloquently in the
Declaration's first paragraphs. Upholding those principles and com-
mitting "our lives, our fortunes, & our sacred honor" made revolutionary Americans a people. And thanks to the sacrifices of the
revolutionary generation, succeeding generations would inherit the
opportunity to govern themselves as a free people, presumably while
recognizing their responsibility to secure the same inheritance for
their successors.

One way to interpret the history of the United States is to see
it as a struggle over the extent to which the American people have
lived up to those ideals. Throughout the nation's history, margin-
alized and oppressed groups have invoked the Declaration to call
for greater rights. To be sure, this is how many Americans, both
Jefferson's admirers and critics, have interpreted the Declaration
since his death in 1826. The history of the United States is therefore the story of whether Americans have succeeded or failed to
live up to the ideals that Jefferson articulated in the Declaration. We

sympathize with this interpretation but believe it obscures a critical dimension of Jefferson's legacy.

Debates about whether Americans are, to borrow Parton's language, "right" or "wrong" about Jefferson, or whether they have lived up to what they conceive of as the ideals of 1776, miss the point. For Jefferson the Declaration of Independence signified the beginning of a new national narrative. Crucially, Jefferson had faith in the capacity of future generations to write their own histories and correct the mistakes of the past. As he wrote to John Adams in 1816, "I like the dreams of the future better than the history of the past."[13] He believed that every generation of Americans is sovereign and, guided by the lessons of the past, must confront its own unique challenges. While the Declaration articulated universal principles of equality grounded in natural rights, Jefferson appreciated that circumstances would change and challenge traditional principles and practices. The year 1776 was an important moment, but not the only moment, for Americans to write their own history. It was a beginning, not an end. This is why the survival of the republic had to take precedence over everything else.

Franklin Roosevelt understood this key, though often neglected, aspect of Jefferson's thinking. When he spoke at Monticello on July 4, 1936, Roosevelt delivered his address from the West Portico of Jefferson's home. Roosevelt recognized the significance of that place. The doors of the portico face west, where Jefferson believed the limitless future of the United States lay. Roosevelt declared, "[Jefferson] applied the culture of the past to the needs and the life of the America of his day. His knowledge of history spurred him to inquire into the reason and justice of laws, habits and institutions. His passion for liberty led him to interpret and adapt them in order to better the lot of mankind." Roosevelt continued, "Our problems of 1936 call as greatly for the continuation of imagination and energy and capacity for responsibility as did the age of Thomas Jefferson and his fellows." Consider the problems which beset the United States that year: a prolonged economic depression, political polarization, and an international crisis. The Spanish Civil War began only a few weeks after Roosevelt delivered his address, triggering a decade of armed conflict in Europe (and beyond) between the forces of liberal democracy, fascism, and communism that culminated in one of the most devastating wars in world history. Roosevelt did not believe that Jefferson had the answers to these challenges but rather that the way Jefferson and his generation responded to its existential crisis was a model and inspiration for future generations.[14]

Roosevelt, like Jefferson, believed Americans should not be constrained by a static view of the past. In 1816, Jefferson wrote, "With the change of circumstances, institutions must advance also to keep pace with the times. We might as well require a man to wear still the coat which fitted him when a boy as a civilized society to remain ever under the regimen of their barbarous ancestors." We should not be bound by the beliefs of Jefferson's time. Roosevelt was a political partisan in his own time, but he recognized that the true power of Jefferson's legacy was civic, not partisan. Jefferson's bequest to posterity transcends the partisan issues of our day, just as it did his own. Nationhood cannot be taken for granted. Every generation must struggle to define and preserve itself against unanticipated and unprecedented threats at home and abroad. Jefferson's generation had a common cause and many enemies on many battlefronts. But what do "we"—if we imagine ourselves to be a people—have in common that is worth fighting for?

Does Jefferson Matter?

Does Thomas Jefferson matter? At most times in American history the answer would have been an unequivocal yes. If we consider the accomplishments that Jefferson had engraved on his tombstone— "Author of the Declaration of American Independence, of the Statute of Virginia for Religious Freedom, and Father of the University of

Virginia"—each of these would seem worthy of commemoration and celebration at almost any point since Jefferson's death in 1826. Yet such is not the case today.

We live in an age of uncertainty, polarization, and crisis. We are told daily that Americans are divided into irreconcilable camps that see the world in completely different ways. We rarely live with or even encounter people who think or believe different things from ourselves. Wars abroad divide Americans at home. Just about every issue, large or small, from decisions over public health policy to the choice of which books should be available in our libraries, seems to open yet another front in an ongoing and never-ending culture war that in turn reinforces political polarization and alienation. Some fantasize about secession while others raise the specter of another civil war. Americans appear to be more divided than at almost any other time in our history. Many now question whether our experiment with republican government can, or should, continue.

Thomas Jefferson offers Americans a way to think about the challenges we face. During his lifetime he challenged us with the question that every generation must confront: Are we capable of governing ourselves? Jefferson had an optimistic faith in the ability of each generation of Americans to surmount the challenges they faced. He did not believe that our success was guaranteed— Americans could not rely on providential intervention to guide our progress—but rather that each generation, adhering to the principles of republican government, *could* succeed and transmit democracy to posterity. For Jefferson, the real challenge confronting each generation is to exit the stage gracefully, passing a better country and a safer world to its successors. Each generation deserves to live in the memories of those that follow *if* it meets its challenges.

The critical term in Jefferson's thinking about generations is "living." Each generation is mortal, like every one of its individual members. Jefferson's democratic theory thus synchronized with the passage of time, embracing the mortality of generations as well as

individuals, all equally fated to pass into history. The practical implication of this fundamental premise was that the laws enacted by a
duly authorized majority of the people at any given time could not
be perpetually binding. As citizens die, the body politic is transformed. Collective consent can no longer be assumed once a critical proportion of those who originally gave it pass away. Jefferson
thus conceived of majority rule in a temporal dimension. Democratic
self-government is limited by the time-sensitive principle of generational sovereignty, not because the long-dead founders decreed that
their original intentions must be fulfilled, as if the Declaration of
Independence and the federal Constitution were sacred texts.

What exactly did Jefferson mean by a "generation"? The answer
is not self-evident. He could not simply mean everyone alive in a particular place—the new United States—at any given moment. The
term became important to him in the context of the nation-making
crisis of the Revolution. When he imagined the nation's unfolding
history in generational terms, Jefferson very much had his own generation of revolutionary patriots in mind. The transprovincial political
and military mobilization that led to independence was aspirationally inclusive—winning the war depended on persuading as many
Anglo-Americans as possible to support the revolutionary common
cause—yet at the same time necessarily exclusive, for many of their
countrymen and countrywomen had (sometimes very good) reasons
to refuse their consent to the patriot project.

"Political nation" might better define what Jefferson meant
by "generation." As he wrote to James Madison, each "generation
is to another as one independant nation to another," underscoring
the civic dimension of his term.[15] So, too, when he imputed a patriotic spirit, virtue, or simple common sense to the "people," he did
not mean everybody; indeed, those characteristics signaled a readiness to mobilize against the people's enemies, foreign *and* domestic.
Following Jefferson's lead, we might conclude that a "generation"
only becomes conscious of itself, and therefore comes into being, as

it confronts the potentially existential crises of its own times—precisely when there are deep divisions within the general population.
The tension between inclusivity and exclusivity is dynamic, animated by the aspiration to make and keep an always elusive republican peace.

Fears that the republic would fail were endemic after the
Revolution, when Americans no longer had a common enemy and
were free to promote their interests at each other's expense. For
Jefferson the readiness of patriots to mobilize yet again, renewing
their commitment to republican principles and to each other, was
the generational solution to such fears.

What connected Jefferson's generations, as he defined them? The
answer for Jefferson was in the inheritance held in trust by each living generation for its successors. This would include private properties, fairly acquired, that would pass from loving parents (mostly
fathers in his world) to their children (mostly sons). The attachments
fostered in a free society within and among families, friends, and
neighbors would give rise to an enlightened love of country or patriotism. Americans would cherish the homeland, the nation's great
continental estate, because it enabled both productive private pursuits in familiar places and opportunities for future generations in
distant places. Thinking generationally meant thinking of all the
children of future generations as their own, just as the enlightened
pursuit of common, public purposes reinforced a sense of solidarity
and identity within each generation. The country that patriots loved
was where private and public interests and aspirations merged in
enduring and enlightened attachments, the civic space within which
republican self-government takes place. This is what Jefferson meant
when he talked about what we call democracy: an intergenerational
peace plan that would enable the new nation to preserve itself, as
the first law of nature and nations enjoined, into a boundless and
uncertain future.

Each "living generation," Jefferson insisted, must reconstitute itself as a people, responsible for sustaining "a more perfect union" across time. But Americans are now shirking that responsibility, tak-ing their status as a people for granted and failing to recognize that republican self-government is a great and ongoing experiment. Rather than following the example of the revolutionaries who launched that experiment, many patriotic Americans imagine that a providen-tially sanctioned new nation miraculously emerged from the war in the nation-making words of the Declaration. They assume that the republic is fixed and permanent. Assuming an enduring collective identity, they look back to the founding and find strikingly familiar images of themselves in Jefferson and his fellow founders.

In the pages that follow we will repeatedly return to Thomas Jefferson's conception of generational sovereignty as we seek to show why what he said and did should matter to us today. Before we can make sense of what Jefferson has to say, though, we must liberate him from the grip of anachronistic characterization and special pleading, celebration and condemnation. A surfeit of conflicting and confusing noise drowns out the slave-owning Virginia planter and soft-spoken politician. We hope to situate him in his own long-lost world, listen-ing carefully to what he meant to say and do then, when he surely did matter.

Revolutionary Americans were anxious about the future. They knew their bid for independence could easily fail. They asked them-selves difficult questions. Could their bold experiment in republican self-government possibly succeed in a world of hostile monarchies? Were they capable of governing themselves? Americans have been troubled by such questions throughout their history. What we now conceive of as "democracy" has been periodically threatened by existential crises, whether from foreign foes, sectional conflicts, or seemingly irreconcilable ideological and cultural divisions among Americans themselves. Democracy is always at risk.

Anxieties focus on collective identity. What—if anything— binds Americans to each other? Has it ever truly made any sense to speak of an American "people" or "nation"? How could the Second Continental Congress presume to declare independence on July 4, 1776, on behalf of a "people" who had not previously recognized its own existence? Eleven years later, when the Philadelphia framers invoked the authority of "We the people of the United States" in the preamble to the federal Constitution, their language was equally aspirational. Who authorized them to speak with such authority? Nationhood was yet again—and always would be—a work in progress, as self-declared Americans imagined and struggled to create that "more perfect union."

If democracy is a work in progress, it is by definition not a fixed thing, an ideal state outside of history. There never was a golden age of democratic (or for that matter constitutional) perfection; nothing can be restored in its unblemished original condition. For better or worse American democracy is a product of history. The daunting prospect of making that history is the past's gift and burden to the present generation.

Thomas Jefferson understood the challenges his generation faced in terms that resonate with us now. Revolutionary patriots did not originally aim to break away from the British Empire, nor did they seek to establish an enlightened, liberal, federal republic that would transform the modern world. They mobilized instead to resist imperial administrative reforms and fiscal policies that threatened the jurisdiction of provincial legislatures and the rights and liberties of overseas Britons. When King George III sought to coerce compliance and resistance turned to rebellion, British Americans faced an existential crisis on a continental scale. Making war against their sovereign, mobilizing a broadly politicized public to vindicate their claims on the battlefield, and drafting new state constitutions to facilitate and legitimize that mobilization led inexorably toward independence and the democratization of American politics.

Wartime political and military imperatives gave birth to "democracy." Elite patriots were reluctant to use the term, instead emphasizing the rule of law, property rights, social contract theory, and enlightened moral philosophy. Jefferson was a gifted synthesizer, crafting a broadly appealing language in the Declaration of Independence that bridged class and sectional distinctions and celebrated the capacity of the American people to win the war and keep the peace. He was not a philosopher who envisioned what was best for the people from a lofty, otherworldly position. He instead participated in and responded to a fundamental transformation of American politics, on the ground in a revolutionary age. Jefferson's faith in the people—and his conception of democracy—proceeded from the bottom up, focusing on citizens' ongoing and active participation in their own government.

What we see as Jefferson's limitations and failures reflect the privileged and prosperous slave-owning planter's embeddedness in his own small, provincial world, situated on the far periphery of Britain's great and expansive empire. Identifying with his neighbors, Jefferson shared their interests and their prejudices. Yet he did not believe the character of his countrymen and -women was static. The American revolutionaries' patriotic willingness to sacrifice all in order to secure the liberty and prosperity of a free people testified eloquently to their virtue and enlightenment. Regime change was predicated on changes in the hearts and minds of British subjects that transformed them into self-governing American citizens. Surely future generations, born free, would be still more enlightened than the generation that launched the nation's history?

We might admire and respect Jefferson more if he had been a philosopher, if he could have transcended his own moment, anticipating ours and affirming us in our own interests and prejudices. But then he would not have anything useful to say: He would not matter.

Three Essays

We argue that Jefferson matters both for familiar reasons—those well-known achievements inscribed on his tombstone—and for ones that are less obvious. We suggest that in his major writings Jefferson outlined a coherent vision for a hopeful future for the United States based on democratic principles. His thinking was not always consistent, and his actions often fell far short of his words. Nonetheless, Jefferson matters two centuries after his death because he was the foremost advocate among the revolutionary leadership for an optimistic, democratic future for the new nation. That vision emerged from his thinking about history in response to the crisis in British–colonial relations prior to independence. Based on his reading of history (and his understanding of the British constitution), Jefferson came to believe that independence was the only answer for Britain's estranged North American colonists. When he composed the Declaration of Independence in the summer of 1776, he declared that Americans were a separate people, distinct from their British forebears. Having won their independence, citizens of the new American republic would write their own history. This republican vision extended across time—to future generations—and space as the American republic expanded geographically. Jefferson's was a capacious and coherent vision that still offers hope for Americans today, however fractious and divided they may seem to be.

We develop these themes through a series of interrelated essays that situate Jefferson in his own world. Samuel Johnson, the great English lexicographer and Jefferson's contemporary, defined an essay as an "attempt" or "endeavour."[16] These essays present neither a comprehensive biography of Jefferson nor a detailed study of the Declaration of Independence or Jefferson's other major writings. Rather they offer our reflections on what Jefferson thought and how he confronted the major challenges of his time in order to offer us an opportunity to confront the major problems of our time.

Historians never have the last word, even though many of us would like to believe that "history"—presumably meaning *future* historians—will render final judgments on the heroes and villains of our times. We are taught to be more modest. Trained to be revision- ists, we know we will be revised, if not before we close the books on our own careers, then certainly when those future historians rework the fields we have cultivated. We are acutely conscious that our inter- pretations of the past—the questions we ask, the stories we tell—are inevitably shaped by our present circumstances. Like all historians, we are writing in a particular moment in time. The questions that inform our study of the past are informed by the concerns of our time. Just as Jefferson thought and wrote about the past (and the future) while constrained by the limited perspectives of his time, we, too, are simi- larly limited in our time. But making a good-faith effort to avoid anach- ronism and treat our sources with respect, we hope to be forgiven for the unavoidable, generational biases that will become apparent to our successors. We seek a fresh perspective on our own world by engaging with Jefferson's. By looking forward with him, we gain a clearer idea of where we now find ourselves and how we arrived here.[17]

Our first essay considers how Jefferson's understanding of his- tory shaped his response to the crisis of his own time and his faith in the future. It shows that Jefferson's somewhat conventional read- ing of British history, mediated by the history of North American settlement, eventually led him—with the help of Thomas Paine— to conclude that the British constitution did not apply in the col- onies. Reaching this conclusion led him to support independence. In a series of writings between 1774 and 1776, culminating in the Declaration of Independence, Jefferson drew on his understanding of history to effectively rewrite the history of America. In so doing he developed two lasting themes: the need for the American people to mobilize in support of independence, and his belief that each genera- tion would, like his generation of 1776, overcome the challenges they faced through mobilization in a common cause.

What makes a generation is not biology but attachment to a particular place. Our second essay considers Jefferson's expansive conception of the American homeland. In his first inaugural address in 1801, Jefferson congratulated his countrymen on "possessing a chosen country, with room enough for our descendants to the thousandth and thousandth generation."[18] He mapped the new nation's endless future history onto a seemingly boundless continent, a great tabula rasa on which to inscribe the progress of mankind. This hyperbolic vision can only seem absurdly exaggerated to us now: The space was hardly empty, the outcome hardly assured, the ecological and human costs immense. But what was most remarkable in 1801 was Jefferson's confidence that a union that had barely survived the turbulent politics of the 1790s and his own deadlocked election (not to mention the constitutional crises of the 1780s) would survive at all, much less for so many more centuries. We might offer a translation: "If we have survived *this* crisis, future generations *can* survive theirs."

Scholars have interpreted Jefferson's idealization of the geographic expansion of the United States as laying the foundation for a republican empire in North America, anticipating and justifying the rapid and bloody expansion of the American republic during the nineteenth century. It is not our intention in this essay to revisit that process, important though it is. We both have written extensively about it elsewhere.[19] Rather, we seek to demonstrate that for Jefferson, the country, the physical entity that became the United States, came before the people. It is the civic space within which self-government flourishes. It is the space in which the transition from one generation to the next, the process according to which "history" unfolds across time, takes place. Generations might come and go, but that space, that country, would allow the republic to survive into an indefinite, open-ended future—if each generation meets its challenges, thus remaking and perpetuating the republic. Although the survival of the republic is not guaranteed, a recognized homeland gives Americans the best possible chance of meeting their own generational challenges.

Which brings us to the American people. In our third essay we focus on how Jefferson articulated a new national identity in the Declaration of Independence. The success of the Americans' republican revolution depended on the active, spirited commitment of citizen-soldiers to the common cause. Patriots' sense of belonging was bounded and exclusionary, forged in a protracted struggle against external and internal enemies. The Declaration thus evoked a dynamic, aspirationally inclusive image of the American people, promising "to hold the rest of mankind, Enemies in War, in Peace Friends." This applied at home as well as abroad.[20] Promulgated in the midst of war, the Declaration inspired or coerced reluctant provincials to make a choice: The republic aspired to inclusivity, but it defined those who withheld their support as enemies of the newly self-declared people; and no meaningful choice was offered to Indigenous or enslaved populations—who, patriots feared, might be enlisted in the British Crown's counterrevolutionary cause.[21] The shifting fortunes of war and uncertain loyalties of people on the ground often blurred the boundary between friends and enemies. For Jefferson the identity of the American people was never fixed or ascriptive.[22] Having vindicated their independence, Americans would welcome waves of immigrants—refugees from Old World tyranny—to their new republican world. Each generation of citizens would have the opportunity and responsibility to preserve and perpetuate the republic.

Taken together, these three essays demonstrate that Jefferson, when confronted with a political and constitutional crisis culminating in a long, bloody, destructive war, articulated a capacious, forward-looking, optimistic, coherent vision of a democratic and inclusive future for the new American people. He did not prescribe a course of action for the future as much as lay down broad principles that might guide future generations as they sought to navigate their own crises.

The familiar, hopeful, egalitarian vision that Jefferson articulated in the Declaration of Independence (and elsewhere) was premised on unfamiliar and unappreciated elements in his thinking. Most notably, Jefferson envisioned the historical process unfolding across time and space. While the Declaration of Independence called the American republic into being, its promise of equality and self-government is not guaranteed to every generation as a birthright.

Jefferson was a gifted prose stylist. One of the reasons that he endures is because his words, carefully crafted and deliberately preserved, continue to speak to us across the centuries. Our argument rests on the vast corpus of Jefferson's writings. The published versions of Jefferson's papers are available via the *Papers of Thomas Jefferson: Digital Edition*, which is the main source for our quotations from Jefferson's writings. Most of the documents we cite are also available on Founders Online compiled by the National Archives. In this book we, as Jefferson scholars, offer our reflections on Jefferson's legacy. In a sense we have been engaged in a dialogue with him, through his writings, for several decades. We invite our readers to engage directly with Jefferson with us. We write about him in the past tense but invite you to consider him in the present tense through his own words, and to this end we have provided extracts from Jefferson's writings, the main texts on which our argument rests, in Part IV.

We know how the history of Jefferson's era played out, even if we cannot agree on what it means. Events take on a coherence and meaning in retrospect that they conspicuously lack in the present moment. For contemporary Americans, 1776 marks a clear beginning, and it is that beginning which we observe on its semiquincentennial in 2026. National histories are premised on myths of origin. The United States, as a country with a relatively short national history (though a long prenational history) has a richly documented, recognizable starting point in 1776. The problem with such a beginning is that it renders history linear and simplifies complex events, exaggerating the roles of key figures in the narrative. This has certainly been the case with Jefferson, who as we have suggested is often reduced to a simple binary: the heroic genius who championed democracy and articulated the nation's creed or the hypocritical enslaver, failing to live up to the ideals he enshrined in that creed. Such a choice does a disservice to the past.

We are not seeking to render a final judgment on Jefferson's character or determine his position in the national pantheon. Nor do we presume to plumb the depths of Jefferson's capacious and elusive mind. Our goal instead is to situate our subject in the complicated and confusing contexts of his own time. We hope to clarify the choices he made in the light of what he could—and could not—see or imagine. As we explore some of the main themes in Jefferson's thought, we will focus on the challenges his generation confronted: constituting stable and legitimate republican governments, eliminating or mitigating the existential threat of racial slavery, and expanding what he called the American "empire of liberty." We will not find comforting answers to the questions our generation faces, however much they now resonate.

Attacking or defending caricatured versions of Jefferson reduces history to a parlor game, fueling our overheated quarrels and obscuring whatever light our past might shed on the history we now live. Our intention is to move beyond debates over whether Jefferson was "good" or "bad." If history is a scoreboard, Jefferson would now be losing. But the way we keep score—the way we think about the past—is itself a contingent product of our present moment. Too many of us think we know how American history will end. We present Jefferson's thinking about the history of his time in order to inform how we might think about our time.

Jefferson did not know what the future would bring. Despite or perhaps because of his ignorance and uncertainty, he cherished an abiding belief in the capacity of the American people to illuminate the way forward for a benighted world. Those hopes, we can now see, bore (and bear) increasingly faint resemblance to realities on the ground. Yet Jefferson's optimism would not be shaken, for it did not reside in an exalted, unrealistic sense of what the revolutionary generation had accomplished in its own fleeting moment.

Jefferson had more faith in us than we have in ourselves as we seek to uphold—or reject—imagined standards laid down some 250 years ago. The current contrasting interpretations of Jefferson suggest this may be yet another moment when Americans question their existence as a single people. In doing so they strike at the heart of Jefferson's conception of generational sovereignty and his hope for the future of the United States. Jefferson asks us whether we can govern ourselves and maintain republican principles. The answer is not clear.

More than all his many, increasingly conspicuous shortcomings, Jefferson's optimism makes him seem like an alien figure today. But his belief in progress is crucial to understanding him in his own time. It is also one of his most important legacies for our time. What we call democracy emerged from the existential crisis Jefferson's generation confronted. His conception of generational sovereignty remains challenging: a hopeful prediction, a provocation, perhaps a prayer.

❂⟩⟩⟩⟩❂

GENERATIONS

F or more than a century a seven-foot statue of Thomas Jefferson "towered over the members of the New York City Council in their chamber at City Hall," the *New York Times* reported in October 2021. The council had just voted to remove the statue from its customary place in response to a request from its Black, Latino and Asian Caucus (BLAC), marking the culmination of intensifying Black Lives Matter protests across the United States and beyond in the wake of George Floyd's murder in Minneapolis on May 25, 2020. During the council's deliberations BLAC cochair Adrienne Adams asserted that "Jefferson embodies some of the most shameful parts of our country's history."[1]

But Jefferson had equally passionate defenders in New York and across the country. In May 2024 a member of the board of the Conroe, Texas, Independent School District opened a new front in the culture wars, declaring that it was "completely inappropriate" for a biology textbook to feature Jefferson's controversial relationship with his mixed-race slave Sally Hemings when explaining DNA testing. Most experts took that relationship as a matter of fact, though a wide range of conservative commentators—including some prominent scholars—begged to differ. Their concern was not only with the assumed "fact" of Jefferson's paternity but with the judgments Adrienne Adams and other hostile critics reached on his character and therefore, by extension, on the historical narrative within which Jefferson played such a crucial role.[2]

Jefferson is yet again the focus of an ongoing, never-ending clash of historical narratives that express and exacerbate contemporary political disputes. Jefferson would have been horrified to know that his relationship with Hemings would be taught in American schools (he believed that his private life was nobody's business) but would not have been surprised that history, including the history of his time, is the subject of political dispute. He recognized the power of history, acutely conscious that historical interpretations—the stories we tell our children and ourselves—reflect and reaffirm political commitments. Jefferson certainly wanted to be fairly remembered for his contributions to the revolutionary cause, as the inscription of his gravestone—a most succinct autobiography—makes clear. Like contemporary Americans he deployed history to address the political controversies of his own time as well as times to come.

"History" is generally understood as a sequence of events, in short, "what happened." We assume we know the facts—Congress voted for independence on July 2, 1776, and adopted the Declaration of Independence two days later—though we expect ongoing research will yield new or forgotten and sometimes surprising information about the past. "History" also consists of what we, at any moment, make of those facts and, to further complicate matters, what our subjects made of the events they experienced. Discussions about what history means are what make it relevant. By themselves, facts are meaningless; only when mobilized in historical narratives do meanings emerge. Inevitably, narratives are contested, becoming meaningful in conflict with other narratives. It is therefore not surprising that Americans have repeatedly been drawn into history wars throughout their contentious history as a people, anachronistically confusing the imperatives of their own historical moment with the history previous generations experienced and sought to understand. "The past is a foreign country," as the English novelist L. P. Hartley so aptly put it: "they do things differently there."[3] Listening carefully to Jefferson, fairly translating his language into ours, and avoiding anachronism will not initiate a new era of peace and love. But it could offer us a fresh and illuminating *historical* perspective on our own fractured world to better understand how we got to be where we now find ourselves.

In this essay we ask what history meant to Jefferson. We explore a number of themes, beginning with how Jefferson thought about the past. Like many of his fellow provincial patriots, Jefferson was attracted to the Whig interpretation of British history, chronicling the ongoing struggle between liberty and tyranny. Jefferson drew on this history when he sought to justify resistance to British tax policy in the colonies, which in turn led him to question Parliament's pretensions to absolute authority—or sovereignty—throughout the empire. When American patriots appealed to Whig history, their goal was not to overthrow British rule in North America but to reform and improve it.

The War of Independence began in Massachusetts on April 19, 1775, when Jefferson was a thirty-two-year-old planter and lawyer living in the Virginia Piedmont. A steadfast critic of British rule in America since he was first elected to serve in Virginia's assembly in 1769, Jefferson had gained recognition as one of the more fervent and articulate defenders of colonial rights with the publication of his pamphlet *A Summary View of the Rights of British America* in 1774. Elected to represent Virginia in the Continental Congress on March 27, 1775, shortly before the outbreak of war in New England, Jefferson helped draft several addresses and declarations during the following months that outlined the colonial critique of Parliament's right to rule the colonies, including Congress's "Declaration of the

Causes and Necessity of Taking Up Arms," as well as resolutions in response to a reconciliation proposal advanced by the British prime minister, Frederick, Lord North.

Jefferson developed a distinctively provincial version of Whig history in these early writings to justify his defense of Virginia's rights in the escalating imperial crisis, our second major theme. The young author and politician developed his historical thinking most fully in his *Summary View* and in an incomplete, unpublished essay drafted in January 1776. Jefferson sought to show that the British constitution had extended to the colonies from their first settlement. By 1776 that position was no longer tenable. George III rejected the idea that there could be any constitutional limitations on his author-ity or that of the imperial Parliament in his dominions overseas. In *Common Sense* (1776), expatriate radical Thomas Paine denied that Britain had a proper constitution, calling the king's authority into question. The British king commanded great power—as embattled Americans well understood—but he did *not* exercise legitimate authority.

Failing to resolve the crisis between Britain and the American colonies by appealing to their shared history, Jefferson then deployed a compressed historical account of recent events to justify the final break with Britain in the Declaration of Independence. In so doing he began to craft a new history for an independent people. This is our third theme. No longer focusing on Virginia's provincial claims within the British Empire, Jefferson and his fellow revolu-tionaries began to construct a transprovincial, *national* narrative. Although he never completely jettisoned Whiggish notions of his-tory and continued to emphasize the contest between liberty and tyranny, for Jefferson, British history now functioned as a negative reference or counterpoint for independent Americans. Freed from Britain's despotic rule, the new nation charted its own course for-ward, a beacon of progress for a benighted world. The new national narrative began with the history of the American Revolution, the history Jefferson and his fellow patriots were making when they declared and waged war for independence, a history that anticipated the future course of events for the people who emerged from that long conflict.

History

To better understand Jefferson, we need to understand his approach to the past. We must ask ourselves how his historical consciousness maps onto our history. It is not enough to put Jefferson's ideas in context, for context itself can be a trap. We are too prone to assume that we, with our ostensibly Olympian perspective, can see the whole picture, failing to realize that we are doing exactly what Jefferson did with respect to British history: choosing an interpretation that suited his contemporary needs. Ultimately, our appreciation of Jefferson's understanding of the past is limited by what we know or think we know about that past. We may have the advantage of hindsight, knowing what Jefferson did and failed to do and therefore concluding that his intentions are "self-evident." But we need to put ourselves in his place and try to see his world through his eyes to understand how he understood the past.

Jefferson was a lifelong student of history. He owned more than five hundred books on ancient and modern Europe, Britain, and America when he offered his library for sale to the United States to replace the congressional library burned by the British in 1814.[4] In 1813, Jefferson, living in retirement at Monticello, expressed his disgust for politics. "I turn from the contemplation [of current events] with loathing, and take refuge in the histories of other times."[5] For Jefferson, history was not simply a diversion; it offered a guide to the present and moral and political lessons for the future. The history he most valued enabled readers to take the long view, offering them a collective, cross-generational judgment on characters and events. Such a perspective came naturally to a lawyer like Jefferson, steeped in the common law. History was also vitally important, he believed, to rising generations in the new American republic.

Nearly three decades earlier in *Notes on the State of Virginia* (1785), Jefferson outlined a plan for state-supported education for white children in his native state. He recommended that all free children in Virginia, boys and girls, be educated for three years in local schools, "wherein the great mass of the people will receive their instruction, [therefore] the principal foundations of future order will be laid here." He called for the teaching of Greek, Roman, European, and American history. Young Virginians should study history: "Apprising them of the past will enable them to judge of the future." Jefferson elaborated, "It will avail them of the experience of other times and other nations; it will qualify them as judges of the actions and designs of men; it will enable them to know ambition under every disguise it may assume; and knowing it, to defeat its views." All governments were susceptible to corruption and would eventually degenerate. The people, properly educated, were the best defense against corruption and decay, which happened more rapidly when rulers had too much power. Jefferson's education plan emerged from his assumptions about Virginia (and latterly the United States) as a place and its residents as a single "people." Jefferson assumed that Virginians—free, white Virginians—shared a common history that bound them together as subjects (and, after independence, citizens) who enjoyed certain rights and liberties, particularly the right to govern themselves according to the rule of law. These assumptions were the product of Jefferson's own study of history and his experience as a British planter.[6]

Just what were the lessons that history should teach young Virginians? Jefferson's historical thinking derived from the Whig interpretation of British and American history that was common among educated people on both sides of the Atlantic during the eighteenth century. The main lesson that history taught was that liberty was always under threat and that it could only be protected by a virtuous, informed, and vigilant citizenry. Knowledge of history was essential if citizens were to recognize the dangers that tyranny posed to liberty. Jefferson was well-versed in this interpretation of history. As a fourteen-year-old he inherited Paul Rapin's *History of England* (1732) from his father, a book he greatly admired, calling it decades later, "the best history of England." Rapin presented the Whiggish interpretation of English history that underpinned Jefferson's writings culminating in the Declaration of Independence.[7]

There was a close correlation between history and the agglomeration of legal and political precedents and acts of Parliament that comprised Britain's unwritten constitution. As such it was indistinguishable from the political and legal history of the kingdom. Whig historians chronicled the great constitutional struggle culminating in Parliament's ultimate triumph over royal prerogative in the Glorious Revolution of 1689. According to their thinking, the Glorious Revolution restored the traditional liberties of England's "ancient constitution" that had been subverted by the Norman Conquest and assaulted by successive dynasties of would-be despots, most recently the Tudors and Stuarts. Whig gospel held that Parliament was the bulwark of British liberty. But a growing chorus of skeptics in Britain as well as its distant North American provinces warned that the sovereignty claims of a corrupt and unrepresentative Parliament signaled the emergence of despotic prerogative in an insidious and unforeseen new form.[8]

Americans feared that Parliament, in unholy alliance with the king, could threaten liberty. Jefferson and like-minded patriots claimed that their rights as overseas British subjects were secured by their own legislatures ("little Parliaments") under the aegis of Crown charters and provincial constitutions. It followed that British Americans owed their allegiance directly to a king whose protective prerogative spanned his far-flung dominions—and who was represented in them by royal governors and lesser officials. For metropolitan critics, American constitutional claims smacked of heresy, displacing the imperial legislature, the king-in-parliament, from its supreme position and thus reversing the outcome of the Glorious Revolution: The presumption that the American colonies had constitutions (or that the empire as a whole had one) was the logical absurdity of *imperium in imperio*. Yet if the British constitution were nothing more than what Parliament said it was, what sort of constitution was that?[9]

Jefferson Writes

During the summer of 1774, Jefferson drafted a lengthy set of instructions for Virginia's delegation to the Continental Congress. The Congress was due to meet in Philadelphia in September to coordinate a colonial response to the so-called Coercive Acts adopted by Parliament in the spring of 1774 to punish the residents of Massachusetts for the Boston Tea Party. Although Jefferson had not been elected to the Congress, he had been elected to the Virginia Convention, which was charged with determining the Old Dominion's response to the political crisis. He was en route to Williamsburg when he was incapacitated by a bout of dysentery and forced to send his enslaved body servant, Jupiter Evans, to deliver copies of his proposed instructions to fellow delegates, including convention president Peyton Randolph, the most powerful man in Virginia politics. Balking at their radical tone, Randolph tabled Jefferson's instructions.[10] But other delegates were so favorably impressed that they arranged for their anonymous, unofficial publication as a pamphlet entitled *A Summary View of the Rights of British America*. Jefferson had not planned to publish his instructions, but his failure to attend the convention led to the publication of one of the most radical colonial pamphlets prior to the appearance of Thomas Paine's *Common Sense* in January 1776.

In *A Summary View*, Jefferson rehearsed the history of the British–American dispute, looking back to the earliest settlements

and offering a novel theory of the empire's origins. "Our ancestors," he observed, "before their emigration to America, were the
free inhabitants of the British dominions in Europe, and possessed a
right, which nature has given to all men of departing from the country in which chance, not choice has placed them, of going in quest
of new habitations, and of there establishing new societies, under
such laws and regulations as to them shall seem most likely to promote public happiness." Jefferson drew a direct comparison between
British settlers in America and the ancient Saxons who migrated to
England.[11] The Saxons did not cede their rights when they migrated,
nor were they subordinate to the indigenous Britons they encoun-
tered. Crucially, they were not beholden to their mother country.
Like the ancient Saxons, English settlers in America retained their
rights when they migrated. Jefferson argued that the relationship
between Britain and the colonies was no different than that between
England and Scotland prior to the 1707 Act of Union: They had
a common executive in the person of the king but otherwise "no
other necessary political connection." A *Summary View*, grounded
in Jefferson's understanding of history, was a fundamental challenge
to British rule in America; it was an Americanized version of Whig
history.[12]

By the summer of 1775, Jefferson represented Virginia in the
Continental Congress. He owed his election in part to the prominence
he had acquired as the author of A *Summary View*. Owing to his reputation as a writer, he was given his first important committee assignment a few days after arriving in Philadelphia. In the aftermath of the
outbreak of war in Massachusetts, Jefferson and John Dickinson, the
author of *Letters from a Farmer in Pennsylvania* (1767–1768), were
added to a committee working on a statement defending the colonists' recourse to arms. Jefferson and Dickinson, arguably the most
celebrated political pamphleteers then in Congress, exchanged drafts
before the Pennsylvanian prepared the final text of the "Declaration
of the Causes and Necessity of Taking Up Arms," which was

adopted by Congress on July 6, 1775. That declaration reviewed familiar colonial grievances and recent British military actions to justify congressional mobilization of patriot forces. Congress vigorously denied any intention to seek independence, affirming its continuing fealty to the British constitutional principles that had animated the resistance movement since 1765. The Declaration also embraced the controversial version of colonial history set forth in Jefferson's *Summary View*: "Our Forefathers, Inhabitants of the Island of Great Britain, left their Native Land, to seek on these Shores a Residence for civil and religious Freedom. At the Expence of their Blood, at the Hazard of their Fortunes, without the least Charge to the Country from which they removed, by unceasing Labour and an unconquerable Spirit, they effected Settlements in the distant and inhospitable Wilds of America."[13] This was tantamount to saying that the colonies had always been, in an original and fundamental sense, independent and that the imperial connection had always been and would continue to be consensual—that is, if the empire managed to survive.[14]

On October 26, 1775, George III addressed both houses of Parliament in London, offering a response to the "Declaration of the Causes and Necessity of Taking Up Arms." After the outbreak of the war in Massachusetts the previous April, the steps taken by the Continental Congress to raise an army, and the breakdown of British rule in other parts of the empire, the king declared the colonies to be in a state of rebellion that he vowed to suppress: "The object is too important, the spirit of the British nation too high, the resources with which God hath blessed her too numerous, to give up so many Colonies which she has planted with great industry, nursed with great tenderness, encouraged with many commercial advantages, and protected and defended at much expence of blood and treasure." The king, furious, denounced his erstwhile American subjects as "rebels" and declared that they were no longer entitled to his protection. The king in essence called the Americans' bluff. He declared them outlaws and traitors, warning that they would waste their "fortunes" and spill much more "blood" unless they submitted to his legitimate authority.[15]

Jefferson read the king's speech after it appeared in Alexander Purdie's *Virginia Gazette* on January 19, 1776. In angry response he hastily drafted a "Refutation of the Argument that the Colonies were Established at the Expense of the British Nation," demonstrating—at least to his own satisfaction—that England had borne none of the costs of settling the American colonies and could not claim them to be its legitimate possessions. British Americans who mobilized in defense of their constitutional rights were patriots, not rebels, loyal subjects of a misguided monarch. Outraged at George III's claim that Britain had the authority to govern the colonies because England had borne the expense of settling them, Jefferson turned to the historical record, evidently still imagining an imperial future even as the British Empire in America verged on collapse. In a new notebook he drafted a twenty-page account of the early history of the English colonization in North America, paying particular attention to the Roanoke colony and the history of Sir Walter Raleigh's patent to settle what became Virginia. Jefferson relied heavily on Richard Hakluyt's *Principal Navigations*, the definitive source on the topic, published in three volumes between 1598 and 1600, which he kept in his library.[16] Constructing a detailed timeline from Hakluyt, Jefferson demonstrated that Raleigh (and others) "received no assistance from the crown in any of these enterprizes." Indeed, according to Jefferson, Raleigh had invested £40,000 of privately raised funds, including his own, in the venture. Jefferson thus decisively concluded that the claim that the colonies had been settled at British expense was simply a "palpable untruth."

Yet in January 1776, Jefferson was not quite ready to criticize the king directly. The blame instead lay with "those ministerial writers, who, in order to prove that the British parliament may of right legislate for the colonies," had misled the sovereign. George had launched a war against the colonists, but Jefferson still held back. "Kings are much to be pitied," he continued, "who, misled by weak ministers, and deceived by wicked favourites, run into political errors, which involve their families in ruin." Perhaps the king could be forgiven for making such a mistake. But if "error is to be pitied and pardoned," vice is nonetheless "a foul blemish" and "not pardonable in any character." A reluctant Jefferson thus inched closer and closer to condemning his acknowledged sovereign: "A king who can adopt falsehood, and solemnize it from the throne, justifies the revolution of fortune which reduces him to a private station." If George III denied the plain facts of the case as Jefferson presented them, he deserved to lose his empire.[17]

Jefferson's discomfort is clearly palpable in this tortured production. He was much more comfortable returning to the archive than directly addressing the king's faults. He believed that another fifty pages of documents—royal ordinances, grants and commissions relating to Virginia during the seventeenth century—would clinch the argument that Virginia had been settled without support of the English state. It comes as no surprise that Jefferson never published this essay, as it reveals more about his equivocating state of mind than about the state of the war then in progress. Historians, too, have tactfully ignored it, focusing instead on Jefferson's momentous stints in Congress in 1775 and 1776.

Yet the "Refutation" should give us pause, for it calls into question the conventional wisdom that the visionary Jefferson was desperate to break from the empire. A Summary View, the argument goes, anticipated the radical views that supposedly made independence inevitable in 1776. We would be better advised to read the "Refutation" as an imagined conversation between Jefferson, a provincial on the western edge of the British Empire, and the king he still recognized. Jefferson initiated the debate about settlement of the colonies in A Summary View and the "Declaration of the Causes and Necessity of Taking Up Arms"; the king responded in his speech to Parliament, and Jefferson offered a redundant rejoinder in his unpublished "Refutation." Both men appealed to history, with the Virginian also invoking the "future page of history" as he indicted the confused monarch for deliberately misleading Parliament. History, he hoped, was on his side: His words would be the last words.

In 1775–1776, George III did not know that he was locked in a debate with Thomas Jefferson, an obscure subject from a faraway province. The very idea that the two men could possibly encounter each other as equals was absurd. The king was responding to Congress, an unauthorized, illegitimate body that was at least *acting* like a sovereign—and would soon seek to be recognized as one by the "powers of the earth." But their exchange is important for two related reasons. First, both the humble provincial and his sovereign understood that history mattered. Their divergent historical interpretations justified radically distinct conceptions of the British constitution, that collection of laws and precedents—and the constitution of the British Empire. As far as the king was concerned, there was no such thing as an imperial constitution. Colonists, dependent on the Crown for their survival, owed him their loyalty and thus their tax revenue. Patriots in North America, on the other hand, were convinced that their identity as a free (British) people depended on vindicating their constitutional claims. Jefferson continually pressed those claims, even as they proved countersuggestive, spurring advocates of parliamentary sovereignty to exaggerate the capacity of an almighty but overstretched British state to impose its will on recalcitrant rebels. The exchange is also important because it signaled that even in late 1775 and early 1776 both men—and they are avatars for the two sides in the British–American dispute—believed that the other might be persuaded (or intimidated) if they would just recognize the strength of the evidence (or preponderant military force) presented to them.

Debate is only possible if each side believes that the other is listening. It is likely that Jefferson did not publish the "Refutation" because he recognized that the moment for such an exchange, or for any meaningful negotiation, had passed. By January 1776 the king's troops and his rebellious colonists were killing each other. Acting as a de facto government, the Continental Congress raised an army to wage war against the mother country. British authority had broken down across the continent, except where occupying, now "foreign," troops commanded submission. The time was ripe for a new conversation and a timely new voice.

Independence

On January 10, 1776, a Philadelphia printer published an anonymous pamphlet titled *Common Sense*. Its author, later revealed to be Thomas Paine, was an English migrant from a modest background who arrived in Philadelphia in late 1774 at the age of thirty-seven. If George III and Thomas Jefferson offered conflicting elite perspectives—metropolitan and provincial—in the imperial dispute, Paine provided a radically different perspective, compellingly pitched to a broad popular audience. Paine wasted no time making himself at home in Philadelphia, soon taking a leading role in mobilizing the city's artisans and opposing British rule. Physician-patriot Benjamin Rush recognized Paine's abilities as a writer and encouraged him to address the question of independence.[18] When Paine began drafting *Common Sense* in the autumn of 1775, the king's speech had not yet circulated in the colonies. In the pamphlet's second edition, published soon thereafter, Paine, unlike Jefferson, impatiently dismissed the monarch's oration: "The Speech, if it may be called one, is nothing better than a wilful audacious libel against the truth, the common good, and the existence of mankind; and is a formal and pompous method of offering up human sacrifices to the pride of tyrants."[19]

Paine had no interest in maintaining—or, more accurately, restoring—the link between the Crown and the colonies. He loathed the England he had left and had no attachment to the empire that provincial British Americans like Jefferson idealized. *Common Sense* thus made an unsentimental and uncomplicated case for independence. Paine's key contribution was to demolish the colossal edifice of the British constitution, however it might have been defined in the protracted debate over its character. The idea that British— and therefore American—liberty was the product of enlightened mixed government, with the glorious synthesis of king-in-parliament transcending historic struggles among the branches was, to Paine, a bad joke. With the possible but dubious exception of the House of Commons (hardly a truly representative institution given the very small number of qualified voters), the branches were rotten, and the mixture was putrid. If Britain's constitution was not a true constitution, then the patriots' imperial constitution was chimerical; in this, Paine and the king agreed. Denying them his protection, George III was treating Americans like an "independent" foreign people; these were facts on the bloody ground of the revolutionary battlefields. Declare your independence, Paine enjoined.

Paine wrote in a forceful, direct style, eschewing the classical imagery and ornate language characteristic of most contemporary pamphlet writers in favor of biblical allusions and simple language. He developed his argument in four sections, beginning with an examination of the origins of government. Stressing the familiar Lockean theme that government was a contractual relationship made necessary by human selfishness, Paine offered a concise account of the development of monarchy, aristocracy, and hereditary succession, all marks of the progressive degradation of modern polities—a secularized version of sinful humanity's fallen state that resonated with Protestant readers. The final two sections of *Common Sense* consider the current state of war between Britain and the colonies, concluding with a sanguine analysis of colonists' ability to gain the independence they had not yet declared, plus suggestions for establishing republican governments.

Paine also appealed to English history to make his case. "I offer a few remarks on the so much boasted constitution of England," he wrote, demolishing the Whiggish belief that the constitution was the bulwark of British liberty. "That it was noble for the dark and slav-ish times in which it was erected, is granted." But, declared Paine, "the plain truth is that the antiquity of English monarchy will not bear looking into." Since the Norman Conquest, England "hath known some few good monarchs, but groaned beneath a much larger number of bad ones." Paine decried William the Conqueror as a "French bas-tard landing with an armed Banditti and establishing himself king of England against the consent of the natives, is in plain terms a very paltry rascally original. It certainly hath no divinity in it." Paine then asserted that the monarchy failed to fulfill its most basic requirement: to protect its subjects. "Thirty kings and two minors have reigned in that distracted kingdom since the conquest, in which time there has been . . . no less than eight civil wars and nineteen Rebellions. Wherefore instead of making for peace, it makes against it, and destroys the very foundation it seems to stand upon." He concluded, "In short, monarchy and succession have laid (not this or that kingdom only) but the world in blood and ashes. 'Tis a form of government which the word of God bears testimony against, and blood will attend it."[20]

Like Jefferson, Paine challenged the assertion that Britain had protected the colonies. Yet while Jefferson argued that the colonies had borne the costs of settlement and self-defense, Paine made the more radical claim that Britain endangered the colonies by drawing them into wars with other powers. Empire was a protection racket: "But she has protected us, say some. That she hath engrossed us is true, and defended the continent at our expence as well as her own is admitted, and she would have defended Turkey from the same motive, viz. the sake of trade and dominion." Paine argued that Britain always acted in its own interest, drawing the colonies into conflict with its enemies. If the colonies were independent, they would not be threat-ened by Britain's enemies and therefore would not require Britain's protection, "security" that the current war made mockery of.[21]

The first edition of *Common Sense* was published as Jefferson was drafting his "Refutation," though he did not receive a copy of Paine's pamphlet until February.[22] It is possible that Jefferson gave up on his examination of early colonial history after reading Paine's treatise. Jefferson's "Refutation" is nonetheless important because it represents the culmination, or final expression, of a historical vision that Jefferson had articulated since he wrote what became *A Summary View* almost two years earlier. Jefferson with his Whiggish version of colonial history had sought to demonstrate that British Americans were free-born, self-governing Britons who lived on the western side of the Atlantic. He believed that this history would help him to heal and indeed improve the governance of the whole British Empire. The unfinished, unpublished "Refutation" represents the last attempt by Jefferson to remake and reform the empire based on his reading of its history and that of his own colony. Six months later Jefferson would review the history of the British–American dispute in his most famous writing, the Declaration of Independence, which can be read equally as a paean to the birth of a new order *and* as an obituary for the British Empire in North America. It was as much a declaration of the failure of Jefferson's imperial vision as it was of the new nation's independence. Thomas Paine clearly spoke common sense to Jefferson and his fellow patriots when he told them that the time for reconciliation had passed. There was no turning back now; the illusion of a constitutional connection between Britain and America was finally, fatefully demolished.

If there was no imperial constitution, independence logically followed. Yet this did not mean that British Americans were precariously poised on the brink of an anarchic abyss. On the contrary: The imperial scaffolding may have collapsed, but British American ground was well prepared for regime change. Even before the Continental Congress could muster the votes for independence, congressmen were urging their home provinces to revamp or replace their governments, in most though not all cases by drafting new constitutions and eliminating royal or proprietary governors. It was a heady moment for law-giving lawyers like Jefferson, but the foundations of new jurisdictions were already well laid. Paine recognized this in *Common Sense* when he offered a striking image of the original social contract, with citizens coming together under a great tree—a metaphor for the origin of government and a version of the history Jefferson elaborated at such great length in his "Refutation."[23]

No more need be said on the imperial question, Paine proclaimed in January 1776, and most homegrown patriot leaders agreed. Over the next few months, Jefferson and his colleagues more or less patiently waited for consensus to form and a people (or peoples) to become fully conscious of their collective identity. Revolutionaries' energies were now directed toward their home provinces: Jefferson was eager to return to Williamsburg to draft a proper constitution for Virginia.[24]

As Americans grappled with the urgent problems that the break with Britain brought to the fore—establishing legitimate governments in the breakaway states, perfecting a postimperial union, providing for collective security in a war-torn world—they set to work with familiar materials. On the geopolitical level, as Jefferson later told the English radical Joseph Priestley, the federal republic represented something "new under the sun."[25] But on the ground, where ordinary Americans defended their homes and pursued happiness, continuities were more conspicuous. American history began long before independence. In the nascent national imaginary, the history of settlement and colonization continued to loom large, as did British, English, and Saxon history before America's "discovery."

Whig history marked the way toward independence for the revolutionary generation. Law-minded patriots took the long view as they sought to vindicate British American rights within the empire. Jefferson and his congressional colleagues defended what they took to be the British constitution's fundamental principles, in essence claiming to be better Britons than their metropolitan counterparts. In *Common Sense*, Paine provided a fresh historical perspective on the deepening imperial crisis, focusing on the war in progress and impatiently dismissing colonists' lingering attachment to the mother country and its vaunted constitution. The English radical compressed the "course of human events" into a single decisive moment, invoking universal, transhistorical principles and emphasizing the urgent need for collective action.[26] Paine's reframing of the crisis enabled patriots to imagine themselves *outside* the empire and seek recognition as one of "the powers of the earth."

The Declaration of Independence was indebted to Paine's intervention. The exhaustive catalog of grievances that constituted the body of the Declaration's text evoked the origins of the imperial crisis in the various colonies, but those histories converged in the more recent past and resonated most powerfully after the onset of hostilities in April 1775 at Lexington and Concord.[27] Military mobilization fostered a continental, protonational consciousness and geopolitical reframing of the crisis that made independence seem increasingly plausible, even imperative. Yet the separate provinces did not disappear at this nation-making moment, for Congress itself represented an alliance or union of state republics. The Declaration was not a constitution, but Congress's status as collective successor to George III depended on the legitimacy of the self-constituted states whose representatives authorized the text Jefferson authored on behalf of their peoples. Britain, as Paine provocatively concluded, might have no constitution, but the separate states and the new union of states would have *many* constitutions, written (and eventually ratified) by the people's representatives at successive founding moments. The Declaration was the original, generative source of this extraordinary outburst of constitution writing.

Jefferson adapted British Whig history and its provincial variants to the imperatives of state-building and nation-making, offering novel and controversial ways to project federal and republican principles through time and space, across generations and a vast continental domain.

"The Earth Belongs to the Living"

The new American nation's birthday, July 4, 1776, was a pivotal day in Thomas Jefferson's personal history. The young lawyer and patriot cast off his provincial identity, denounced his former king, and proclaimed himself a self-governing citizen of the free and independent Commonwealth of Virginia. This was not the Virginia of Jefferson's youth, for the vindication of American independence and destruction of the British Empire cast the Old Dominion adrift. The empire had been Jefferson's "imagined community," the distant metropolis that nurtured his ambitions and defined the expansive horizons of his world.[28] The patriots who affixed their signatures to the Declaration of Independence recognized the fatal finality of their bold act. In a passage his congressional editors suppressed, Jefferson acknowledged a deep sense of loss in the violent rupture of the imperial body politic. "We might have been a free & a great people together," he pathetically exclaimed: George III's war against his American subjects, this "last stab to agonizing affection," marked the ultimate failure of patriot dreams of imperial greatness.[29] Thwarted in their campaign for a closer, constitutional union with the mother country, reluctant revolutionaries now turned away from Britain and toward each other, seeking an ever "more perfect union" among the renegade provinces—what George Washington would deem, with ratification of the federal Constitution hanging in precarious balance, "the wretched fragments of empire."[30]

"Union" was a protean term for Jefferson, evoking private sentiments as well as public meanings. Students of law and politics deployed the term to variously describe the product of a negotiation resulting in a contract, compact, or—"among the powers of the earth"—a treaty.[31] Marriage, the result of a "treaty" between families, produced a conjugal union, simultaneously a public, legal fact and, for enlightened sentimentalists like Jefferson, the private affective attachment that constituted the foundation of family life.[32] The union that congressmen sought to consummate with their Declaration signified on both levels, sealing a transprovincial, continental alliance and indicating an openness to alliances with foreign powers in the ongoing war. Military mobilization and battlefield success turned on deeper attachment to the "common cause," a reciprocal recognition among autonomous, disconnected state-republics with their distinctive and often conflicting interests and cultures.[33]

The Declaration did not create an enduring or legitimate constitutional union, but it did provide the foundation and framework for nation-making, convincing "Americans" that they constituted a single people who could negotiate alliances (or unions) with foreign powers, win the war, gain recognition from Britain in the 1783 Peace of Paris, draft a federal constitution, and establish a new, postimperial continental government—all problematic, nearly failed projects.[34] But Jefferson kept the faith. Declaring independence was the "fundamental act of union," the necessary, nation-making predicate of subsequent constitutional construction projects. The Declaration was the point of departure for an unfolding national history—the history that an enlightened people would inscribe on the continent—and the point of return, to the first principles of republican government laid down for the ages in the Declaration and to the "spirit" that animated Jefferson and his generation in their great struggle to fulfill its promise.

The people came first and the constitutions that enabled Americans to govern themselves and secure their independence followed. The fundamental, "self-evident" principles of republican government were timeless, outside of history; constitutions, drafted under contingent, constantly changing circumstances, were the time-sensitive products of particular historical moments. This for Jefferson was the American Revolution's obvious lesson. Constitution-writing

was the hallmark of regime change as Americans created new governments to meet the immediate and compelling challenges of political
and military mobilization. The now-conventional view is that the
Declaration was an extraconstitutional and ephemeral wartime man-
ifesto, hastily and belatedly drafted to meet the exigencies of the
moment and lacking the legitimacy and authority of contemporaneous constitutions. Jefferson thought differently. When, in an 1816
letter to Samuel Kercheval, he likened the federal Constitution to a
"coat," serviceable for its moment but long since outgrown, he point-
edly distinguished between enduring republican regime principles
and the constitutions successive generations would choose to live
under.[35] Jefferson did not want to be remembered as a law-giving
founder—perhaps, a skeptic might suggest, because he had not
played an important role in drafting Virginia's 1776 constitution and
was on the wrong side of the Atlantic when his close friend James
Madison and his fellow "demigods" met in Philadelphia to draft a
new federal charter in 1787.[36] He instead fashioned himself a servant
of the people, deploying his skills as a draftsman to articulate the
principles that animated American revolutionaries to overthrow a
despotic king and to recognize each other as a new people.

Mobilization of the American people in the Revolution was the
template and inspiration for Jefferson's democratic constitutionalism.
It was *not* the precursor of what would later be called a "living constitution," drawing its vitality from the supreme wisdom of justices
who would discover new (or putatively "original") meanings through
tortured interpretations of an obsolescent text.[37] To "ascribe to the
men of the preceding age a wisdom more than human" was a great—
antidemocratic—mistake, violating the fundamental principle that
"all men are (and were) created equal" and submitting to the past's
dead hand. Long since retired from public office, Jefferson counted
himself among those merely "human" revolutionaries. "I knew that
age well," he told Kercheval. "I belonged to it, and labored with it.
It deserved well of its country." Yet every generation had to meet

its own distinctive, unpredictable challenges: His generation "was very like the present" living generation, but "without the experience of the present: and 40 years of experience in government is worth a century of book-reading: and this they would say themselves, were they to rise from the dead."[38]

Jefferson thought in generational terms because of the way he experienced the Revolution. Sons and daughters of liberty and brothers-in-arms forged strong attachments through common patriotic commitments that transcended provincial boundaries and transformed abstract principles into facts on the ground. Wartime political and military mobilization had a profoundly democratizing effect on Jefferson's nation-making generation, but succeeding cohorts had the inestimable, practical advantage of governing themselves thereafter. Of course, as historians have emphasized, independence depended on the emerging communication networks that enabled a diverse, widely scattered but broadly literate population of newspaper, pamphlet, and book readers to become a people.[39] As Jefferson told Henry Lee in 1825, his "object" as the Declaration's draftsman was "not to find out new principles, or new arguments, never before thought of, not merely to say things which had never been said before," but rather to set forth "the common sense of the subject" in an "expression of the American mind."[40] Literacy constituted a common ground, operationalizing equality, enabling consent, and giving birth to a nation. An able worker in words, Jefferson played a modest but important role in the process of mobilization that made contemporaries conscious of their collective, generational identity.

When revolutionaries thought of themselves as a distinct "people" and declared themselves sovereign successors to King George III, they shook off the past and focused on the present. For patriots, popular sovereignty was a largely accurate description of a people at war, declaring their independence and forming new governments. Self-governing republicans rejected the genealogical premise of monarchical government: The right to rule did not descend through successive generations from a dynasty's founding but instead remained latent in the people, its original source. Jefferson and his colleagues appealed to this fundamental "right of revolution" in the Declaration, borrowing the language of their favorite philosopher, John Locke, in his *Two Treatises of Government* (1689).[41] Wartime military and constitutional mobilization made British American patriots conscious of their identity and sovereign authority. In a nation-defining moment of collective self-recognition, Jefferson and his fellow revolutionaries—his "living generation"—sought the world's recognition in their Declaration on July 4, 1776.

Jefferson's conception of generational sovereignty, most fully elaborated in a long letter he wrote to James Madison on September 6, 1789, constituted his great effort to map a progressive national narrative for the American people by renewing and perpetuating the patriotic spirit of 1776 through successive generations.[42] His crucial move was to conflate the conventional idea of a generation as it applied to particular families—whether modest property owners, aristocratic landlords, or royal dynasties—and the all-inclusive family of families, the people or nation. In a formulation that must have mystified Madison, Jefferson announced that "between society and society, or generation and generation there is no municipal obligation, no umpire but the law of nature." If their generation could legitimately make a revolution, subsequent generations could lawfully claim the same right. "We seem not to have perceived," he provocatively concluded, "that by the law of nature, one generation is to another as one independant nation to another."

Madison *was* at a loss for words.[43] Was Jefferson imagining an intergenerational "state of nature" or, in common parlance, a state of war between one generation and the next, fathers and mothers against their sons and daughters? This was an astonishing doctrine for a conscientious common lawyer to embrace. Securing the regular, predictable descent of property—particularly real estate in an agricultural society—was the major concern of municipal law, and

every good republican acknowledged the critical importance of fidelity to contracts of all sorts. But Jefferson was far from being a libertarian or anarchist, nor did he naively believe that natural law was
self-executing. Quite to the contrary, his message to Madison was
that constitutional renewal on a predictable, generational schedule
would preempt future conflicts that would inevitably result from
the increasingly conspicuous illegitimacy of constitutions—and laws
enacted under their aegis—that failed to express the will of future
populations. Like clothing, constitutions had to fit an ever-changing
and expanding body politic.

Unlike his more cautious contemporaries (including Madison),
Jefferson did not see constitutions and the rule of law as bulwarks
against the "excesses of democracy" or tyrannical majorities. More
democracy, not less, was the answer. Jefferson insisted that the success of American experiments in self-government depended on con-
tinuously mobilizing citizens to draft, ratify, amend, and replace
the constitutions that secured and sustained their collective identity as a people. *Common Sense* persuaded patriot constitutionalists that the so-called British constitution was no constitution at all,
precisely because its archaic branches—the House of Lords and the
monarchy—were alien excrescences, cancers on the body politic.
The House of Commons alone could pretend to be representative,
though only a very small percentage of the British population—and
no Americans—were qualified to elect its members.

Jefferson agreed with Paine that the British government was an
institutionalized—or constitutionalized—state of war that enabled a
corrupt and predatory ruling class to exploit the mass of ordinary folk
who produced the nation's wealth. That characterization would have
seemed absurd to loyal provincial subjects before George III declared
them rebels and the empire collapsed. When the king outlawed them,
patriots in the newly independent states mobilized on behalf of the
constitutional principles the mother country had betrayed. Wartime
political and military mobilization democratized British American

constitutional thought and practice. Jefferson's conception of generational sovereignty reflected the nation-making choices he and his countrymen made in the midst of war. His generation was the nation, but that nation could only survive if succeeding generations replicated the sense of self-conscious solidarity and reciprocal recognition that Jefferson and his fellow revolutionaries experienced. The challenge was to provide a framework for regulating intergenerational relations that would enable the new republican regime to avoid the crisis of legitimacy and constitutional failure that destroyed the British Empire.

Jefferson's democratic constitutionalism reflected the binary oppositions that characterized his political thought. The Revolution was an epochal struggle between patriots' soaring hopes for the future and the dead weight of the past, under an old regime that perpetuated the despotic rule of the privileged few—monarchs and aristocrats—over the just claims of the people. Property and power descended through the generations, accumulating in the degenerate hands of king and courtiers, throttling the ambitions of the best and the brightest—the "natural aristocracy"—of every succeeding generation. The animating, life-giving principle of republican self-government was equality, the antithesis of the deadening effects of old-regime inequality.[44]

For a generation of patriots who subscribed to the fundamental principle that "all men are created equal," the self-evident solution to unconstitutional assaults on their liberties was majority rule. But that commonsensical axiom was predicated on the prior commitment that all citizens would submit to the determinations of superior numbers on specific policy questions. As Jefferson wrote in the first draft of his 1801 inaugural address, "Absolute acquiescence in the decisions of the majority" is "the *vital principle* of republics." But being in the minority was not a permanent and therefore unequal status. In the version he finally delivered, Jefferson asked his countrymen to "bear in mind this *sacred principle*, that though the will of the majority

is in all cases to prevail, that will, to be rightful, must be reasonable; that the minority possess their equal rights." Majorities were
evanescent, subject to changing circumstances, while the political
communities within which they formed (and reformed) endured.[45]
Consent, not the accidents of birth or residence, thus marked the
boundaries of the American republics: Citizenship was "volitional,"
not ascriptive.[46]

Free citizens pledged their allegiance to each other, not to former
fellow subjects who remained loyal to George III—or to their dead
ancestors. Jefferson projected the majoritarian logic of revolutionary
mobilization into the future, across generations. For consent to be
meaningful, every successive generation had to be guaranteed a clean
slate, or tabula rasa, with the freedom to return to the Declaration's
"first principles" and reconstitute their republics. The "living" generation should not squander resources, plunge into debt, or waste the
collective estate, thus shackling its successors with life-threatening
burdens and commitments and making a mockery of the republican
promise of self-government. The challenge for Jefferson was to precisely define what he meant by "generation" and sustain or replicate
the patriotic attachments revolutionaries forged with each other in
a nation-making war with Britain that was also a civil war among
British Americans. His seemingly impracticable, even absurd solution
was to determine life expectancy in America by consulting actuarial
tables for France (the best available proxy), concluding that the majority of the nation's (or state's) population at any specific moment—
for instance, when it declared independence or constituted a new
government—would be dead, thus making survivors a minority of
the population, nineteen years later. At that point the people should
draft a new, better-fitting constitution, and public debt should be
appropriately serviced. For Jefferson this was yet another, critically
important application of the majority rule principle.

What was most remarkable about this most remarkable proposal was the way it deployed the aristocratic logic of perpetuating

dynastic wealth, privilege, and power across generations on a national scale, merging particular families into one great and inclusive republican family of families.[47] All families were created equal, and though their fortunes would diverge, a wise commonwealth provided social goods—education, access to public land, a truly free market—that would equalize opportunity for young citizens to accumulate property and form new families. Property rights must be scrupulously upheld under the law, Jefferson thought, but only if they served the higher purpose of preserving the republic.[48]

Jefferson's democratic commitments reflected his understanding of the crisis of legitimacy that subverted the British government's authority in the thirteen contiguous mainland provinces that became the United States. The mobilized people were the authors of constitutions that established their collective identity. Popular political and military mobilization of rights-conscious provincials in turn prepared the way for declaring independence and implementing new constitutions. Self-constitution thus was the predicate of self-government; the ongoing legitimacy of republican rule depended on each succeeding generation fulfilling its sacred responsibility to reenact the revolution, declare its independence, and affirm its sense of itself as a people. Nationhood was not the legacy of venerated founders in a far distant past but the achievement of each living generation to be passed on to its successors.

Jefferson's democratic constitutionalism pivoted on a revolutionary conception of intergenerational relations and therefore of national history. If nations and individuals were equally bound by the ethical and moral imperatives of natural right, the logic of legitimacy required that nations respect the independence—the capacity to consent—and rights of each citizen. In other words, self-preservation was the first and highest law of nature for citizens—claiming equal rights with fellow citizens—as well as for communities. Jefferson's constitution was not the "living" constitution of modern (antidemocratic) theorists, who look to the wisdom of unelected judges to adapt the

constitution to changing times through creative, or "loose," interpretation of the constitution's text. What gave the constitution life
was the will of the living generation, expressed in the text that the
requisite republican majority wrote and ratified.[49]

The constitution was not a sacred text, or "ark of the covenant,"
as Jefferson told Kercheval, but republicans who were true to their
own words would hold it in the highest regard, as if it were sacred—
until it was superseded by a new constitution in generational due
course.[50] These constitutions were of course written, and this is
generally supposed to be the great American contribution to constitutional theory and practice. But the point of writing constitutions, Jefferson insisted, was to make them legible and legitimate to
the people who lived under them. Like the Declaration, the constitutions revolutionaries wrote were projects and products of their
times, providing frameworks for future change, inaugurating a new
epoch in what was now national history. Future generations would
not have to mobilize against moribund constitutions and unresponsive governments, thus making war—as Jefferson's generation did—
to reclaim their liberties. That, at least, was what Jefferson believed.

In the future Jefferson envisioned, the constitutional generation was an artificial, man-made mechanism to sustain an ongoing,
predictable process of republican renewal. Revolutionary patriots
had become conscious of themselves as a generation in the context
of war and regime change that they had not expected or intended.
The constitutional calendar would give rise to future self-conscious
generations. Mobilizing to revise, remake, or replace outmoded
constitutions, they would peacefully reenact the original nation-
making moment. In contrast to the private, familial experience of
generational change, constitutional generations would be public
and political, embodying the whole people. The aim of Jefferson's
scheme was to protect families from the disruption and devastation
that failed constitutions—like the British constitution in America—
had inflicted on subject populations. Constitutional renewal in a

self-governing republic could not secure families from economic failure or the hazards of the life cycle, but it would keep the peace and
preserve the commonwealth.

Passing the great national estate unencumbered to its successors,
all the families that constituted the living generation could envision
a happy future for their children and children's children. Liberated
from the past's dead hands, grateful future generations would freely
acknowledge the incalculable debt they owed to their prudent predecessors. Jefferson's conception of generational sovereignty thus
would preempt the chronic conflicts between generations—and
within families—that threatened the republic's survival. It was an
intergenerational "peace pact," analogous to the consensual union of
free states expanding across the continent.[51] Jefferson's generations,
"independent nations" in peaceful succession, would extend across
time, thus fulfilling the promises he so eloquently articulated in the
Declaration of Independence. "*The earth belongs in usufruct to the living*" and would continue to do so—until the end of national history.[52]

"Take Care of Me When Dead"

As he approached his death in 1826, Thomas Jefferson consoled
himself with the thought that succeeding generations of Americans
would set things right, completing what his hopeful generation had
left undone and correcting its mistakes. But hope betrayed fear.
Would each succeeding generation fulfill its historic responsibilities?
How would future Americans look back on their past? How would
he be remembered?

There was no place for great men, conquering heroes, or larger-
than-life lawgivers in Jefferson's conception of generational sovereignty. In a free republic the people were their own sovereign,
liberated from the despotic chokehold of the past. Modestly casting
himself as the people's servant, acknowledging his limitations and
prejudices, eschewing pretensions to greatness, Jefferson assumed a

time-bound civic identity as a member of his own generation. No individual deserved to be venerated beyond the grave, as if he or she were more than a merely mortal human being. Yet Jefferson did want to be remembered as a faithful republican who played a modest role in his own generation's great work. To be remembered in this way depended on the nation's survival, and the nation's survival depended on the accuracy of the stories Americans told themselves and their fidelity to the timeless principles of republican self-government that defined the new nation.

Jefferson withdrew from public life when he completed his second presidential term in 1809, having served as governor of Virginia, American minister in Paris, secretary of state, vice president, and president. Though no longer playing an active role in national politics, he was determined to set the historical record straight. Jefferson was also convinced that his congressional editors had introduced flaws in the Declaration of Independence that misrepresented his—and therefore the people's—originally intended meaning.[53] It was critically important for successive generations to grasp the fundamental principles that may have seemed "self-evident" to the American people when they declared independence but had become increasingly obscure with the passage of time. Jefferson did not see fellow members of the Continental Congress as proxies for the people, fairly representing the diverse perspectives of their respective states. He instead imagined *himself* speaking for "the people out-of-doors," patriotic Americans who were already fighting the good fight—and dying—on revolutionary battlefields; he did not see himself as the thin-skinned, self-protective author of the Declaration but rather as the people's penman, expressing "the harmonizing sentiments of the day."[54] The mouthpiece of his generation thus found himself at odds with factious, temporizing, and insufficiently patriotic colleagues—as he would throughout his later career as the people's partisan champion.

In January 1821, Jefferson began writing a retrospective account of his public life. Later identified as his autobiography, the incomplete manuscript only covers his career to 1790, when he joined George Washington's cabinet as secretary of state.[55] Over the next few years he edited the text, expanding his account of the drafting of the Declaration of Independence based on his own contemporaneous records. "I took notes in my place while these things were going on," he wrote, "and at their close wrote them out in form and with correctness."[56] There were several versions of the Declaration: Jefferson's "original Rough draught" presented to Congress on July 2, 1776; the edited version adopted on July 4; and an intermediate version edited by the committee that charged Jefferson with preparing the original draft.[57] Congress removed nearly a quarter of Jefferson's original draft, yet Jefferson always believed that that draft was a more faithful rendition of the sense of the people than—and therefore superior to—the version adopted by Congress. He was careful to include his full draft in his autobiography, along with commentary based on relevant documents.

Jefferson's documentary history of the Declaration demonstrated that he was the primary author of the founding document of the United States. Preserving and circulating his version of the Declaration, along with his account of its drafting, was not merely an exercise in authorial vanity on Jefferson's part. Rather, he hoped to offer future generations a more accurate account of his role in articulating the new nation's republican ideals and thus assure that those ideals would be preserved and reaffirmed from generation to generation and across the continent. As his tombstone indicated, he wanted to be remembered as the "author of the American Declaration of Independence."[58] Authorship in this case signified fidelity to the sense and sentiments of the revolutionary generation, expressed with "the proper tone and spirit called for by the occasion." The Declaration's authority originated with the people, not Jefferson; it would be a touchstone for subsequent generations as they renewed that spirit and reaffirmed the nation's first principles.[59]

In his final days Jefferson looked anxiously to the future. He could take comfort in the friendships that had sustained the republican cause for a half century, particularly with James Madison. "The harmony of our political principles and pursuits," Jefferson told his old friend a few months before his death, "have been sources of constant happiness to me thro' that long period." Madison was a "constant" for Jefferson, as were the "principles" they shared during their ongoing political "pursuits," the source of his "happiness." "It has also been a great solace to me," Jefferson confided, "to believe that you are engaged in vindicating to posterity the course we have pursued for preserving to them, *in all their purity*, the blessings of self-government, which we had assisted too in acquiring for them." Contemplating the cessation of activity, Jefferson testified to his belief that his younger friend would remain active, continuing—as long as he lived—to vindicate their commitment to republicanism. "If ever the earth has beheld a system of administration conducted with a single and steadfast eye, to the general interest and happiness of those committed to it, one which, protected by truth, can never know reproach," he eloquently concluded, "it is that to which our lives have been devoted."[60]

Why should the old man be so anxious? Appealing to the "earth" itself and all the political systems it had ever "beheld" and insisting on the truthfulness of his irreproachable claims, Jefferson betrayed his doubts. The success and survival of America's republican experiment depended on the spirit that animates each generation and brings abstract principles to life. At the end of his day and in the last sentence of his letter, Jefferson had a simple yet momentous request to make of his good friend: "Take care of me when dead."[61] Still living, Madison was Jefferson's bridge to posterity. Yet if Jefferson could be confident of Madison's posthumous care, he also knew—and feared—that the waning commitments of future generations to the republican cause might lead posterity to forget the sacrifices and achievements of their predecessors.

Although he did not believe that past generations should bind and control their successors, Jefferson was anxious that future generations might misunderstand or abandon what his generation had achieved. He had sought to transmit to posterity an accurate record of his generation's achievements so that future generations could meet their own challenges. We have suggested that the Declaration of Independence might be read as a testament to the failure of the British constitution to meet the needs of British settlers in North America. From that failure a new people emerged. Jefferson began the Declaration by acknowledging that Americans and Britons were becoming two peoples: "When in the course of human events it becomes necessary for one people to dissolve the political bands which have connected them to another, and to assume among the powers of the earth the separate & equal station to which the laws of nature and nature's God entitle them, a decent respect to the opinions of mankind requires that they should declare the causes which impel them to the separation."[62] Jefferson's faith in generational sovereignty and hope for the future was premised on the belief that Americans were a single "people," a people created by Jefferson's generation of 1776, a people that emerged from the wreckage of one empire whose successors would create a new, republican, empire, but only if they had learned the lessons of 1776.

Our History

Thomas Jefferson prayed that the new nation that emerged from the American Revolution would survive forever. As he envisioned the American future, Jefferson constructed a version of the provincial past that pointed inexorably toward a republican future, combining a progressive, Whiggish conception of the British constitution with his faith in the virtuous commitment of liberty-loving patriots across the continent to mobilize in defense of their liberties, forge a more perfect union, and declare themselves an independent people.

The existence of an American people was the product of mobilization, not its predicate. Patriots mobilized to vindicate their rights as overseas Britons, identifying—and claiming an equal status—with their metropolitan counterparts, insisting on their allegiance to the British king even when he declared them rebels and sought to force them into submission on American battlefields. When George III betrayed his trust to loyal provincial subjects, they had to justify their violent resistance to legitimate authority. Recasting the principles that animated resistance in terms of universal, natural rights, revolutionaries disclaimed responsibility for the empire's collapse, portraying themselves as victims of an alien, unnatural, and illegitimate foreign power. The bid for independence thus required a new understanding of the provincial past and a new framework for making and interpreting the nation's unfolding history.

Our history may not be Jefferson's, but the challenges his generation faced in its great nation-making project resonate with and help illuminate the challenges we now face—or evade—in another moment of existential crisis. Indeed, Jefferson would say that *every* generation must engage with the distinctive circumstances that always threaten to subvert republican government, even and especially when it might seem to be most securely established. "The earth belongs to each of these generations, during it's course," he wrote James Madison, "full, and in their own right." Each "living generation," during "it's course," occupied the same space—or "country"—for a limited time, conscious of its own mortality and therefore of its indebtedness to prior generations and responsibility to its successors. "One generation" might be to "another *as* one independant nation to another," but because they did not coexist, they could not be in the "state of nature"—or state of war—that characterized contemporary international relations.[63] Past generations were beyond claiming or fighting for anything. "The dead have no rights," Jefferson told Samuel Kercheval. "They are nothing; and nothing cannot own something." Future generations would have to wait their turn. "This

5858

corporeal globe, and every thing upon it, belongs to it's present corporeal inhabitants, during their generation."[64]

Jefferson's "independant" generations came together in the civic and historical consciousness of patriotic Americans. Patriots loved the country that preceding generations held in trust for them, and their gratitude for this glorious legacy extended beyond independence to the founding settlers of their respective provinces. All might easily have been lost, however, when patriots mobilized in defense of the transprovincial, continental country they all shared, ultimately finding themselves forced to break with Britain and declare themselves a separate, independent people. Jefferson's revolutionary generation certainly deserved to be cherished in historical memory. Yet in the fullness of time the same would be said of every generation that fulfilled its trust, keeping its successors in mind as they defended the country against foreign and domestic threats and secured an ever more perfect union, across the continent and to the "thousandth and thousandth generation."[65] Acutely conscious of the many ways they—and the republican experiment—could fail, history-minded patriots bore the extraordinary burden of staying the course from generation to generation.

Contemporary Americans often think about generations in terms akin to Jefferson's. They speak of the "Greatest Generation," born in the early twentieth century, that won the war against fascism, or the Baby Boomers who were born in the aftermath of that conflict. They've named each generation that followed: Gen X, Millennials, Gen Z, and, most recently, Generation Alpha (born after 2013). Jefferson believed that each generation would confront its own challenges and that it must surmount these and transmit the democratic government and healthy civic institutions to its successors. Some generations might be called, like his (and the Greatest Generation), to wage wars while others might face social and political challenges such as extending civil rights or confronting pandemics. One reason that Jefferson was able to postpone taking significant action to end slavery in his lifetime, a failure we see as abject, was because he thought in generational terms. *His* generation had won independence, created the union, and established republican government. It had given future generations the tools they would need to solve the problem of slavery, and he was hopeful, though not certain, they would do so. The success of each generation was (and is) not guaranteed. Indeed, each generation must undertake to renew and defend the nation's republican experiment.

Far from being exempt *from* history, as exceptionalists then and now have imagined, the new nation came into existence—and could only continue to exist—*in* history, or what Jefferson called in the Declaration of Independence "the course of human events."[66] The Declaration's author prayed that future generations would fulfill the Revolution's promise, implicitly acknowledging the limits of what he and his generation could accomplish in their own, all-too-brief moment on earth. The only fixed points in the arc of the new nation's future course were the timeless principles of republican self-government that became "self-evident" to patriots as they mobilized in defense of their liberties and their country against a formidable array of counterrevolutionary enemies at home and abroad.

Jefferson's faith in the future reflected anxious forebodings about the contingent commitments of his own generation. The ultimate success of the republican experiment depended on faithful adherence to the promises citizens made to each other in the present moment and across succeeding generations. In this sense, what we call "democracy" was merely procedural, a technology for decision-making pointing in no certain direction. But all outcomes were not created equal for the moral philosopher and national historian; for Jefferson the emergence of a truly self-governing people was an epochal moment in world history. If self-preservation was the first and preeminent law for *all* nations, it was all the more compelling for the United States, the first great modern republic. Patriotic "rebels" had created something "new under the sun," exulted Jefferson, setting a new standard of legitimacy and state capacity for the benighted nations of the Old World.[67]

These expectations may seem hopelessly, even perversely exaggerated from our disenchanted contemporary perspective. In our history, Jefferson's history—the way the young Whig rewrote America's colonial past and imagined its national future—may no longer illuminate pathways to the present or plausibly map the way forward. But it is worth remembering that Jefferson hoped that Americans, whoever they might be, would learn from the experiences of successive generations, that they would struggle to imagine and sustain their more perfect but always fragile union under unimaginable circumstances, that they would mobilize in unprecedented ways to meet new challenges. In short, Jefferson tells us, we Americans are history's people, as of course all peoples are, although perhaps with a distinctive sense of our own ongoing responsibility for the history we make—for better and for worse.

II

MY COUNTRY

O n April 30, 1913, Henry W. Kiel, the mayor of St. Louis, Missouri, dedicated the first national memorial to Thomas Jefferson. Located in the city's Forest Park, the Jefferson Memorial Building, now the Missouri History Museum, featured a nine-foot statue of Jefferson seated and holding state papers, carved from a forty-ton slab of marble by Karl Bitter, an Austrian American sculptor. More than two decades later, President Franklin D. Roosevelt took an interest in the efforts to memorialize Jefferson in the city. In June 1934, nine years before he dedicated the Jefferson Memorial in Washington, DC, the president signed the legisla-tion to establish the United States Territorial Expansion Memorial Commission. The commission created what became the Jefferson National Expansion Memorial, a ninety-acre park on the banks of the Mississippi River in St. Louis that since 1965 has been the site of the Gateway Arch designed by Eero Saarinen.[1]

Why did politicians like Kiel and Roosevelt associate Jefferson with St. Louis—a city the Virginian never visited? The first Jefferson memorial was funded by the proceeds from the 1904

World's Fair, held to mark the centenary of the Louisiana Purchase. It had been at Jefferson's behest that Meriwether Lewis and William Clark set out from St. Louis in 1803 to explore the trans-Mississippi West. Although Jefferson never traveled beyond the Appalachian Mountains, he had faith that the future of the American republic lay in the West. We have seen that Jefferson promoted republicanism across time through his conception of generational sovereignty. He also believed that the success of the new nation's bold experiment in republican government depended on commanding sufficient space to accommodate the expansive energies of future generations in their own "pursuits of happiness." A generation only had meaning if it had a common attachment to a particular place. Americans needed a shared and recognized geographic space in which to practice self-government.

In this essay we consider the role of space in Jefferson's thinking about the future of the United States. We show that Jefferson and many of his fellow revolutionaries thought continentally prior to declaring their independence from the British Empire. The failure of the British constitution to encompass territories beyond Britain itself led settlers in North America to embrace their identity as "Americans," a capacious character that extended far beyond the borders of their colonies, later states. We show that Jefferson believed that the model for future American expansion beyond the Appalachian Mountains and eventually beyond the Mississippi River was premised on his confidence in what we call democratic federalism, a constitutional arrangement in which new territories were permitted to join the American federal union on an equal basis with the nation's original states. This arrangement, impossible under the former British regime, facilitated the expansion of the new American republic seemingly *ad infinitum*. Consent, we show, was all-important in Jefferson's vision. While Jefferson conceived of an expansive and expansionist American republic, new territories should only join the union if a majority of their citizens gave their explicit approval. That expansion benefited citizens of the new United States but came at the expense of North America's Indigenous peoples. Late in Jefferson's life the nation's geographic growth caused dissension among American citizens over the future of slavery, threatening the very union that Jefferson had dedicated so much effort to making and sustaining. And it was in Missouri, the very place where Jefferson's contributions would later be celebrated, that America's republican experiment was most severely threatened.

It was a commonplace belief in the eighteenth century that republics could only survive and flourish on a small scale, with limited boundaries and virtuous, self-sacrificing citizens and closely knit, homogenous populations.[2] Jefferson had a different view, envisioning republicanism in dynamic terms, on a much grander scale. His generation of patriots recognized that securing their rights as Britons depended on forging a "continental" union among their provinces to counter the massive force of the British imperial state. Therefore, long before independence and the consolidation of power, Americans began to think and act as an empire. They channeled the energies of freedom-loving patriots in a continentwide mobilization. The goal of this democratizing mobilization was simultaneously "conservative"—seeking to restore constitutional government, rule of law, and rights protections—and unprecedentedly "radical," acknowledging the stake ordinary folk had in the war's outcome and enabling future generations to pursue their own happiness.

Jefferson's evolving conceptions of democratic federalism reflected the distinctive circumstances of empire-breaking and nation-making in late colonial British America. The conceptual framework at this moment of existential crisis was *spatial*, for when the war came, "Americans" were predisposed to think big, drawing on the histories of their colonies within the empire and focusing intensively on the relationship between the center and the provincial periphery—the customary "imperial constitution"—during the decade before independence.[3] The United States, Jefferson hoped, would emerge as a stronger, vastly improved version of the old British Empire, stripped of its historic, distinctively British corruptions and a model for free, self-governing peoples everywhere.

───

The country came before the people. Self-declared "Americans" took their name from the continental landmass named for the Italian explorer Amerigo Vespucci that successive waves of settlers and their native-born descendants occupied and cultivated.[4] Americans mobilized in defense of their country *before* they thought of themselves as a separate people. Indeed, the revolution was precipitated by the British government's refusal to recognize British American claims to equal rights, as Britons, *within* the empire. As Jefferson wistfully put it in his "original Rough draught" of the Declaration, "we *might have been* a free & a great people together."[5] If the transatlantic constitutional connection had been preserved and perfected, the country that patriots defended would have remained an integral part of the British Empire. That was what Americans originally intended.

The revolution unfolded in distinctive ways in the various British American colonies.[6] Increasingly impatient policymakers in London sought to centralize administration, reorganize colonial governments, and impose new taxes and regulations across the continent. These ill-fated initiatives—among them the Stamp Act, Townshend Duties, Tea Act, and Coercive Acts—prompted patriots to correspond, cooperate, and identify with each other, recognizing the existential threats they all faced and embracing their common cause. Overreach by the government in London threatened American liberty and fostered an emerging and expansive continental consciousness. British American patriots—still loyal subjects of their protector-king— hoped to save the empire, even after it unleashed its armies against them. Declaring independence in 1776 constituted a sudden, radical, and irreversible change for colonial British Americans, bringing forth a new people and effectively turning their world upside down. Yet the protracted progress of political and military mobilization on a continental scale provided Jefferson and fellow patriots with a geographic framework for nation-making. If the continent was their country, they could mobilize against unconstitutional assaults on the rights of their countrymen, while holding out hope—perhaps naively—for their patriotic king to intervene on their behalf. If the king turned against them, they could as a last resort imagine and declare themselves to be an independent people.

The terms *America* and *American* were widely used on both sides of the Atlantic long before the Revolution, but they took on new meaning for Jefferson and fellow provincial patriots in the years leading up to the break with Britain. As resistance leaders forged ties with one another across provincial boundaries, they became increasingly conscious of the common ground they occupied and sought to defend. Their goal had been to secure recognition of their constitutional rights as subjects of King George III and equal members of a greater British, transatlantic people; to do so, they would have to transform the empire's customary constitution into something approximating a treaty or grand alliance among independent states, a written constitution with explicit guarantees of the autonomous jurisdiction of their respective legislatures.

Patriotism

In 1776 a London printer produced a British edition of *Massachusettensis*, a series of anonymous letters written in support of British rule by a New England loyalist. In a preface the publisher delineated the terms used by the author. According to the publisher the terms *Whig* and *Tory* "have very different significance in Old and New England." In Britain the words denoted two political parties, but in America, a Tory supported "*the supremacy of the British constitution over all the empire*," while a Whig favored colonial independence. The editor further explained, "In the present controversy, the King and People of the British islands have, and can have but *one* interest; which American independence, aiming first at the *unity* of our constitution, then at the *extent* of our commerce, and lastly at the *dignity* of our power, attempts to destroy." According to the editor the constitution applied only in "the British islands," that is, the home islands, and was threatened by American independence, which they disdained as "the mock patriotism of the day—a patriotism, founded on the ignorance of some, urged by the artifices of others, and tending the ruin of all." According to the printer of *Massachusettensis*, "Patriot," too, was a proper noun, like Whig—a political label applied to those who opposed British rule and eventually supported independence, which is how we use the term.[7]

In defense of their rights American patriots thus aimed to negotiate an imperial constitution that would define and secure the boundaries of legislative authority within the empire. Attempting to constitutionalize such lines would destroy the empire, as Governor Thomas Hutchinson warned the Massachusetts legislature in 1773. For advocates of parliamentary supremacy, the result would be to unleash the many-headed monstrosity of *imperium in imperio*, a "state within a state." Hutchinson's interlocutors remained unconvinced. They believed the customary constitutions of Massachusetts and the other American provinces had long since defined the territorial jurisdiction of their governments while setting local limits on royal—and parliamentary—authority.[8] The boundless authority or "sovereignty" Hutchinson claimed for Parliament was unconstitutional. It was akin to the despotic power that provincial enslavers exercised over their human chattel. This was the irresistible implication of Hutchinson's logic: Stripped of their English rights, British Americans would either become "Americans" taking their stand on their natural rights or slaves to their British masters.

Patriots loved and defended their country. During the decade before war broke out in 1775, patriots became increasingly conscious of the continental dimensions of the territory they shared with counterparts in the other British American provinces. The term *patriotism*, in use since the early seventeenth century, would become indistinguishable from *nationalism*, a coinage that emerged in the wake of the nation-making age of democratic revolutions, beginning in America.[9] British American patriots, mobilizing in defense of rights they shared with their metropolitan fellow subjects (in the mother country), therefore could not be "nationalists." They patriotically identified with their continental homeland at a time when nations—or peoples—were not necessarily understood as fixed in place; they could move, or be moved, from place to place. The political and legal circumstances governing that movement—its consensual or coercive character—would determine the geography of slavery and freedom in America.[10]

The coming of the revolution threw British Americans on the defensive, prompting them to think and act continentally. By threatening the authority of provincial legislatures and the integrity of colonial jurisdictions as well as the property rights they authorized, misguided efforts to reform imperial administration fostered a new historical and constitutional consciousness in the various colonies while simultaneously promoting union among them. The histories of the separate colonies converged in the continental cause with the distinction between "America" and its "mother country," between new world and old, ultimately superseding distinctions among the provinces and the constitutions that had tied them separately and directly to the metropolis. The new state republics that succeeded the old British provinces would play a key role in the transformation of American constitutionalism. These self-governing states had the capacity to constitute the kind of union that the patriots had sought within the empire. This is why Jefferson longed to be in Williamsburg in 1776, drafting a constitution for the Commonwealth of Virginia, rather than in Philadelphia, where the Second Continental Congress had tasked him with drafting the Declaration of Independence on behalf of the postimperial "country" as a whole.

If Jefferson later claimed that the Declaration of Independence was the "fundamental act of union of these states," it was personally more significant at the time for affirming his fundamental values.[11] "If any doubt has arisen as to me," he wrote his old college friend William Fleming on July 1, 1776, "my country will have my political creed in the form of a 'Declaration &c.' which I was lately directed to draw." Jefferson thus offered "decisive proof that my own sentiment concurred with the vote" the Virginia delegates "instructed us to give."[12] In other words, his signature on the document would be as important as his authorship of it. Properly constituting Virginia and the other new states was the predicate of constituting the more perfect union that Jefferson had originally sought within the empire. He turned toward Virginia not because he was an advocate of state sovereignty but because the commonwealth was committed to independence for all the states, so setting the stage for creating a continentwide federal constitution. "My country" *was* Virginia, but it would also be, as it already was for Jefferson, "America."

Thinking of America as his country offered Jefferson and his fellow patriots a new framework to consider Virginia's provincial past and its future as an independent commonwealth. The original settlement of Virginia by "farmers"—or "laborers," as Jefferson called them—epitomized the process of colonization throughout "British America." Carrying their rights with them from their native country and left largely to their own devices, settlers established governments under the aegis of Crown charters, negotiated ongoing relations with the metropolis, and extended the bounds of empire.[13]

When, in the wake of Britain's great victory over France in the Seven Years' War (1756–1763), imperial reformers began to undermine these customary arrangements, lawyers like Jefferson were compelled to translate the experience of prior generations into legal and constitutional language. The histories of Virginia and the other British American provinces allowed patriots to identify with each other and mobilize in defense of their homeland. Sustaining and perfecting union depended on constitutional developments in the new state republics: drafting new constitutions (or, in the case of Connecticut and Rhode Island, modifying charter governments) to erase any vestige of the Crown's executive and protective role. The revolutionaries thus created a vacuum of authority that extra-constitutional continental congresses and the quasi-constitutional Confederation Congress would fill before the states authorized and the American people, convened in their respective states, ratified the federal Constitution.[14] The people and their country were then finally, *constitutionally* joined, though their patriotic attachment— to the land and to each other—was long since established.

Americans imaginatively possessed a vast imperial homeland before the break with Britain. Their conception of a common, continental space underwrote a characteristic optimism about the future that helped justify the dreadful costs of the protracted war for independence. Britain's failure to embrace the empire that colonizing provincials had helped win for them—owing to the insular mentality and narrow provincialism of the metropolitan governing class—had destroyed the old empire. Far from a radical break with the past, independence would permit Americans to sustain a transgenerational continuity linking them equally with the settler-founders of their colonial past and with future founders of self-governing states on the ever-expanding frontiers of their federal republican empire.

Jefferson's belief that colonizing settlers carried the rights of their "native country" with them to a new country across the Atlantic Ocean—his theory of expatriation—was a variation on a familiar theme. The Crown made a similar claim, demanding allegiance from its subjects wherever in the world they might land. Settlers developed patriotic attachments to the new lands they collectively occupied and cultivated, but that did not make them aliens or foreigners at home in their country of origin. Attachments developed by conscious choice and the hard work of building property and creating a civil landscape; by contrast the rights these colonizers claimed were their inextinguishable birthright *as* Englishmen—a genealogy of liberty implicit in the persistent claim to "the rights of Englishmen" in British America.

The empire was *British*, but the settlers were still *English*, in the same deep historical sense that their language and common law—with provincial adaptations—were also English.[15] When George III turned against his *American* subjects, refusing to protect their rights and declaring them rebels, patriots turned to each other, mobilizing in defense of the property rights that secured the possession and improvement of their common country. Reluctant revolutionaries declared themselves to be an independent people and legitimate possessors of a continental country. The patriots' defensive love of country now merged with an aggressive assertion of the new nation's place in the world: Patriotism and nationalism converged, becoming indistinguishable.

Patriotism—"love of country"—was traditionally grounded in particular places; revolutionary Americans, by contrast, identified with the entire continent.[16] Thomas Jefferson was a patriotic Virginian, dedicated to the interests and progressive improvement of the commonwealth throughout his life. Yet he harbored no imperial ambitions for Virginia, even after independence was declared. Jefferson instead sought to include a provision in the 1776 state constitution for dividing Virginia's ample territory and creating self-governing republics.[17] These new states would be incorporated into the union on equal terms, thus expanding the limits of the country Jefferson shared with his *American* countrymen.

Although Jefferson's proposal failed—one of many defects in a hastily enacted and radically imperfect document—Virginia proceeded to shrink, both in absolute and relative terms, when it ceded its charter claims to the Confederation in 1784 and sponsored formation of the new state of Kentucky in 1792. Meanwhile the United States grew, annexing new territory and adding new member states, thus fulfilling the young Jefferson's patriotic goals for the British Empire, the original template for his "empire of liberty."[18] Americans now contemplated different and complementary countries: the places they came from—their "native" countries—and the places where they or their children would make new homes and form new attachments. The dynamic of settlement from old home to new, one country to another, marked, they believed, the progress of civilization across generations and across the continent. Patriotism was a potentially limitless resource, renewed and refreshed by the ongoing process of developing and improving new lands, making new homes, and forming new communities.

Nation

Jefferson tracked the relationship between the American people and their homeland in iconic images of the good republican citizen. American colonists, he contended, transformed "the wilds of America" into *their* country. "America was conquered, and her settlements made, and firmly established, at the expence of individuals," Jefferson wrote in his *Summary View of the Rights of British America* (1774): "Their own blood was spilt in acquiring lands for their settlement, their own fortunes expended in making that settlement effectual." In English philosopher John Locke's classic formula, individual colonists became property owners by mixing their labor with the land; by adopting "that system of laws under which they had hitherto lived in the mother country," they affirmed and confirmed their property rights while preserving their continuing "union" with the English people under the protective aegis of "the same common sovereign."[19] Acutely conscious of their rights, colonists were already mobilizing in defense of their country in 1774. But they were much less clear about where their allegiances lay.

Jefferson expressed patriots' ambiguity in the title of his pamphlet: *A Summary View of the Rights of British America*. The "rights" he sought to vindicate were imputed to a distinct and separate part of the British Empire, the continental "country" that constituted the common ground for patriot resistance. Patriots were still "colonists" who acknowledged constitutional ties and some (rapidly diminishing) degree of subordination—through the king—to Britain. But Jefferson's use of the terms "America" and "American" was threatening, for the "British" status of a vast territory that colonists had conquered and claimed as their own was increasingly tenuous, as was the supposedly subordinate status of colonists who refused to be governed. The constitutional battles that set the stage for American independence were still playing out in the respective colonies in 1774 and would finally depend on constructing a constitutional union that could accommodate a new, continental people.

In the meantime Jefferson offered Congress a revisionist account of Virginia history that spoke to the protorevolutionary moment, emphasizing developments in the commonwealth that were relevant everywhere. Looming large in this account was the dynamic figure of the settler-founder, emigrating from a distant homeland, investing blood and treasure in the conquest of "America" (not just Virginia), and promoting the progress of settlement in an expanding hinterland. Cast in humble terms as "farmers," the first settlers left a precious patrimony to their descendants, fostering patriotic attachments to home and country. Establishing settlements required an extraordinary degree of collaboration among consenting individuals, under primitive conditions that anticipated the challenges Jefferson's generation of patriots now faced on a continental scale. The version of Virginia history he offered in A Summary View was reductive. But it was crucially important for Jefferson to emphasize Virginians' independence and their collective capacity to negotiate the colony's ongoing relationship with London and, as the imperial crisis deepened, the other British American provinces.

The convergent colonial histories previewed in A Summary View culminated in the collective experience of the "American" people that was chronicled in the Declaration of Independence. Increasingly sensitive to assaults on their constitutional rights, patriots interpreted developments in other provinces as precedents for their own, diminishing and eventually transcending the distances that separated them. Embattled patriots shared each other's pain, as if they collectively constituted a single body politic, marching together toward a glorious future as they made their own history. If Americans proclaimed themselves a people at a precise moment, on July 4, 1776, declaring independence was also an intensely personal, often agonizing experience, taking place at different times in radically different social and political contexts for every prospective "American." Many refused; many more hesitated or changed their minds.

Citizens as well as soldiers lost their way in the "fog of war." Their choices were radically limited, their "consent" often brutally coerced. Existential threats were ubiquitous and unpredictably present. Signers of the Declaration of Independence understood that they might be signing away their lives; indeed, large numbers of the men-in-arms they claimed to represent had already forfeited theirs. The very idea of a "people" was an aspirational fiction, a spur to mobilization—as well as a club to beat (and silence) dissenters. But it proved to be a compelling idea for growing numbers of patriots because it mapped so neatly onto the capacious, continental conception of the country they had long since mobilized to defend. By this logic loyalists and other dissenters did not belong in the "land of the free." They could either flee the country or submit to civil disabilities and internal exile in the land of their birth. In either case these "enemies of the people" chose to *expatriate*, betraying their country and reversing the imagined arc of British American history.

The profound, patriotic attachment of a people to its country has come to seem axiomatic in a modern world of nation-states. However, provincial British American patriots had no original, abiding intention to become a separate, independent people. John Dickinson of Pennsylvania and Delaware, a precocious continentalist and a (if not *the*) most influential patriot in the run-up to independence, did not think the break with Britain was self-evidently justified on July 4 or at any other time, unless and until there was absolutely no possibility of reconciliation. The premature Declaration did not lead Dickinson to withdraw from the war effort or turn against his countrymen. To the contrary, despite principled scruples and prudential misgivings—misgivings shared but suppressed by reluctant signers— he bent all his energies to the Revolution's success.[20] As Dickinson's case shows, the fit between people and country that the Declaration of Independence affirmed was far from perfect, but it performed significant political and cultural work for the imperiled common cause. For ordinary Americans the escalating constitutional quarrels that engaged Dickinson and other leading patriots only hit home when war endangered their country and threatened *their* homes.

The key figure in the embattled country Jefferson evoked in the Declaration was that of the citizen-soldier who rose in defense of home and homeland. "Declaring us out of his Protection and waging War against us," King George III sought to establish "an absolute Tyranny over these States." His erstwhile subjects could no longer rely on autonomous provincial governments to secure their constitutional rights. Jefferson's catalog of grievances, drawn promiscuously from different British American colonies, made it compellingly clear that those provinces no longer existed as British colonies. The Crown had destroyed their governments and dissolved the boundaries that previously divided them. Now it was urgently "necessary" for Americans "to dissolve the political bands" that connected them with Britain, affirm their union with each other as a people, and "assume among the powers of the earth, the separate and equal station to which the Laws of Nature and of Nature's God entitle them."[21] By withdrawing allegiance from the king, self-declared, freely consenting Americans played the critically important, originating role in the nation-making drama.

The homeland Americans defended from assaults by internal as well as external enemies was the basis of their emerging common identity. Uncertain and volatile loyalties often made it difficult to distinguish friends from foes, but patriots' claims to their country were clearly defined—most conspicuously when counterrevolutionary forces occupied *American* territory, including every major city, often for extended periods. Jefferson and his congressional colleagues waged their war for America on complementary fronts, mobilizing men and materiel for conventional battlefield engagements while urging member states to reconstitute legitimate governments in order to strengthen their union and sustain the war effort.[22] But Americans' conception of their country extended beyond the effective jurisdiction of member states, or even the implausibly expansive claims of colonial charters: Virginia's charter claims extended to the Pacific Ocean. As John Adams drafted a Plan of Treaties for the new nation's future foreign relations in September 1776, patriots looked to the far limits of the British Empire in the West Indies as well as North America. The United States thus claimed "the sole exclusive, undivided and perpetual possession of all the countries, cities and towns on the said continent and of all islands near to it, which now are or lately were under the jurisdiction of or subject to the king or crown of Great Britain, whenever they shall be united or confederated with the said United States."[23]

The geopolitical revolution in British North America expanded patriots' horizons across and beyond the continent, transcending the local boundaries of their familiar provincial worlds. "Give me liberty or give me death!" the great patriot Patrick Henry proclaimed on March 23, 1775, as he assessed the dimensions of the impending crisis. It was "an awful moment" for "this country," he told his fellow Virginians. This country was clearly not Virginia, as it would have been not very long ago, for the imperial crisis now engulfed the entire continent. But Henry did not stand alone, for the "God of nature" endowed America, "our country," with immense potential power. "Three millions of people, armed in the holy cause of liberty, and in such a country as that which we possess, are invincible by any force which our enemy can send against us," Henry averred. Jefferson admired Henry's patriotic spirit in the midst of an extraordinary military mobilization that swept up thousands of patriots (every man, woman, and child was included in the hyperbolic Henry's "three millions") who chose freedom over the slavery of submission to a despotic king. Virginian soldiers marching to distant battles would leave their homes and native country behind them, moving through and toward the more capacious country or homeland of their future. "Almighty God," according to Henry, "the God of Hosts," the "just God who presides over the destinies of nations," would be marching with them.[24]

Both Jefferson and Henry invoked "nature's God," the deity whose presence was mediated through the laws governing the natural world, but Henry—ever the martial Christian—did not hesitate to call on a more personal, less mediated, interventionist God. Still Jefferson and Henry, in complementary ways, emphasized the fundamental importance of the consenting and committed individual. All the customary institutional and constitutional safeguards of British Americans' rights and liberties had been stripped away, leaving them naked and unprotected in the face of the British state's almighty power. Standing alone, every man with the weight of his world and the future of his country on his shoulders, naturally and spontaneously—perhaps prayerfully and providentially—turned toward their fellow patriots.

The geography of the expansive country within which the United States was formed and the American people declared itself into existence was the foundation for the Declaration of Independence. The mobilization that Jefferson and his fellow committeemen celebrated and sought to sustain may have marked the beginning of national history, but it is better understood as a culminating moment in an ongoing process. The patriotic citizen-soldier was already in the field, long since committed to the cause, animated by his love of country. Of course, the Declaration of Independence performed other critically important functions, most notably in promoting the reconstitution of legitimate authority in the new state-republics, creating a progressively more perfect union among them, and negotiating wartime alliances abroad. On the home front and the battlefront, however, the challenge was to sustain the waning morale of citizens and soldiers as they lost ground to a formidable alliance of counterrevolutionary forces, internal as well as external. The initial burst of martial enthusiasm that sustained the patriots after the outbreak of the war in Massachusetts in the spring of 1775 began to wane as Britain marshaled its army, navy, hired mercenaries, loyalists, Indigenous, and enslaved soldiers to suppress the rebellion in 1776. The contagious enthusiasm of 1775 might not sustain the resistance until independence could be declared. British forces had already attacked, occupied, and governed American seaports—a demoralizing portent of things to come.[25]

The Declaration's most important message was that the *people* must be united in order to secure the territorial integrity of their *country*. Nationhood may have been an "invention" and aspirational ideal. But it was also the product of war's brutal logic, drawing a bright, bloody line between friend and foe. If the Crown outlawed colonial patriots, dubbing them rebels, independent Americans returned the favor, ostracizing former countrymen who refused to defend their country, driving them into exile and branding them traitors. Aligning the people with their country was the "self-evident" imperative, enabling them to envision a future worth fighting for.

Continental Country

Jefferson the Virginian embraced a capacious conception of British America as a country in the years leading up to independence. By 1776 the customary constitutional framework that had defined and sustained the British Empire and the governments of its American provinces had been demolished. Denied their constitutional rights, the king's former subjects stood exposed to his unlimited, despotic power, facing the awful prospect of being reduced to the condition of an enslaved people. The iconic image of the citizen-soldier rising up in defense of his country, consenting to sacrifice everything on behalf of the cause, was inscribed in this *free* people's declaration of independence. Popular sovereignty thus was the consequence of popular political and military mobilization, the collective result of the decisions of myriad individuals to invoke the first and fundamental law of nature: self-preservation. Patriots' commitments were motivated by the thick weave of attachments that tied them together as kin, friends and neighbors, fellow worshippers, and workers of the soil, not by the libertarian delusion of self-sovereignty.

Jefferson's "American" stood on home ground, in direct unmediated relation to his country, a vast expansive homeland of imperial dimensions. The American was not a solitary figure. In Query XIX, on "Manufactures," in *Notes on the State of Virginia*, Jefferson explained how "those who labour in the earth are the *chosen people of God*, if ever he had a chosen people, whose breasts he has made his peculiar deposit for substantial and genuine virtue."[26] Because the self-subsisting farmer was not dependent on fickle customers or feudal superiors, he could exercise his own free will. Equality and independence constituted the threshold of true consent, enabling naturally sociable individuals to form families and forge closer attachments—more perfect unions—with one another.

Ostensibly a short essay on Virginia's political economy ("let our work-shops remain in Europe"), "Manufactures" was also, and more importantly, a parable of mobilization and nation-making. The farmer was not a peasant (or a slave) fixed in place, forced to labor in the earth, but rather a free citizen—free to move from place to place. "We have an immensity of land courting the industry of the husband-man," Jefferson intoned, evoking the vast country that excited the enterprise of market-oriented farmers. The latent, unselfconscious virtue that spurred successive waves of new settlement was made manifest in the Revolutionary War effort. This was the empowering paradox in Jefferson's celebration of the yeoman farmer: Equal and independent citizens, conscious of their rights—and vigilant in their defense—came together freely and spontaneously to form a new peo- ple. Animated by "that sacred fire, which otherwise might escape from the face of the earth," the self-governing American people's sov- ereign power was and would be irresistible.[27]

Mobility and the concomitant capacity to form attachments in new places and sustain them from place to place across the continent were the key characteristics of Jefferson's archetypal American. As Jefferson well knew, the people's potential would be limited as long as they deprived the captive nation of enslaved Africans of its liber- ties, corrupting the morals of patriot enslavers. In Query XVIII, on "Manners," immediately preceding his discourse on the patriotic vir- tue of farmers, Jefferson leveled an unusual indictment at the "degen- eracy" of plantation society in *his* "native country." There could be no "amor patriae"—or love of country—among enslaved Blacks, "for if a slave can have a country in this world, it must be any other in pref- erence to that in which he is born to live and labour for another."[28]

Jefferson surely loved Virginia, but it was much easier to love the country America promised to become. Looking beyond present- day Virginia and toward the continent's grand prospects, Jefferson could assure himself that the new nation would find a way to rid itself of slavery, the immoral, corrupting legacy of the colonial old regime. An unjustly enslaved labor force, not the vicious and unruly "mobs of great cities," constituted the most immediate and compel- ling threat to the new commonwealth. When he reflected "that God is just," Jefferson could only "tremble for his country." The trem- ors were particularly pronounced in Virginia, "considering numbers, nature, and natural means only," where "a revolution of the wheel of fortune" might leave white enslavers to the tender mercies of insur- rectionary Blacks.[29]

The far horizon portended a more benign future. Drawn westward, "husbandmen" from long-settled eastern states would outnum-
ber other, less virtuous "classes of citizens" in the new settlements,
securing the civic health of an expanding body politic. "The mass of
cultivators" was an orderly army of citizen-settlers, focusing its energies on liberating a "savage" wilderness from its Native proprietors and
transforming "free" land into productive property. Jefferson's iconic
image of the yeoman farmer emerged from a dynamic process of military mobilization that exalted (and exploited) the independence and
virtue of ordinary folk, democratizing patriotism by redefining the
relationship between the people and their country. Citizen-soldiers
rose to a new level of civic respectability, demonstrating their love
of country through dedication to the cause. In Jefferson's optimistic
imagining, frontier settlers—once despised as violent, lawless, and
semisavage outcasts of civilized society—were fighting the "good
war" against the "merciless savages" George III unleashed on his former American subjects; some marched east to join the Continental
Army's siege of occupied Boston, gaining instant celebrity as exemplary patriots.[30]

Love of country leveled distinctions and fostered generational
solidarity. For Jefferson the revolutionary valorization of the people
fit neatly with—and helped inspire—a new history of Virginia (and
by extension America) that emphasized the ongoing process of settlement and the modest virtues of its unsophisticated farmer-founders.
Working the land rewarded "laborers," making them property owners; freed from the tyranny of feudal tenures, the land made men
free. With land enough for the "thousandth to the thousandth generation," President Jefferson proclaimed in his first inaugural address
in 1801, Americans *could* redeem their continental country's great
promise.[31] Yet this happy outcome was by no means certain.

The new nation's destiny was not yet "manifest" for Jefferson
and his auditors as it came to be for later exponents of American
exceptionalism. His hyperbole instead expressed his enormous relief

that the union survived the partisan strife of the 1790s and his own deadlocked election—barely a generation after the new nation's birth. How many such constitutional crises could the country survive? "Nature's God" made no providential promises: Every generation would face the challenge of adapting to changing times. There was "land enough," but would Americans forfeit their country's bountiful endowment? If Americans were a "chosen people," their future would be secured. But Jefferson did not know the mind of God and could not know "*if ever he had* a chosen people." That Americans would continue to be a people—that their country would not be torn asunder, as the British Empire had been—was and would be their choice, from generation to generation, for all those thousands of generations.

Jefferson believed that Americans would be inspired by the continental dimensions of their country to develop a correspondingly capacious patriotism. The expansive character of this "rising nation" was shaped by the land that made them free. The new president was particularly struck by the energy and enterprise of his countrymen, "*spread* over a wide and fruitful land, *traversing* all the seas with the rich productions of their industry, *engaged* in commerce with nations who feel power and forget right, *advancing* rapidly to destinies beyond the reach of mortal eye."[32] Americans thus disproved the conventional wisdom that republican government could only survive, much less flourish, in small states where like-minded citizens formed strong local attachments.[33] Jefferson's countrymen were constantly in motion, fostering new, more inclusive attachments, collapsing distances and conquering space. Far from being a reactionary opponent of a modern market economy, Jefferson was a "commercial republican" who eagerly embraced its expansive potential.[34]

Jefferson's fellow citizens were primed to scan distant horizons and respond immediately to existential threats. "Every man, at the call of the law," he predicted, "would fly to the standard of the law, and would meet invasions of the public order as his own personal concern." The citizen's identity was drawn from—and would "fly to"—the far limits of his country, anywhere it was threatened.[35] Jefferson expressed the same thought in 1816, when he promised his young colleague Joseph Cabell, a former Virginia state legislator and Jefferson's chief lieutenant in his campaign to create a state university, that the creation of democratic "ward republics" in a new state constitution would generate patriotic sentiments that could no longer be taken for granted. Actively participating at all levels of government, the good citizen would "let the heart be torn out of his body sooner than his power be wrested from him by a Caesar or a Bonaparte."[36] Though Caesar was long dead and no threat, Napoleon's recent designs on American territory made a more powerful impression. Perhaps another Napoleon was looming on the horizon? Many Americans thought so—perhaps in the person of a home-grown avatar such as military hero Andrew Jackson.[37]

In the wake of his ascendancy to the presidency in 1801, Jefferson breathed a great sigh of relief. "The storm is now subsiding & the horison becoming serene," he wrote the English scientist and philosopher Joseph Priestley. "The great extent of our republic is new. It's sparse habitation is new. The mighty wave of public opinion which has rolled over it is new." Most gratifying was "the order & good sense displayed in this recovery from delusion, and in the momentous crisis which lately arose, really bespeak a strength of character in our nation which augurs well for the duration of our republic."[38] But there would be many more "storms" to come. Size alone would not guarantee the ultimate survival and success of the new nation's experiment in republican self-government.

Love of country—the identification of a "chosen people" with its "chosen country"—would repeatedly be tested by conflicting loyalties and interests and the unpredictable vagaries of human nature itself. Born in war and manifest in political and military mobilization against existential threats at home and abroad, the patriots' "sacred fire" might flicker out and die. Jefferson was always acutely aware of

the dangers that lay ahead. His proposed solutions focused on recon-
ceiving and reconstituting the spaces within which the people participated in their own government and patriotism flourished.

Divide and Subdivide

When Jefferson looked westward, he looked to the future. Succeeding
generations of his countrymen would advance the progress of civilization in the wide-open spaces of their vast continental domain, coming together to make their own history. Revolutionary Americans
had justified their bid for independence by revoking their common
attachments as colonial peoples and subjects of George III. In the
new republican regime, colonizing settlers would carry their rights
as American citizens with them—as, Jefferson argued, their forebears had arrived on American shores with the rights of Englishmen.
But American settlers would also find themselves in future new
states. When their populations crossed predetermined thresholds,
the "peoples" of these preconstituted spaces would automatically
claim equal, independent status in an expanding federal republic.
They would not have to suffer the trauma of another Revolutionary
War to vindicate their rights.

Yet Jefferson had no illusions about the natural and spontaneous
emergence of civic community and social order on the frontiers of
settlement. "Free" land did not make the American people free. The
continental domain Jefferson evoked in his inaugural address was a
legacy of the revolutionary generation, freed from the clutches of
other imperial powers by its heroic sacrifices and held in trust for
succeeding generations. It was not, however, free of other peoples:
Indigenous communities with claims on the land that British and
American governments could not ignore, and Euro-American squat-
ters and speculators who routinely *did* ignore or cynically exploit
Native property rights, thus sustaining a near-anarchic "state of
nature" in highly contested frontier regions.[39] Taking the long view,

Jefferson overlooked complicated realities on the ground, instead offering a "peace pact" for future new states that would preempt the constitutional conflicts that had destroyed the British Empire.[40] His plan for the constitutional organization of space was complementary and equivalent to his design for peace across generations, freed from the past's dead hand. The peace Jefferson imagined in both cases was grounded in his capacious, continental conception of the United States as a country. Defense of that country against internal as well as external enemies could—and of course did—lead to an ongoing American "way of war" to secure the peace Jefferson and his fellow revolutionary patriots envisioned for future generations.[41] Making American land "free" was a messy, violent business, best viewed in anticipation and from a distance.

Jefferson offered his original prospectus for the creation of fourteen new western states in a committee report adopted by the Confederation Congress in 1784; he also served on the committee that recommended imposing the famous checkerboard grid on public lands before sale and settlement. Neither ordinance was implemented during Jefferson's brief congressional tenure from 1782 to 1784, but Congress subsequently embraced the principles he articulated in its Land Ordinance of May 20, 1785, and the Northwest Ordinance of July 13, 1787, projecting the creation of from three to five new states in the trans-Ohio region.[42] The goal was to direct (and monetize) settlement in an orderly fashion, thus preempting the conflicts over property titles and jurisdiction that fostered widespread squatting, land speculation, violence, and separatist projects. In the short term the territorial system fell far short of Jefferson's expectations: The new federal congress lacked the administrative and coercive capacity to keep the peace and win (or buy) the loyalties of enterprising settlers in contested frontier regions. In the longer term, however, the prospect of eventually securing land titles and joining the union on equal terms effectively countered the centrifugal tendencies unleashed by the progress of settlement, particularly as external threats from imperial neighbors receded. Divided into states; subdivided into counties, townships, and cities; and populated by market-oriented property owners, contested frontiers became settled places—and settlers fashioned themselves as patriotic Americans.

The federal republic's expansion did not depend on the central government's coercive capacity. The land was *made* free, cleared of Indigenous peoples through a chronic state of settler-initiated warfare that wary federal officials generally sought to avoid. Yet this was not "conquest" in the conventional sense. Following the prescribed pathway to statehood, territorial citizens acted collectively—as self-constituted "peoples"—to form new governments and become members of the federal union, by their own free and uncoerced choice. No longer dependent on territorial governments, new state citizens claimed the full benefits of state *and* federal citizenship. Progress toward new statehood replicated the history of the original American states in their protracted struggle for independence. The crucial difference was that the colonies' quest for constitutional union with Britain culminated in a war that fractured the British Empire. The American union was instead designed to expand, whether by adding other British colonies to the Confederation—with a specific invitation to Canada, its continental neighbor—or by dividing the national domain into prospective new states in anticipation of their future settlement.

Insisting on its sovereign supremacy and the logical absurdity of *imperium in imperio*, the British Parliament demonstrated the impossibility of constitutional union. As the London editor of *Massachusettensis* complained, "To be a patriot in mode, is to aim at a separation of the state into *twenty* or *thirty* different parcels, instead of seeking a consolidation of several provinces into *one* empire. People of this stamp are for saving our enemies the trouble of enforcing the difficult part of the motto—*divide et impera*—by attempting the *first* for them."[43] This was precisely the kind of union Jefferson and his fellow American patriots sought to construct: The perfection of their union, and its capacity to mobilize the power of the American people, was premised on dividing and subdividing authority in a multiplicity of jurisdictions. Unlike the European state system, the Americans' federal union was not a zero-sum game of winners and losers. Citizens' attachments to multiple, nested jurisdictions—one within another, from local to national—would buttress their patriotic love of the whole continental country, including a vast unsettled and uncivilized (though hardly empty) hinterland onto which Jefferson projected his inspiring image of the new nation's future.

Whereas advocates of parliamentary sovereignty in Britain (and a later generation of nationalist centralizers and "consolidationists" in America) sought to erase lines, Jefferson was eager to draw them—on maps and around jurisdictions. The genius of the federal system was to secure the autonomy of governments at all levels and in their respective sphere of authority: All townships, counties, and states were equal to and independent of each other, and their subordination to higher authority was strictly defined and constitutionally limited. Ascending upward, the citizens who were constitutionally mobilized at the local level were represented at each higher level; gaining a progressively broader perspective, their representatives identified with each other and formed new solidarities while promoting and defending the rights and interests of their constituents. The American people thus expanded to the imagined limits of the country they called their own. "We can no longer say," Jefferson told Priestley, that "there is nothing new under the sun."[44]

Jefferson envisioned federalism as a constitutional structure of mediation, connecting the individual citizen and fostering identification with fellow citizens across the country. If they could "trust" one another, as they believed they had in the Revolution, patriotic Americans might justify Jefferson's bold assertion in his first inaugural address that their "Government" was "the world's best hope"—looking beyond the gridlocked, nearly failed union of a few short weeks previous and envisioning "the Strongest Government on earth."[45] The "energy" that powered the government would come *from* the people, not, as his archenemy Alexander Hamilton thought, by imitating the engorged, corrupt, and overcentralized British government that had alienated Americans and driven them from the empire.

Throughout his career Jefferson invoked his gospel of dividing to unite, of bringing government closer to the people in order to broaden their horizons and deepen their patriotic commitments.[46] But it was only in 1816, in the midst of yet another failed effort to draft a proper constitution for Virginia, that he fully elaborated his conception of federalism. (The Virginia constitution of 1776 had *not* been drafted by a duly elected convention, nor had it been ratified by the people's vote.) "The way to have good and safe government," he wrote Joseph Cabell, "is not to trust it all to one; but to divide it among the many, distributing to every one exactly the functions he is competent to." Harking back to the revolutionary era when he unsuccessfully proposed a plan for taxpayer-funded local schools, the now former president urged his loyal lieutenant to take the education issue directly to the people: "Declare the county ipso facto divided into wards, for the present by the boundaries of the militia captaincies," the administrative unit that came closest to the New England township. Cabell should "explain the object of the law to the people of the company, put to their vote whether they will have a school established, and the most central and convenient place for it; get them to meet & build a log school house."

Combining local knowledge with a broadly inclusive, forward-looking patriotism, the citizen-soldier—recently returned perhaps from service on the northern frontier in the War of 1812, the new nation's second war for independence from Britain—was Jefferson's republican ideal. Who was better equipped to provide for the rising generation's education than the homecoming farmer-in-arms? Some might believe these "elementary schools" would "be better managed by the Governor & council, the Commissioners of the literary fund, or any other general authority of the government, than by the parents within each ward," Jefferson concluded, "but it is a belief against all experience." By the same logic, the autocratic logic of parliamentary sovereignty, the state government should take on "the management of all our farms, our mills, & merchants' stores."[47] Such a consolidation of authority would signal the republic's demise—and the pointlessness of the revolutionary generation's sacrifices.

Constitutional reform was imperative to channel and contain a spirited people. If Jefferson "like[d] a little rebellion now and then," as he famously assured James Madison and Abigail Adams in early 1787, he also recognized that the chronic rebellions fostered by inadequate constitutions like Virginia's would ultimately subvert any regime, even a republic.[48] It was therefore critically important to give popular political energy an appropriate sphere of action and authority, to constitutionalize the "spirit" that gave birth to the republic and sustained it across generations. "Making every citizen an acting member of the government, & in the offices nearest & most interesting to him," Jefferson wrote Samuel Kercheval, "will attach him by his strongest feelings to the independance of his country, and it's republican constitution."[49] Subdivision enabled expansive sentiments, a surplus of patriotism that would secure both Virginia and the whole "country" against all threats.

Federalism in the new United States was a legacy of the old imperial regime. The separate British American provinces were irreducible geopolitical facts that any postimperial regime would have to accommodate. But Jefferson, more than any other revolutionary patriot, recognized ways in which distinctions among and within these jurisdictions and new ones could be exploited and improved to expand and perfect a federal republican union. The answer to supposed democratic excesses was *more* democracy; the bulwark against consolidated and despotic power was a thoroughly democratized constitutionalism.

The genius of American federalism was to secure the liberties of a great and far-flung people without concentrating authority in a strong central government: The United States would be a *republican empire*, an empire *without* a metropolis.[50] Having eliminated the king and his court, Americans no longer needed a single, all-powerful legislature like the British Parliament to protect them. "By dividing and subdividing these republics from the great National one down thro' all it's subordinations, until it ends in the administration of every man's farm and affairs by himself," the people protected themselves. The classic rationale for mixed government, pitting monarchy against aristocracy, one social order against another, branch against branch, no longer made sense in a republican regime where "all men were created equal." In the traditional, top-down logic of British American constitutionalism, the great desideratum was—and for many still is—"checks and balances." Jefferson's broad-based, bottom-up federal constitutionalism would secure the same ends. "The elementary republics of the wards, the county republics, the State republics, and the republic of the Union, would form a gradation of authorities," he told Joseph Cabell. Each would stand "on the basis of law, holding every one it's delegated share of powers, and constituting truly a system of fundamental *balances and checks* for the government."

The reversed word order in Jefferson's formulation, with "balances" coming before "checks," suggests a reversal of the constitutional order, with the "elementary republics" providing the enduring foundation for the rule of law. The ongoing surveillance of an engaged citizenry, beginning with the ever-vigilant citizen-farmer, was the best check on the abuse of power. It was "by placing under every one what his own eye may superintend," the enlightened observer concluded, "that all will be done for the best."[51] Administrative and jurisdictional "subordinations" were functional, as the people's representatives at successively higher levels grappled with more complex and specialized problems involving the whole country and its relations with others. Patriotic citizens remained the best judges of their representatives' fidelity to first principles, all the way up.

They could see the fundamental connection between their homes and "our country," the homeland, the source and site of their collective American identity.

Americans' patriotism extended to their country's distant frontiers. But it was not disinterested, for self-governing Americans knew that the rights they had fought for were grounded in the property they claimed—and hoped to accumulate—for themselves and their respective families. Jefferson emphasized the prime importance of property ownership for forging enduring attachments in a republic. Though he was "conscious that an equal division of property is impracticable," as Jefferson wrote Reverend James Madison (his good friend's cousin), he recognized that unequal land distribution produced "so much misery to the bulk of mankind" that "legislators cannot invent too many devices for subdividing property, only taking care to let their subdivisions go hand in hand with the natural affections of the human mind."[52] "The true foundation of republican government," as Jefferson explained to Kercheval, "is the equal right of every citizen in his person, & property, & in their management." This was the standard for assessing "every provision of our constitution": "See if it hangs directly on the will of the people."[53]

American patriots looked beyond their home provinces as they envisioned the settlement of the vast new country they claimed in the wake of the empire's collapse. Many patriots actually did move, or speculated in the movement of their land-hungry, market-oriented countrymen. The challenge for patriots like Jefferson was to construct a dynamic postimperial constitutional regime that would enable them to "conquer space," both by forging a more perfect union among the original states and by organizing new ones to extend their republican empire into—and eventually beyond—vulnerable and contested frontier regions. Federalism would serve national purposes, thus vindicating patriots' original, frustrated ambitions for Britain's expanding American empire.

To conquer space, Jefferson thought, the new republican regime would have to constitutionalize federalism, thereby empowering citizens to move and trade freely across state boundaries and establishing pathways to the West for successive waves of settlement within territories and new states. Harnessing and depending on the energy of enterprising citizens, a federal system of nested and reciprocally reinforcing jurisdictions would foster patriotic devotion to the union. Its "balances and checks" thus would expand the ambit of popular political participation, providing safe channels for an unprecedented "release of energy" in Jefferson's "empire of liberty."[54] National independence depended on mobilizing the people; "dividing and subdividing" as they moved forward in time and across space would sustain their ongoing mobilization in peaceful pursuits, demonstrating the extraordinary benefits of democratic constitutionalism and federal union for their continental country—and for the emerging order of the modern, progressively more enlightened world.

Consequences

The American Revolution remained a touchstone for Thomas Jefferson for the rest of his life. In 1776 the Declaration of Independence evoked an inspiring image of union among and within deeply divided British American provinces in the grip of a protracted existential crisis as they organized to resist the invasion and occupation of their embattled country. A generation later, partisan and sectional divisions among Americans exposed the union's fragility. Jefferson, the newly elected president, rose to the rhetorical occasion, reminding his countrymen of their common commitments—we are all "brethren of the same principle. We are all republicans: we are all federalists"—and enjoining them to redeem the boundless promise of their bountiful homeland. Discounting, if not trivializing, profound political and ideological differences, Jefferson emphasized more fundamental attachments that made Americans into "a rising nation," a great and expanding republican family of families.

Nothing was more important than the vast country they shared, looking westward, "spread over a wide and fruitful land, traversing all the seas with the rich productions of their industry, engaged in commerce with nations who feel power and forget right, advancing rapidly to destinies beyond the reach of mortal eye."[55] This was an inspiring prospect for every enterprising American, channeling the spirit that had won independence into securing its fruits forever.

The visionary Jefferson asked his auditors and readers to over-look recent turbulence and put their recent quarrels into perspective. In directing their gaze to the west, he also overlooked inconvenient facts on the ground. Hostile European powers—Britain to the north, Spain to the south and west—contested the new nation's expan-sive dominion: Before the Louisiana Purchase, the trans-Mississippi remained foreign territory, and separatist settlers within America's nominal borders speculated in alternative political futures. More importantly, Native peoples continued to mobilize in defense of *their* homelands, forging alliances, relocating, seeking protection and support from competing empires—including the United States. The future could be seen as a blank slate, but the continent was any-thing but one.

Jefferson had glimpsed the future in his inaugural address in 1801. As he approached the end of his life, he imagined himself rising above it all, gaining a more than mortal perspective on the progress of civi-lization across the continent. In retrospect everything looked differ-ent. The "philosophic observer" looked eastward in 1824, back on the future he had once envisioned, equating the span of his own life with the history of mankind through progressive stages of develop-ment. "Commence a journey from the savages of the Rocky moun-tains, Eastwardly towards our seacoast," Jefferson advised William Ludlow, and there "he would observe" man "in the earliest stage of association living under no law but that of nature, subsisting and covering themselves with the flesh and skins of wild beasts." Moving on, the "philosophic observer" would encounter people "on our frontiers in the pastoral state, raising domestic animals to supply the defects of hunting," followed by "our own semibarbarous citizens, the pioneers of the advance of civilization," before finally reaching man's "as yet, most improved state in our seaport towns."[56]

Jefferson's time- and space-traveling philosopher would see what the visionary overlooked. The progress of civilization was irresistible and irreversible, the "natural" course of things, and Americans thrilled to be at its leading edge. But the philosophical Jefferson betrayed misgivings about the costs of progress. The displacement and removal of Indigenous peoples was the dark, destructive underside—and the now dominant image—of the supposedly benign history of expansion. Before the European onslaught, Jefferson believed, sociable "savages" lived peacefully in small groups, under the law of nature: They were "natural republicans." Free from the heavy hand of too much government and "too many laws" in their natural state, Native "associations" offered an idealized model for the wards or townships Jefferson advocated. The waves of white settlers Natives encountered were "semibarbarous," lawless and violent "pioneers" on civilization's bleeding edge, advancing into Indigenous territory.[57] Despite the "horrors" they committed, these settlers were "our" citizens and could therefore call on the federal government to protect them, "covering" their crimes and mobilizing federal forces on their behalf. Jefferson knew that Americans' claim to their country was in some sense originally defective. This was the knowledge he carried with him on an imaginative journey *eastward* to the nation's "infancy" and his own childhood, before Native Americans "vanished" in the wake of civilization's progress.

There was a tension between Jefferson's optimism about the future of republicanism in the West as envisioned in the imaginings of his eastward-looking philosopher and the reality on the ground in the region. Jefferson was aware of this tension, and it has run through the attempts of Americans across generations to make sense of the region and its history. In February 2018, President Donald J. Trump signed a bipartisan bill to change the name of the Jefferson National Expansion Memorial in St. Louis to Gateway Arch National Park. A new visitors' center opened on July 3, 2018, giving more attention to Indigenous displacement as well as the role of slavery in Missouri and less to a heroic narrative of western expansion. According to a report in the *Washington Post*, the renaming "honors historical events that are now understood as deeply problematic within the larger trajectory of American history, including the dispossession of Native American land, cultural genocide, the extension of slavery, centuries of conflict and ill will with Mexico, environmental degradation and the emergence of a myth of American exceptionalism."[58] The progressive development that Jefferson envisioned unfolding across time and space in the West was apparently giving way to—or at least making space for—a vision of degradation, genocide, and slavery. It is fitting that this reckoning took place in Missouri because it was in Missouri that Jefferson's vision of western progress and democratic federalism nearly collapsed in the crisis that unfolded there from 1819 to 1821.

Jefferson's great hopes for the American people were shadowed by fears that the republican experiment would fail. The broad distribution of authority in the federal republic would keep the peace in an expanding union of self-governing states, fostering the patriotic attachments of enterprising citizen-settlers to each other and their country. Secure in their own well-defined rights, Americans would combine forces in peaceful and productive pursuits—as they had in securing the new nation's independence. Yet this was necessarily a dynamic peace, constantly recalculated and recalibrated under ever-changing circumstances; it was not, as Jefferson's conception of generational sovereignty acknowledged, a permanent settlement, frozen in time. Americans sacralized the union—and sought to make it "more perfect"—precisely because it was so fragile and contingent. The union was always at risk, disunion and its attendant horrors always a pregnant possibility.[59]

The patriotic imperative to defend the country's integrity against internal as well as external threats depended on a willingness to compromise. Patriot-heroes of the postrevolutionary era therefore were compromisers, prepared to make great sacrifices for the greater good of securing the union.[60] But some sacrifices, Jefferson understood, were too great to make. In the Missouri controversy of 1819, *he* would not compromise on what he claimed was the constitutional principle of state equality. If the self-governing citizens of Missouri were not free to decide for themselves on the future of slavery in their new state—as they did decide, unequivocally, in favor of the "peculiar institution" in the constitution they drafted in their bid to Congress for membership in the union—then the union itself was fundamentally flawed and inevitably would suffer collapse. For a slim congressional majority to restrict slavery in Missouri against the declared will of the (white) people of that state was to impose "a geographical line of division" between slave states and free, North and South. This was "the most portentous crisis I have ever contemplated," Jefferson wrote James Monroe.[61] Far from a mere local issue, the unconstitutional assertion of authority by a sectional "party" in Congress affected the whole country. "A geographical line," Jefferson told a sympathetic congressman from the Maine District of Massachusetts, was totalizing: To divide the country in this way was to create two distinct peoples. Because the line—a national boundary—would coincide "with a marked principle, moral and political, once concieved and held up to the angry passions of men, [it]} will never be obliterated."[62]

Jefferson's conception of democratic federalism was turned on its head in his hyperbolic response to the "Missouri question." The new boundary he envisioned negated the permeable lines among and within states that promoted free movement and patriotic sentiments, fitting the American people to its country; it was incompatible with the "right of Expatriation" that supposedly justified American independence. Just three years earlier, Jefferson had taunted John Manners and "the whole body of English Jurists to produce the map on which Nature has traced, for each individual, the geographical line which she forbids him to cross in pursuit of happiness."[63] Jefferson was tracing just such a line in 1820. Rallying to the cause of his "native country," Virginia, and the other slave states, he revealed— even reveled in—the destructive potential of a truncated federalism: The only government that now mattered was Virginia's (despite its defective constitution); the ward republics remained figments of his imagination; and the federal government had been captured by an insidious, alien, partisan conspiracy. The "angry passions of men" now reigned supreme: As the public reason of patriots gave way to anarchy, demagoguery, and mob rule, democracy would die.

Jefferson was passionate and angry. Contemplating the union's destruction, the old man regretted that he would soon "die in the belief that the useless sacrifice of themselves, by the generation of '76. to acquire self government and happiness to their country, is to be thrown away by the unwise and unworthy passions of their sons, and that my only consolation is to be that I live not to weep over it." The conflict raging over what he dismissed as an "abstract principle"—the future of slavery in America's republican empire— was cast as "treason against the hopes of the world," for surely emancipation would come in due course if the union survived. "I can say with conscious truth that there is not a man on earth who would sacrifice more than I would, to relieve us from this heavy reproach, in any *practicable* way," Jefferson told John Holmes. "The cession of that kind of property, for so it is misnamed, is a bagatelle which would not cost me a second thought, if, in that way, a general emancipation and expatriation could be effected."[64]

Jefferson's selfserving logic is astonishing to us. To present himself as an opponent of slavery and exponent of emancipation ("in any *practicable* way") as the peculiar institution tightened its stran-glehold on the nation strains credulity beyond the breaking point. But as in his eastward account of civilization's progress, Jefferson's response to the Missouri question disclosed a darker narrative of the new nation's unfolding history. The aging Virginian defended his good faith and fealty to the federal republic's first principles in order to sustain his belief in the common sense and patriotic virtue of the American people. When he depicted the controversy as a *constitu-tional* crisis, he emphasized the fundamental distinction between the body of the people and their torn and tattered constitutions, "cloth-ing" that was no longer fit to wear. The revolutionary generation created a new nation—and a model for the peoples of the world—in a sustained moment of extraconstitutional turmoil, taking their bearings from the country they defended. Perhaps, as Americans found themselves on the brink of another war, "they would pause before they would perpetrate this act of suicide on themselves."[65] Of course, the war they would make on each other would be about slavery. They could secure lasting peace only by eliminating slav-ery, that chronic and demoralizing state of war between enslavers and enslaved.

Divisions among Americans could not be displaced, nor could they be resolved in the West. The West itself became the arena and object of sectional conflict, threatening to demolish the union: A sup-posedly boundless region—and America's future—was bounded by irreconcilable conflict over the future of slavery. Americans turned against each other as hostile sectional blocs sought to capture the union, thus bringing on its destruction.

Prayers

Jefferson never doubted that the American people would reunite in the aftermath of the constitutional crises that periodically tore them apart. In September 1819, before the Missouri controversy raised the specter of disunion, he reflected on his ascension to the presidency a generation earlier. The peaceful transfer of power vindicated "the true principles of the revolution of 1800," he told Virginia judge and polemicist Spencer Roane, "for that was as real a revolution in the principles of our government as that of 76. was in it's form." This second revolution was "not effected indeed by the sword, as that, but by the rational and peaceable instrument of reform, the suffrage of the people."[66] Though in the months that followed, Jefferson feared the sword would be unsheathed, he hoped his countrymen would come to their senses and come back together again.

Recognizing the costs of disunion, northerners would "think better" of their misguided effort to ban slavery in Missouri, Jefferson assured South Carolinian Charles Pinckney, "and return to the embraces of their natural and best friends."[67] The original union of the American people followed the collapse of constitutional government in the British Empire and antedated the Confederation and federal Constitution. Jefferson's sentimental language evoked a primal, extraconstitutional, nation-making scene at the beginning of American time—a scene that would be reenacted across the generations. Writing to Richard Rush, son of his fellow patriot Benjamin Rush and the American ambassador in Britain, Jefferson predicted that any separation would be "for a short term only" before the estranged partners were brought back together, "like quarelling lovers, to renewed embraces, and increased affection." Americans would renew their vows and keep the faith: "Were we to break to pieces, it would damp the hopes and the efforts of the good, and give triumph to those of the bad thro' the whole enslaved world." Jefferson should not need to remind his patriotic countrymen that they enjoyed an exalted rank as "members . . . of the universal society of mankind" and that it was therefore "our sacred duty to suppress passion among ourselves." Even in this heartfelt plea for peace, Jefferson could not resist another twist of the rhetorical knife: If the union failed, it was northern restrictionists—feigning solicitude for southern slaves when they sought to ban slavery in Missouri—who would bear the ultimate, awful responsibility for impeding the progress of freedom in "the whole enslaved world."[68]

Jefferson could not extricate himself from the attachments, interests, and prejudices of Virginia, his "native country," even as he embraced a more inclusive continental patriotism that supposedly transcended local (and sectional) differences and located Americans in the vanguard of the progress of civilization, in the West and around the world.[69] Yet he could not escape the knowledge that Americans—and particularly enslavers of the southern states, himself included—were at least implicated in, if not ultimately responsible for, slavery's enduring grip on "the land of the free." That he felt discomfort before the gaze of an increasingly skeptical world was apparent in his letter to Rush. What, after all, was so "sacred" about a union that rational, self-interested compromisers might perpetuate forever, without freeing a single enslaved victim of a radically unjust, constitutionally sanctioned institution?

God was on Jefferson's mind in his last years, and the aging patriot prayed. When James Heaton, a "native of Virginia" who had moved to the free state of Ohio, sought a public statement from him condemning slavery shortly before his death, Jefferson demurred.[70] Recalling the Missouri controversy, he asserted that "a good cause is often injured more by ill timed efforts of it's friends than by the arguments of it's enemies. Persuasion, perseverance, and patience are the best advocates on questions depending on the will of others." Nothing Jefferson could now say—"my sentiments have been 40. years before the public"—would make any difference. Nor did he now claim that the "people" would rise to the occasion in any foreseeable future: When the Missouri controversy subsided, they "embraced" each other—while pledging to remain silent and scrupulously avoid doing anything about slavery that might disturb the fragile intersectional peace. "The revolution in public opinion which this case requires, is not to be expected in a day, or perhaps in an age," he told Heaton, "but time, which outlives all things, will out-live this evil also." Would that wondrous moment arrive within or beyond the nation's time? Jefferson could not know. Yet if there was no public audience for his "stale and threadbare . . . sentiments, they will not die with me. But living or dying they will ever be in my most fervent prayers."[71]

Jefferson, the great Virginian and American patriot, imagined himself in another world, alone with God, knowing he had always been right, leaving his country and its people far behind.

In his penultimate letter, written from his deathbed on June 24, 1826, declining an invitation to join fellow patriots in Washington, DC, to celebrate the new nation's fiftieth birthday on July 4 (the day he and John Adams died), Jefferson struck a more optimistic, upbeat note. Rather than retreat into the privacy of prayer, "I should indeed, with peculiar delight, have met and exchanged there, congratulations per-sonally, with the small band, the remnant of that host of worthies, who joined with us, on that day, in the bold and doubtful election we were to make, for our country, between submission, or the sword."

In this last, hopeful moment, Jefferson donned his patriot garb, returning to earth and projecting a glorious future for the whole world:

> May it be to the world what I believe it will be, (to some parts sooner, to others later, but finally to all.) the Signal of arous-ing men to burst the chains, under which Monkish ignorance and superstition had persuaded them to bind themselves, and to assume the blessings & security of self government. The form which we have substituted restores the free right to the unbounded exercise of reason and freedom of opinion. All eyes are opened, or opening to the rights of man. The

general spread of the light of science has already laid open to
every view the palpable truth that the mass of mankind has
not been born, with saddles on their backs, nor a favored few
booted and spurred, ready to ride them legitimately, by the
grace of god. These are grounds of hope for others. For ourselves let the annual return of this day, for ever refresh our
recollections of these rights and an undiminished devotion
to them.[72]

This was the story Jefferson had in mind as he lay dying. He
would play his appropriate part as it unfolded—"finally to all"
mankind—by praying, in death as in life, for its consummation. Of
course, he knew that "a favored few booted and spurred" trampled
mercilessly on the enslaved masses in America, and he had no reason
to think that "the general spread of the light of science" would ever
bring them to their proper senses. Perhaps Jefferson told himself that
the liberation of the "enslaved world" and inexorable advance of freedom and enlightenment would rebound on its source in America,
that a "revolution in public opinion"—or some other, more violent
revolution—would redeem and rededicate the nation to its first principles before its moment had passed.

We cannot know what was on Jefferson's mind in his last days.
We might suggest, however, that it was enough for Jefferson to imaginatively return to July 4, 1776, before a half century of his country's history complicated and compromised the American people's
prospects. The seemingly limitless horizons of that great continental country framed the future for Jefferson's generation of patriots.
The Declaration of American Independence was then—and has ever
since been—a spur to action, mobilizing the people and serving as
a touchstone for subsequent generations and other nations. In all
these times and places the text of the Declaration has taken on different and distinctive meanings, reflecting the ongoing, never-ending
"course of human events."

Jefferson, the Declaration's jealous drafter, resented what he saw as Congress's heavy-handed editorial interventions. Yet he also understood that it was the American people, not he, who authorized independence and brought the Declaration's words to life, making them meaningful. If this was true in Jefferson's moment, it must be true today.

The Declaration of Independence resounded for Jefferson as he lay dying, louder than ever. What sort of "Signal" does the Declaration send out to us, and the world, so many generations on?

III

⬛░░░░░⬛

THE PEOPLE

or more than sixty years immigrants to the United States have participated in a naturalization ceremony held at Monticello. Each year, on the Fourth of July, new citizens stand on the West Lawn facing the house's portico (the "nickel view" of Jefferson's home) and recite an oath to the United States:

> I hereby declare, on oath, that I absolutely and entirely renounce and abjure all allegiance and fidelity to any foreign prince, potentate, state, or sovereignty, of whom or which I have heretofore been a subject or citizen; that I will support and defend the Constitution and laws of the United States of America against all enemies, foreign and domestic; that I will bear true faith and allegiance to the same; that I will bear arms on behalf of the United States when required by the law; that I will perform noncombatant service in the Armed Forces of the United States when required by the law; that I will perform work of national importance under civilian direction when required by the law; and that I take this

obligation freely, without any mental reservation or purpose of evasion; so help me God.[1]

The oath, with its rejection of monarchy and call to defend the American republic, echoes the Declaration of Independence.

The US citizenship oath, formally known as the Oath of Allegiance, evolved over the course of the twentieth century. Although new citizens have pledged to uphold the Constitution of the United States since 1790, there was no uniform oath until 1906. The requirements to bear arms on behalf of the country and for civilians to "perform work of national importance" were added in 1950 and 1952.[2] That self-governing citizens must be prepared to mobilize for war seemed imperative in the early years of the Cold War. Anxious Americans were duly reminded of the perilous circumstances of the nation's birth, when patriots struggled to vindicate their bid for independence on revolutionary battlefields.

We may now revere the Declaration of Independence for its eloquent statement of timeless, universally applicable political principles, but the first order of business for Thomas Jefferson and his congressional colleagues in 1776 was to sustain popular resistance to King George's invading armies. By transforming rebellious British subjects into self-governing American citizens, independence justified the immense sacrifices patriots would have to make—and had already made—as they rallied in defense of their liberties, homes, and homeland. In retrospect, the patriots' declaration marked the beginning of the American national narrative; in its own moment it constituted the legitimating culmination of the protracted process of popular political and military mobilization that transformed British Americans into a new people. The American Revolution is often described as a "people's war." It might also be said that Americans were the "war's people."

When the war began in April 1775, as we have shown, provincial British Americans thought in continental terms and recognized the need for transprovincial union. Their violent resistance to the king's unnatural and unconstitutional assault on their liberties represented a desperate, extreme, and ultimately doomed effort to negotiate with fellow Britons, to define the terms of a lasting peace *within* the empire. Before Congress's declaration—and the declarations simultaneously emerging from many other places across the continent—patriots defined themselves as British.[3] Making "thirteen clocks, Strike precisely" at the same moment was a daunting enough challenge, as John Adams acknowledged on the eve of independence. But many more clocks were also in play, as declarations resounded and resonated across far-flung locations.[4] We might call this process a feedback loop. Independence was the message, drawing its legitimacy from a people that became conscious of its collective identity through the process of wartime mobilization and the creation of extraconstitutional infrastructure—the ubiquitous ad hoc committees, conventions, and congresses—that coordinated resistance and exercised quasi-governmental authority across the continent. The medium *was* the message, and the "people" were *not* a "fiction" but rather a work in progress, a product of the Revolution itself.[5] The survival and success of this self-declared people depended then on the fortunes of war.

The war's outcome was far from certain in the summer of 1776. The Declaration of Independence defined what was at stake for patriots who embraced the idea that they shared a collective identity with their fellow Americans: Recognizing each other, *they* constituted the people. This new people longed for a peace that would secure the claims they made on behalf of future generations to a continental homeland. The Declaration's boldest, most controversial claim was that this new people knew precisely who they were—that common sense and "self-evident" principles justified their break with Britain and resort to arms, that they waged a "just" and legitimate defensive war against a despotic regime that threatened to enslave them, that their claim to independent nationhood should be recognized and supported by the "powers of the earth."[6]

As we will see, these lofty aspirations bespoke deep anxieties, for the national project was existentially threatened on multiple battlefronts and patriotic commitments were—like everything
else under the sun—subject to changing circumstances, conflicting
attachments, and self-interested calculations. The American "people" never spoke with a single voice and never shared the single
"mind" Jefferson imputed to them as he approached the end of his
life.[7] The simple truth that the very existence of the "people" was a
function of wartime mobilization and collective action confirms the
radically indeterminate bounds of nationhood. Americans—whoever they might be at any given moment—engaged their enemies
on multiple fronts: on revolutionary battlefields, on the high seas,
on distant frontiers, in their own neighborhoods, and in their own
homes. A revolutionary people at war was defined by its enemies.
The Declaration acknowledged this brutal fact, even as Americans
justified their belligerence by invoking universal principles: They
would hold their British cousins as they held "the rest of mankind,
Enemies in War, in Peace Friends."

A "state of war" existed wherever peace could not be guaranteed, which meant practically everywhere. When the new nation
and mother country finally negotiated the Treaty of Paris in 1783,
critical issues remained unresolved, threatening future conflict.
Indigenous peoples were profoundly affected by the treaty's provisions but did not participate in the peace talks, nor, needless to say,
could enslaved or formerly enslaved people claim a place at the negotiating table.[8] And it remained unclear to observers both at home and
abroad whether Americans could in fact govern themselves and preserve (much less perfect) a federal union that could guarantee collective security and prevent the states from making war on one another.
A shared vision of peace—at home, among the states, and with the
world—energized American patriots, reinforcing their solidarity and
promoting an exalted sense of their revolution's world-historical significance. But peace, like happiness, was an aspiration, an imagined

and elusive destination. Getting there depended on creating a new postimperial regime that could effectively harness the power of the people, enabling Americans to make and keep the peace.

It is fitting that new US citizens take their oaths in front of Monticello's West Portico. It is a space redolent with hope and optimism. The portico faces west, where Jefferson believed the future of the United States lay. The ceremony overtly links the modern citizenship oath with the nation's founding, pledging new Americans to defend their country. Opening with a reading from the Declaration of Independence, it evokes the moment when the first generation of US citizens gave voice to the timeless principles—the "American creed"—that justified their break with Britain and transformed them from subjects into citizens.[9] Looking forward, Jefferson imagined a "permanent revolution," an ongoing dynamic of rebirth and renewal, as this protean people took possession of its continental homeland "to the thousandth and thousandth generation."[10] For Americans the past would always be present. The principles that inspired Jefferson's generation would inspire its successors across time and space, as they fought their own wars and sought to make their own peace.

Declarations of War

"When in the Course of human events," patriotic Americans declared, "it becomes necessary for *one people* to dissolve the political bands which have connected them with another, and to assume among the powers of the earth, the separate and equal station to which the Laws of Nature and of Nature's God entitle them, a decent respect to the opinions of mankind requires that they should declare the causes which impel them to the separation."[11] The Declaration was itself an "event." As we have shown, independence was not inevitable. Had the king and his ministers pursued a different course of action there might have been nothing to declare. Britons in Britain and North America might continue to be a single people; independence would have been unimaginable, much less "necessary."

Law-minded Americans knew that the "laws of nature" did not sanction rebellion against legitimate, recognized authority. This was an unpardonable crime deserving death, the ultimate sanction. "Americans" could only plausibly claim to be a people if their acknowledged sovereign betrayed his American subjects, failing in his sacred responsibility to protect them.[12] Their Declaration can be read as an indictment of the king for his crimes against them, "a long train of abuses and usurpations" culminating in his declaration that they were rebels—outlaws, aliens, and enemies—and his decision to launch a war of conquest to strip them of their liberties and reduce them to slavery. One declaration begat another: The king's led immediately to the outbreak of hostilities; in belated response the Americans' declaration sought to persuade the "powers of the earth" that they were not rebels, that their demonstrated capacity to make war warranted recognition by potential allies. For that claim to be credible, revolutionary patriots had to convince skeptical observers, at home and abroad, that they could command the allegiance and marshal the manpower and resources of the "people." The people-in-arms constituted a legitimate, sovereign "power" that other powers must recognize. In other words, only by declaring independence were Americans finally able to declare war. They fought for a just peace with their former sovereign but would never again acknowledge his authority over them. Now "nature" and "Nature's God" enjoined national independence and eternal separation: A people's self-preservation was the first and fundamental law of nations.[13] Securing independence was now the whole point of the war, the patriotic people's "common cause."

The principles pronounced in the first paragraphs of the Declaration of Independence framed a redemptive vision of a peaceful future. In the catalog of grievances that followed, Jefferson invoked the language of family, describing the British as "unfeeling brethren" and lamenting their unnatural, fratricidal assaults on British American liberties. "We might have been a free & great people together," Jefferson acknowledged in a revealing passage excised by his congressional colleagues, "but a communication of grandeur & of freedom it seems is below their dignity. Be it so, since they will have it: the road to glory & happiness is open to us too; we will climb it in a separate state, and acquiesce in the necessity which pronounces our everlasting Adieu!"[14] Americans did not become a separate people for "light and transient" reasons. The new nation would follow its own "road to glory & happiness," gaining glory in war to secure happiness in peace. ("Happiness," in this case, was a collective enterprise, not a private "pursuit.")

When the Continental Congress voted in favor of independence on July 2, 1776, the colonies had been at war with Britain for almost fifteen months. British soldiers and rebellious Americans had slaughtered each other from Massachusetts to South Carolina, and the Royal Navy had burned American ports from Portland, Maine (then Massachusetts), to Norfolk, Virginia. Congress had raised a standing army and appointed George Washington as its commander the previous June. Washington and a combined force of Continental Army soldiers and patriot militia had successfully laid siege to Boston, driving its British occupiers from the city. In July 1776 a huge, thirty-thousand-man British expeditionary force under the command of General William Howe—the largest such force the British had sent overseas to that point—arrived in New York with orders to suppress the rebellion. The war between Britain and its estranged colonies would drag on for another seven long and bloody years.[15] The Declaration of Independence was adopted against this backdrop of existential struggle. Although according to the Declaration "all men are created equal," citizenship for the revolutionary generation was a choice, not a birthright. It would be earned by those who stepped forward, pledging "to each other our lives, our fortunes, & our sacred honor."[16]

The Declaration that Congress formally adopted on July 4 con-
tains a list of twenty-seven grievances against King George III. Most
concern the political and legal disputes arising from British tax policy
between 1765 and 1775; the final five relate to the ongoing war. The
twenty-third grievance responds directly to the king's October 1775
speech pronouncing his former subjects to be rebels: "He has abdicated Government here, by declaring us out of his Protection and
waging War against us."[17] Here lawyer Jefferson chose his words carefully: George III did not declare *war* against the Americans, for to do
so would be to recognize their legitimate status as a belligerent—or
independent—power under the law of nations. He instead outlawed
subjects who rejected his legitimate authority, casting them beyond
his protection into a stateless condition, dismembered from the body
politic. Mobilized in resistance, British American patriots insisted
that their personal identities—as Britons or Americans, subjects or
citizens—antedated King George's malediction. The royal despot
alienated himself from the people, standing alone in his infamy; "*he*,"
unmoored from the Constitution that made his authority legitimate,
"has plundered *our* seas, ravaged *our* coasts, burnt *our* towns &
destroyed the lives of *our people*."[18]

What the sovereign authorized in his infamous speech was in
many ways worse than war. British commanders exercised restraint,
hoping that the display—and limited deployment—of overwhelming force would lead timorous colonists to capitulate.[19] Yet the peace
that the British government sought to impose by force or threat of
arms was radically incompatible with peace within the empire on
terms that reconciliation-minded patriots, including future fire-
brands like Jefferson, had long advocated. Increasingly violent
reprisals to colonial resistance were counterproductive, not only
eliminating the possibility of peaceful negotiation but also fostering cross-class, transprovincial political and military mobilization
and transforming a would-be "patriot king" into a lawless despot.
Nothing could be more abhorrent and unnatural to patriotic British

American constitutionalists—and many "friends of America" in Britain agreed.[20] Driven to desperate extremes, patriots engaged the Crown's forces on land and at sea and sought support from Britain's (and their own) historic enemy, France. In declaring independence, on July 4, 1776, Americans proclaimed that they were not rebels but a new nation or people capable of making war against and with other nations.

Having established that George III was waging war (or something worse) against his American subjects, the Declaration then levels more specific charges relating to his prosecution of the war. "He is at this time transporting large armies of foreign mercenaries to compleat the works of death, desolation & tyranny, already begun with circumstances of cruelty & perfidy unworthy the head of a civilized nation," reads the twenty-fifth grievance, referring to the large number of German mercenaries in General Howe's expeditionary force. According to the twenty-sixth grievance, the king and his officers were coercing Americans captured at sea, "our fellow Citizens," to enlist in the Royal Navy, "to become the executioners of their friends and Brethren, or to fall themselves by their Hands." The Declaration then turned from the ocean to the West, accusing the king of encouraging "merciless savages" to descend on vulnerable frontier settlements.[21]

The Declaration of Independence offered Americans a compelling account of their recent history and a language to justify their bold assumption of sovereign authority—to the world and to themselves. A formally declared war accentuated existential anxieties about ubiquitous threats on multiple fronts, generating and exploiting a climate of fear. But the war Congress asked Americans to keep fighting was not a lawless and anarchic struggle of all against all. The idea that war could ever be conducted "lawfully" might seem confounding. Yet the discipline that fighting wars requires, the customary restraints on its destructive means, the protection it affords negotiators, and the peace warring powers seek to make are all predicated on the capacity or "power" of so-called "civilized" states. As a recognized "power of the earth," the new United States would not only be able to meet external threats—by violent means if necessary—but also to govern its own people and protect them from one another.

State capacity in the new, self-declared nation depended on the legitimacy of republican government as well as the willingness of its citizens to submit to laws of their own making, pay taxes, and fight its wars. This, of course, is precisely what new citizens pledge when they recite the Oath of Allegiance. Jefferson's Declaration celebrated and sought to sustain the ongoing process of popular political engagement that led to the break with Britain. American resistance to an unconstitutional, unresponsive, irresponsible, and therefore "foreign" British imperial state set the stage for constituting new governments and perfecting a postimperial union that would effectively contain and deploy the power of the people in war and in the peace patriots hoped victory would bring.[22]

The Declaration was not a rhetorical sleight of hand, with the people conjuring themselves into existence, as if words alone would do the trick. Jefferson and his congressional colleagues instead held up a mirror to Americans, "our people" and "our fellow citizens," and the extraordinary things they had already achieved. Patriots had successfully improvised the extraconstitutional equivalent of state institutions and were holding their own on revolutionary battle-fields. They endured the assaults of would-be British conquerors as a *people*, not as criminals or rebels; they demonstrated the capacity to make war, even when their initial enthusiasm crested in 1776 and prospects of an early peace faded.

Until they finally declared themselves an independent people, Americans continued to think of themselves as British. When they took up arms in defense of their country, they also sought to defend the constitutional rights of Britons on both sides of the Atlantic. "No taxation without representation" was a clarion call to property-owning and liberty-loving Britons everywhere, not just to British

Americans. Surely the British people would make common cause
with their American counterparts and mobilize against the incipi-
ent despotism of an imperial legislature and royal government that
exercised absolute, unlimited, unconstitutional power over the colonies? British Americans thus hoped for regime change in Britain
even as British imperial reformers sought radical regime change in
the American provinces.

Identifying with the British people and encouraged by the support of articulate "friends of America" in the metropolis, Jefferson
and his fellow patriots were bitterly disappointed by the failure of
the British people to rise to the occasion and mobilize in resistance
to their tyrannical government. Here was sad proof that Americans
were, in fact, a separate people. Many ordinary Britons were indiffer-
ent to the fate of the Americans, and many others patriotically supported the government: All were complicit in the abuse Americans
suffered at the king's hands. "They too," the final Declaration read,
"have been deaf to the voice of justice and of consanguinity. We must,
therefore, acquiesce in the necessity, which denounces our Separation,
and hold them, as we hold them the rest of mankind, Enemies in War,
in Peace Friends."[23] For better or worse, despite their original intentions, Americans were on their own. They now had to defend their
country as the homeland of a separate, independent people.

The Declaration of Independence enabled Americans to make
sense of the converging histories of their separate provinces, providing a new language to describe their collective experience: The continent was their "country," and their willingness to fight and die in its
defense made them a "people." That willingness was fatefully signified by their conscious and conspicuous consent, *public* acts that confirmed their enduring attachment to one another and brought a new
political community into existence. The "union" they thus forged
would secure the precious private and personal attachments they
had once associated with home and homeland in King George III's
formerly flourishing American provinces.[24]

Declaring independence meant distinguishing potential "Friends"—allies in the war in progress—from "Enemies." The process of mobilization had created political communities in the various provinces, and they affirmed an enduring alliance or "union" in the Declaration. Canada and other British American provinces, such as Bermuda and the Floridas, were invited to join (all declined), and individual subjects across the continent were encouraged (in some cases coerced) to affirm their allegiance to the new regime. Enslaved people were presumptive enemies as George III had already "excited domestic insurrections among us," according to the Declaration. Indigenous peoples, like the enslaved, might be enlisted as proxies in the counterrevolutionary cause—although some calculated advantage in aligning with the Americans. The king did not hesitate to exploit enmities in contested frontier regions as well as conflicts within the colonies themselves: "He has incited treasonable insurrections in our fellow-subjects, with the allurements of forfeiture & confiscation of our property," reads the Declaration.[25] Such people must be excluded from citizenship. Indeed, they were worse than slaves who took up arms for the Crown because, Jefferson acknowledged, the cause of the enslaved was just.

Yet these self-declared, self-governing new states could never achieve universal inclusivity. Consent was a high, exclusionary threshold: Citizens were required to abjure allegiance to their sovereign and take up arms against fellow subjects, including family members, however close their former attachment. Conflicting loyalties alienated family, friends, and neighbors from each other in a "state of (anything but civil) war." The paradox of volitional citizenship was that the universal principles the Americans invoked to justify separation from the mother country also separated provincial British Americans from each other.[26] Those principles authorized the peoples of the new states to draft constitutions that would codify and institutionalize exclusions, drawing boundaries around and sanctions against counterrevolutionary enemies.[27] Antiloyalist legislation thus

resembled slave codes in policing those boundaries, with the crucial difference that the vast majority of enslaved people were never
offered the opportunity to pledge allegiance to the new regime—
though a significant number would do so when military manpower
needs so dictated.[28]

The Declaration of Independence seemed to present a clear
choice, cutting through the fog of war, justifying sacrifices already
made and enabling combatants to envision a future beyond war. In
retrospect the document seems to have done its critically important work well, defining the people and providing subsequent generations with a birth certificate attesting to their legitimacy. But
"retrospect" was a distant prospect in July 1776, and the fog only
deepened as the war dragged on inconclusively, year after year, until
Britain's ignominious surrender at Yorktown on October 19, 1781—
and diplomats from the two countries signed a peace treaty at Paris
on September 3, 1783.

Facing new, ever-changing threats, imagined and real, in war and
in peace, a protean people redefined the boundaries of nationhood.

Friends and Enemies

Familial metaphors proliferated during the revolutionary era:
George III was a wayward father-protector, a "patriot king" who
betrayed the people's trust; patriots defended their liberties as
brothers-in-arms; and Britain was the mother country that the colonies' first settlers left far behind, long ago. Jefferson eagerly embraced
the generational idea, exalting sibling solidarity and justifying the
natural separation of children from parents as they made homes of
their own in a new country.

Yet family connections also exerted a strong pull across time
and space. The first families of Virginia constituted a kind of provincial cousinage with enduring ties to their metropolitan counterparts (cousins at some more or less distant remove). These ties were

reinforced by trade and travel and commemorated in genealogies and coats-of-arms.[29] Before the British-American world fell apart, these transatlantic connections accentuated the social distance between proud provincial gentry—that is, prosperous, slaveholding plant- ers like Jefferson—and their humble neighbors. The imperial crisis shattered family harmony, metaphorically and literally. The familial metaphors that patriots deployed were now mobilized in support of the "common cause," breaking up many actual families and turning cousin against cousin. The "people" who emerged in the crisis forged blood ties on battlefields and through the sacrifices they made in defense of their country. Family members who withheld their con- sent were disowned as enemies of the people. They were in a sense the true rebels.

Jefferson had a genius for marking the boundaries that defined the American people. His conception of the people evolved over the course of the imperial crisis and the war that followed. As he mobi- lized support for the patriot cause and sought to preempt and neutral- ize threats from actual or potential enemies, he defined and redefined who the American people were. For Jefferson the nation-making pro- cess began at home, in Virginia, before he drafted the Declaration of Independence, a compendious—but by no means definitive—catalog of the inclusions and exclusions that defined the limits of American nationhood.

The emerging national boundary was a profoundly personal matter for Jefferson. In late August 1775, he arranged to pay his friend and distant cousin John Randolph £13. Several years before, Jefferson and Randolph had entered into an informal agreement that should Randolph outlive Jefferson, he would receive £100 worth of books from Jefferson's library, and if Jefferson outlived Randolph, he would receive his kinsman's violin and £60 worth of books from Randolph's library.[30] What had begun as a jest between two compan- ions became more serious after the Revolutionary War commenced. As summer gave way to autumn in 1775 and the conflict spread across the colonies, Randolph, who remained loyal to the Crown, prepared to go into voluntary exile. He sold his treasured violin to his old friend, the patriot who would in a few months draft the Declaration that severed the colonies from Britain. Jefferson regretted that his friend did not feel he could remain in Virginia but hoped that Randolph and other British American exiles would press for reconciliation between Britain and the colonies. His "first wish is a restoration of our just rights," he told Randolph.[31]

John Randolph wrote a poignant response to Jefferson as he prepared to leave Virginia: "Tho we *may politically* differ in Sentiments, yet I see no Reason why *privately* we may not cherish the same Esteem for each other which formerly I believe Subsisted between us. Should any Coolness happen between us, I'll take Care not to be the first mover of it. We both of us seem to be steering opposite Courses; the success of either lies in the Womb of Time. But whether it falls to my share or not, be assured that I wish you all Health and Happiness."[32] John Randolph went into exile in 1775 and died in 1784, his wish for reconciliation unfulfilled.

Jefferson and Randolph wished each other well but recognized that their friendship would be suspended for the duration of the conflict. Although no less a native Virginian than Jefferson, Randolph alienated himself from his countrymen by continuing to pledge his allegiance to the sovereign of another country. If Jefferson was not yet ready to declare the fateful rupture on a continental scale, on behalf of the *American* people, he and Randolph understood that his cousin could no longer be considered a *Virginian*. At this critical moment patriotic Virginians—defenders of their country—constituted a distinct people. On both sides there was still hope that the distinction might yet dissolve, with the restoration of rights that Jefferson and the Continental Congress prayed for preempting a declaration of independence. The two cousins had already negotiated the terms of their own separation, anticipating the resumption of friendship when peace was finally restored. It soon proved a forlorn wish. At the end of August, when Jefferson and Randolph were corresponding, George III rejected Congress's Olive Branch Petition calling on him to stop the war. In October the king declared the colonies in rebellion, and the conflict spread. Within a matter of weeks British and loyalist troops began raiding the coast of Virginia. Jefferson and his fellow Virginians had not declared independence in November 1775, but they were already performing it on revolution-ary battlefields, in council chambers, and in their homes.

Randolph's voluntary exile contributed to the cause by reinforc-ing the identification of the *people* with their *country*.[33] Jefferson's cousin had many fellow travelers: Approximately sixty thousand loyalists had joined Randolph in exile by the end of the War of Independence.[34] By fleeing to Britain or other loyal colonies through-out the empire, these exiles sought a civil separation and a way to avoid the bitterness of armed conflict. They looked forward to recon-ciliation with estranged kin and former neighbors and hoped for the restoration of their property rights when the war ended.

Randolph and his ilk were ideal "enemies," neatly separated and easily reincorporated in the new republics, "Friends in peace." But for every loyalist who left, there were many of dubious loyalty who stayed behind: Some enlisted in the king's armies, others welcomed British occupation, and many opportunistic "sunshine patriots" were up for grabs as they calculated their chances under one regime or the other.[35] Given the volatility of loyalties in the changing cir-cumstances of the war, it was (and is) often frustratingly difficult to identify these "enemies of the people" and therefore to calculate their numbers. More or less secret loyalists who could easily pass as patriots were in many ways the most elusive, most dangerous ene-mies. British strategy proceeded from exaggerated estimates of their ubiquity and availability (not necessarily the same thing) for counter-revolutionary mobilization. For patriotic Americans, securing the wartime boundary with their loyalist neighbors was thus the key determinant of the Revolution's ultimate success.[36] Disorder on the home front would unleash an anarchic "state of nature" that would incapacitate the American states on the battlefront as they struggled for international recognition.

The War of Independence was a civil war that became a war between nation-states when rebellious Americans declared themselves independent and sought international recognition. The status of a nation depended on the formal recognition of other powers but was predicated on a people's demonstrated capacity to make war, the ultimate test of state capacity. Actions spoke louder than words, however eloquently expressed. The existence of a Continental Congress that could plausibly speak to the "world" on behalf of the people while managing the daunting logistics of a continental war effort constituted a powerful argument for American independence. Yet without the Continental Army there would have been no war to manage. And what Commander in Chief George Washington's army proved—rarely by winning battles, more often by simply surviving to fight more battles—was that a (sometimes barely) sufficient number of liberty-loving Americans were prepared to submit to a modern army's hierarchical structure and absolute disciplinary authority. The intent of the Declaration of Independence was to demonstrate its animating principles—the principles that inspired patriots to overthrow a despotic, unpatriotic king—were compatible with, perhaps even essential to, establishing a functional, recognizable, "treaty-worthy" state that other states could deal with.[37]

Jefferson did not "invent" the American people when he drafted the Declaration. His crucial contribution was instead to articulate a new relationship between the people-in-arms and their government. Not only were ordinary citizens the source of legitimate authority— as the term *popular sovereignty* suggests—but they also constituted the foundation of the revolutionary government's power. The definition of the people itself was transformed, collapsing the hierarchical distinctions of the old regime, according to which the "better sort" were categorically different from and superior to common folk.

The "citizenship revolution" was an inclusive leveling-up, a reimag-
ining of social order on a horizontal rather than vertical plane, animated by the consensual attachments of civic equals.[38] In this bold
reformulation the people were no longer seen as unreasonable and
unruly, a mindless and disorderly crowd that had to be governed.
Popular mobilization in the patriot cause thus was the antithesis of
the mob action that anxious elites customarily found so frightening.
Jefferson's iconic recitation of the "self-evident," common-sense principles patriots shared was a heartfelt tribute to the enlightened state
of the "American mind." For Jefferson popular patriotism was moral
sense in action, the "spirit of 1776" that was manifest in the ongoing
process of military mobilization.[39]

The relative inclusivity of Jefferson's conception of the people was affirmed by the patriot's free choice to embrace the cause.
Citizenship was demanding, for self-sacrificing patriots-in-arms had
to willingly submit to superior authority in order to empower their
government to win the war and secure the long-deferred fruits of
a republican peace—for future generations if not for themselves.
Consent therefore also constituted an exclusionary boundary, distinguishing "friends" from "enemies" on yet another revolutionary
battlefront: Loyal British subjects like John Randolph scrupulously refused the offer, while many others calculated the odds
or changed their minds.[40] For patriots the ultimate rewards were
incalculable, and none was greater than the sense of civic equality,
social solidarity, and collective power in what Jefferson later called
"the strongest government on earth."[41] In the new republican dis-
pensation rulers and ruled, governors and governed, would not be
consigned to separate stations. The mobility of citizens—and their
capacity to mobilize against domestic as well as foreign threats
in response to perceived existential threats—would preserve the
new republic.

For Jefferson the internalized discipline of civic belonging transformed the mass of ordinary people from being seen as a threat to

social order—the object *of* government—into the ultimate source of governmental power in the new republican regime. The self-governing citizen thus supplanted the subject of despotic power. As citizen-soldiers demonstrated their patriotism on revolutionary battlefields, Jefferson cast a critical eye on the ambitious designs of their quondam commanders. "Where should we have been now," Jefferson asked Maria Cosway in October 1786, "if our country, when pressed with wrongs at the point of the bayonet, had been governed by it's heads instead of it's hearts?" The answer was clear to the Declaration's draftsman, for if Congress had failed to follow the people's lead in July 1776, rebellious colonists would all have hung "on a gallows as high as Haman's."[42]

Jefferson's democratic conception of the people emerged from the leveling imperatives of wartime mobilization. Ascending to a new level of civic equality and empowered by the republican constitutions they authorized, vigilant citizens subjected their leaders—*public servants*—to constant surveillance, assuring the faithful discharge of their public responsibilities. Jefferson did not assume that ordinary folk were immune to temptation, and he was aware that they could easily be misled. But the choices they made to support the Revolution and their identification with fellow patriots as a self-governing people guaranteed that their "hearts" would remain in the right place, even when they were temporarily misled by misinformation or dire circumstances.

Popular Patriotism

A patriot, for Jefferson, was not a singular character. Patriotism was a shared sentiment, presupposing a country and a people dedicated to its defense. The vindication of individual rights depended on the people's solidarity. That connection was clear to revolutionary Americans when they mobilized against what they saw as an overreaching British imperial state. But subsequent generations of rights-conscious Americans have missed that fundamental point and therefore misread Jefferson.

The confusion is understandable. The Declaration's "self-evident" principles rehearse the familiar narrative of social contract theory, beginning with individuals in a state of nature who—in the "original contract"—freely agree to become a people. But that state of nature was a conjectural account of what might (or should) have happened long ago, in an imagined moment of founding, not the real-time experience of a revolutionary people at war. Writing and ratifying constitutions can be seen as the ritual reenactment of imaginary original contracts, securing the legitimacy of the new republican regime—and offering lawgiving "founders" a claim to everlasting fame and authority. Jefferson certainly thought that a self-governing republican people should be properly constituted, and that the Commonwealth of Virginia was radically defective in this regard. Individual Virginians—and Americans generally—had long since departed the theorists' state of nature: Their identity as a people was a well-established fact on the ground. If they objected, they could follow John Randolph into exile or, as enemies of the people, face the brutal consequences. The consenting individual, endowed with the full panoply of natural rights, theoretically came before the people. In the state of war that revolutionary Americans experienced, the people came first. Self-preservation, the first law of nature and *nations*, applied to them collectively in their *national* capacity: If their republics failed, former citizens could claim no rights at all, natural or otherwise.

Jefferson had no illusions about the importance of government. A "stateless" people was a contradiction: No nation could exist without the capacity to engage with other powers as a state on equal terms. Societies were organized in one of three ways, Jefferson told James Madison in January 1787: "1. Without government, as among our Indians. 2. Under governments wherein the will of every one has a just influence, as is the case in England in a slight degree, and in our states in a great one. 3. Under governments of force: as is the case in all other monarchies and in most of the other republics." For a modern nation with a growing population, the first option was clearly impracticable, however attractive in theory. In Indigenous communities, custom, kinship, and neighborly attachments might take the place of governments—though Jefferson certainly knew that Native peoples were often at war, with each other as well as European settlers. His second option, the British American option, wherein the "mass of mankind . . . enjoys a precious degree of liberty and happiness," was obviously superior to government by force, as American victims of the "oppressions of monarchy" could testify.[43]

The distinctions Jefferson drew among forms of government described ideal types, not the complicated world he experienced. Not "every one" within the new American republics was included in the civic community and could exercise their "just influence" over their government—a clear if vastly understated, from our perspective, acknowledgment of slavery's injustice and the unjust expropriation of Indigenous homelands. Still, the inclusion of the "mass" of Americans in the citizen body was the ultimate source of the republican regime's power. "Influence" was customarily seen as a top-down phenomenon, with factious leaders corrupting credulous common folk, but the "*just* influence" of ordinary citizens worked in the other direction, serving to check the self-seeking ambitions of the so-called better sort. The American people were incorruptible in the aggregate. Americans might occasionally be led astray, as they were during Shays's Rebellion in western Massachusetts in late 1786 and early 1787 when they challenged legitimate authority and public order. That rebellion tested and confirmed Jefferson's faith in the people. Yet "even this evil is productive of good," Jefferson told Madison. "It prevents the degeneracy of government, and nourishes a general attention to the public affairs. I hold it that a little rebellion now and then is a good thing, and as necessary in the political world as storms in the physical."[44]

The remedy for Shays's Rebellion and other political storms was responsive constitutional government that could command the people's allegiance and channel its power. While Madison and other observers saw portents of anarchy in western Massachusetts, Jefferson reaffirmed his faith in the people. American governments should not repeat the British Empire's tragically misguided policy of making war against supposedly unruly subjects. Overwhelming force was not the answer. Jefferson endorsed Madison's campaign for a federal Constitution because the *absence* of a properly constituted government for the Confederation engendered conflicts among the states and jeopardized their collective security. He could not, however, contemplate establishing a strong central government that would silence and suppress—and thus immobilize—a patriotic, liberty-loving people. Because power flowed upward, *from* the people, republican statesmen should strive to strengthen the people's attachment to their government.

Jefferson was convinced that the counterrevolutionary machinations of ambitious elites, not popular unrest, constituted the leading threat to the survival of the new American republics. In his emerging conception of constitutional politics, a critical mass of vigilant citizens policed the boundary between the patriotic people (or "sheep") and the dangerous minority of pseudo-republican leaders ("wolves").[45] Jefferson thus subverted the traditional hierarchical assumption that all men were created unequal and that the "lower sort" were savage predators, driven by their base appetites. If, as Jefferson declared on behalf of his fellow Americans, all men were in fact created equal, it was the artificial and unnatural privileges enjoyed by the wellborn and well situated that enabled *them* to prey on hapless sheep. Equality depended on governing the wolves; sheep were egalitarians by nature.

When Jefferson defended the Shaysites, he did not celebrate or condone their disorderly conduct. Taken out of context, his extravagant language suggested otherwise. "The tree of liberty must be refreshed from time to time with the blood of patriots and tyrants," he told William Stephens Smith, John Adams's son-in-law. "It is it's natural manure." The point of Jefferson's letter was to counter reports in the British press that the United States had become ungovernable. Compared to monarchical Britain, where popular uprisings and violent reprisals were everyday occurrences, the American states were remarkably peaceful. Jefferson did the math: "We have had 13. states independant 11. years. There has been one rebellion. That comes to one rebellion in a century and a half for each state. What country before ever existed a century and half without a rebellion?" And that rebellion proved to be "little," belying Smith's anxious forebodings, with limited casualties. "What signify a few lives lost in a century or two?" Jefferson wondered.

Jefferson's data demonstrated that the American republics enjoyed a decisive "peace dividend" in comparison with their European counterparts. The few lives lost also stood in stark juxtaposition to the American Revolution, a very big, regime-changing "rebellion" when the blood of patriots flowed freely and the "tree of liberty" first took root. The same "spirit of resistance" that secured American independence was on conspicuous display in Shays's "little rebellion." The tree of liberty—a powerful symbol of a patriotic people's deep-rooted attachment to their country—stood stronger than ever when the storm passed. "The remedy" for this "natural" disturbance, Jefferson concluded, was to "set" the Shaysites "right as to facts" and then to "pardon and pacify them."[46]

Much has been made of Jefferson's sanguine attitude toward popular disorder. Modern antigovernment terrorists invoke Jefferson's words: When the Oklahoma City bomber, Timothy McVeigh, was arrested in 1995, he was wearing a t-shirt emblazoned with a quotation from Jefferson's "tree of liberty" letter. Not long thereafter the Irish diplomat and scholar Conor Cruise O'Brien vilified Jefferson, portraying him as a supremely irresponsible advocate of extreme libertarian violence.[47] Yet for all his many faults Jefferson was no anarchist or libertarian. "Where does this anarchy exist?" he asked Smith. The term did not even properly apply to western Massachusetts, where citizens marched, courts were closed, and taxes could not be collected. This was nothing like the supposed original "state of nature"—or what Americans had experienced in the war with Britain, the closest modern equivalent. "Can history produce an instance of a rebellion so honourably conducted?" He would "say nothing of it's motives," for "they were founded in igno- rance, not wickedness." Shays's followers were misguided patriots, but their patriotism was a precious national resource. "God forbid we should ever be 20. years without such a rebellion," Jefferson exclaimed, anticipating the generational sovereignty theme of his "earth belongs to the living" letter to Madison two years after Shays.[48] The constitutional challenge was to sustain a dynamic, "liv- ing" connection between a patriotic people and their government, reenacting the Revolution—and manuring the tree of liberty with- out any loss of life.

Jefferson did fear that credulous, well-meaning citizens might be misled by unethical leaders. Demagogues might mobilize the people in service of unjust, antirepublican ends. As he wrote of the Alien and Sedition Acts in 1799, the American people "have been the dupes of artful maneuvres, & made for a moment to be willing instruments in forging chains for themselves."[49] Almost two decades later, during his retirement, Jefferson reflected on how popular opinion in New England had been mobilized during his presidency in opposition to his embargo policy, which had adversely affected that region. "I felt the foundations of the government shaken under my feet by the New England townships," he wrote. "There was not an individual in their states whose body was not thrown, with all it's momentum, into action, and altho' the whole of the other states were known to be in favor of the measure, yet the organisation of this little selfish minority enabled it to overrule the Union." Nonetheless, Jefferson marveled at the strength of popular opposition in New England, contrasting it with the relative weakness of support for the embargo in the South and West where he feared only "the drunken Loungers at and about the Court houses" might be mobilized.[50] The danger was twofold: The people might be mobilized for the wrong cause, or they might not turn up at all when needed in defense of liberty. Both possibilities threatened republican government.

Jefferson was aware that unscrupulous leaders might manipulate the people and popular disorder could threaten liberty, but he believed that these risks were preferable to the danger posed by monarchical government. He retained his faith in the people. Although he complained that New Englanders had stymied his embargo policy while he was president, he wrote with admiration about their faith in themselves. "I do believe that if the Almighty has not decreed that Man shall never be free, (and it is blasphemy to believe it) that the secret will be found to be in the making himself the depository of the powers respecting himself, so far as he is competent to them."[51]

Partisans

Jefferson's suspicions about the good faith and patriotism of people of his own "sort," or class, precipitated his turn to the people. If his celebration of virtuous farmers anticipates the romantic nationalist apotheosis of the "Volk," he did not idealize a backward-looking, earth-bound peasantry. Yes, God might consider "those who labour in the earth" his "chosen people," "*if* ever he had" one—if God ever operated in this invidious fashion.[52] In any event the enslaved laborers Jefferson owned were surely, if unjustly, not part of the people Jefferson had in mind, nor were his market-oriented farmers likely to stay put if better land or better markets beckoned. His revolution was not an "agrarian" revolution, either in the classical, redistributional sense or in the Shaysite sense of angry farmers seeking tax relief. The American people forged a new, collective identity in the war, not in the mythic mists of time immemorial; they knew themselves by the values they shared and by their determination to defend their country.

The aggregation of individual choices made resistance to British tyranny and the revolutionary vindication of their country's independence legitimate both to self-declared Americans and ultimately to a "candid" world. As we have seen, there were counterrevolutionary enemies of the people on multiple battlefronts—and they were often difficult, sometimes impossible, to identify before the battle began. Hypervigilant patriots were always on the lookout for signs or symptoms of disloyalty to the cause. Wartime mobilization was an ongoing screening process, forcing consent from reluctant patriots and exposing internal enemies. It was hardly surprising that political mobilization should deploy the same tools. If, as the master strategist General Carl von Clausewitz later observed, "*War is only a continuation of State policy by other means*," the reverse was also the case in postrevolutionary America: Party politics was a continuation of war "by other means."[53] This was particularly true in an era of geopolitical upheaval and endemic warfare in the Atlantic world. Peace was elusive, even for great powers with the capacity to enforce it, much more so for the imperfect union of American republics.

Jefferson's critics—in his own time and ever since—have been puzzled by his leadership of the (Jeffersonian) Republicans, the new nation's first great political party. Agreeing with fellow patriots that partisan divisions jeopardized national security, Jefferson assumed the apparently anomalous if not outright hypocritical role of antipartisan partisan. But the confusion is ours, not Jefferson's. Factions within the government—corrupt coalitions of self-dealing insiders—were clearly illegitimate, most conspicuously in the case of "Federalists" who supposedly had captured the Washington and Adams administrations. When Jefferson and his allies mobilized support out of doors, among the people, they were simply following the script of revolutionary patriots. The people's party was no party at all; it was not a self-interested faction, seeking to advance its interests at the expense of the whole. Quite to the contrary, Jefferson saw the protracted political mobilization of the 1790s that culminated in his ascent to the presidency as a peaceful reenactment of the nation-making war for independence. In the aftermath of adoption of the Alien and Sedition Acts (1798)—laws passed by Federalists in Congress to limit free speech and curb the rights of immigrants in the United States—Jefferson proclaimed that "the spirit of 1776. is not dead. It has only been slumbering." Rising up in resistance to Federalist tyranny, "the body of the American people" showed that it "is substantially republican."[54]

The people spoke decisively when they chose Jefferson to be their president in 1800, affirming their collective identity and expressing their sovereign will. In his inaugural address in 1801, Jefferson sought to assuage Federalist anxieties. After all, the vast majority of Federalists were "honest patriots," bound to their fellow Americans by attachment to "federal and republican principles"—that is, "to union and representative government." When Jefferson identified himself as a "federalist," he defined the term differently than his centralizing opponents, who disingenuously called themselves Federalists even as they sought to destroy the states and thus demolish the union. "If there be any among us who would wish to dissolve this Union, or to change its republican form," he magnanimously concluded, "let them stand undisturbed as monuments of the safety with which error of opinion may be tolerated." There would be no violent purge because none was necessary. Exposed to the light of a new day, erroneous opinions would fade away; their discredited exponents would stand muted, like "monuments," "undisturbed" in their deathlike repose, reminding the people of the horrible fate they had so barely escaped.

Jefferson's dire account of devastating costs of endless war in Europe set the stage for the eloquent and inspiring image of the new nation's glorious future he offered his countrymen in his inaugural address. "During the throes and convulsions of the ancient [not

merely old]] world," he began, "during the agonising spasms of infuriated man, seeking through blood and slaughter his long lost liberty,
it was not wonderful that the agitation of the billows should reach
even this distant and peaceful shore."[55] Jefferson thus acknowledged
that war in Europe *had* drawn "peaceful" America into its destructive vortex. At a time when embryonic political parties could not
yet claim legitimacy, Americans stigmatized their opponents as
"partizans" of either Britain or France—and therefore as enemies
of America—in the epochal European struggle.[56] Defenders of the
administration accused Jeffersonian demagogues of subverting social
and political order, unleashing the anarchic and destructive power
of unruly mobs. In response Republicans assumed the exalted role
of the people's tribunes, vindicating their virtuous character by
mobilizing them—as patriotic Americans had been mobilized in the
Revolution—in defense of their precious liberties.

The resulting war of words was certainly hyperbolic, hysterical,
and ideological, but it was also uncannily reminiscent of the run-up
to the war that had so recently consumed so many American lives.[57]
Yet again the specter of civil war reared its ugly head. Jefferson's
genius in his inaugural address was to shine a bright light on the
future, imploring Americans to forget the recent past and "unite with
one heart and one mind" and so "restore to social intercourse that
harmony and affection without which liberty, and even life itself,
are but dreary things." As he looked westward, into the future, he
depicted the country and its peaceful, patriotic people as innocent
victims of a foreign threat, a contagion or conflagration "billowing"
from abroad.[58]

Skeptics then and now might track the progress of popular political mobilization and revolutionary regime change in the
other direction, with the American Revolution setting the example for France, its "sister republic." Certainly, Jefferson himself
imagined such a transit of liberty, from west to east, in the French
Revolution's early years, and he continued to cherish hopes for the

liberation of benighted peoples around the world until his death.[59] But in 1801 it was critically important to think in exceptionalist terms: to distinguish the new nation from the rest of the world.[60] When Jefferson then conjured up a vision of peace in America, he exaggerated the spatial and temporal distance between the republican New World and its "ancient" European counterpart. So he also looked beyond the differences among Americans that nearly shattered the union and any plausible conception they might have had of their collective, national identity. The antipartisan party leader told his countrymen that parties did not—and could not—really exist in America. Teetering on the brink of war, a patriotic people had finally come to its senses with his ascension to the presidency: The "reign of witches," as he had described Federalist excesses, was over.[61]

Jefferson could not recognize the legitimacy of political parties because he could not distinguish his party from the nation itself. During the increasingly bitter political conflicts of the 1790s, Republicans righteously insisted on their legitimate opposition—as true representatives of the people—to corrupt and factious Federalist administrations. Federalists might mislead credulous "partisans," but they could never mobilize the "people" as a whole. They insisted on quiet submission to their authority between (infrequent) elections, thus demobilizing the people and denying them their revolutionary heritage. As Federalists sought to consolidate and perpetuate their power by distinguishing governors from governed, Republicans raised the alarm: A factious, self-interested, pro-British minority was determined to reverse the Revolution's outcome. Anti-Federalists had "smelled a rat" during the campaign for ratification of the proposed federal Constitution in 1787–1788, and the stench was unmistakable to Jefferson in 1792 when he served as secretary of state in the first Washington administration. "The ultimate object" of Treasury Secretary Alexander Hamilton's corrupt machinations, Jefferson told the president, was "to prepare the way for a change,

from the present republican form of government, to that of a monarchy, of which the English constitution is to be the model."[62]

In their protracted campaign to rouse and mobilize the people,
Jefferson and his allies sought to unmask Federalist administration
supporters, revealing their unnatural attachment to Britain and their
more or less secret hostility to republican government. Federalists
were "anglomen," "monarchists," "tories," "aristocrats," and "monocrats" (Jefferson's coinage)—all enemies of the people.[63] In retrospect the epithets seem ridiculously inflated, particularly when
they implicated the sainted Washington himself. Yet in the context
of geopolitical instability, international conflict, and revolutionary
regime change, the prospect of war was always on the near horizon.
Vulnerable on multiple fronts, the people needed to assess threats,
distinguish friends and foes at home and abroad, and prepare for coming conflicts. The already compelling need to draw lines and define
boundaries was exacerbated by ambiguous loyalties and unpredictably changing circumstances. It was hard to see clearly in such a
foggy state of almost-war. Just as vigilant patriots, fearing the worst,
mobilized politically before the Revolution, so too would Jefferson
and his allies mobilize during the dark days of the Federalist ascendancy. They could not know if the darkness would pass, nor could
they know whether the Federalists would peacefully relinquish
power in the wake of the Republicans' narrow victory at the polls
in the presidential election of 1800. Whatever happened, Republican
patriots were prepared to fight in another, second "revolution" in
defense of their liberties. The "sacred fire" still burned.

The peace Jefferson proclaimed in his inaugural address did
not result from a treaty or compromise between Federalists and
Republicans. Federalists instead capitulated to the new regime, pru-
dently enacting the peaceful submission they had once preached to
unruly Republicans. Federalist nonresistance afforded Jefferson the
opportunity to redefine the bounds of American nationhood in more
generous and inclusive terms, reassuring Federalists that the rights

of minorities would be sacredly upheld now that the Republican majority finally held sway. The very fact that his opponents relinquished control of the federal government and did not mount armed resistance to the new administration demonstrated their fealty to "federal and republican" principles. (Some high-flying Federalists might have preferred a reversion to monarchy, but this was, by 1801, clearly a hopelessly lost cause.) Performance trumped long-festering suspicions. Where conspiracy-minded Jeffersonians had once sought sinister meanings and evil intentions in everything the "monocrats" said or did, they celebrated the advent of peace and the end of partisan rancor. When he drafted the Declaration, Jefferson had conjured up a unifying "American mind." Now, in his inaugural address, he humbly implored Americans—as their "servant"—to "unite with one heart and one mind."

Jefferson's inaugural address was an invitation to partisan opponents to capitulate—an amnesty to imagined enemies. Yet exalted expectations were shadowed by irrepressible anxieties. Although the "people" had once again risen to the occasion, mobilizing against the Federalists' counterrevolutionary, neomonarchical plot against America, Jefferson feared that his followers' patriotic fervor would give way to complacency and so lead them to let down their guard. Peace was the great desideratum, but it was also dangerous. Demobilization set the stage for new divisions—for schisms within the party and delusions of "free security" in a war-prone world. Changing circumstances at home and abroad could give moribund "monocrats" a new lease on life. For Jefferson, counterrevolutionary Britain remained an existential threat, made worse by the revival of commercial, cultural, and kinship connections to the former metropolis. The return of many loyalist exiles to their former American homes after the 1783 Peace of Paris previewed the imagined reintegration of Federalist "Anglomen" in the Jeffersonian Peace of 1801. In both cases, national boundaries blurred. If peace made former enemies "Friends," another war might reveal their evanescent loyalties. This was the problem with defining what it meant to be an "American," for the individual identities of a dynamic people—originally determined by their willingness to fight for the new nation's independence—were fluid and contingent. How different, after all, were these Americans from their British cousins or from their British American predecessors?

In his inaugural address a public-facing President Jefferson projected a peaceful and inclusive mobilization of enterprising citizens across the continent, blending streams of settlement from Europe as well as the eastern and southern states. But in private correspondence over the course of his presidency and beyond, he betrayed persistent misgivings about the new nation's relations with its imperial and Indigenous neighbors and foreign trading partners. For Jefferson, Britain loomed large as the ultimate existential threat to American independence—except during the Louisiana crisis of 1802–1803, when Napoleon's territorial ambitions in the West threatened to dismember the union.

In a remarkable letter to Philadelphia newspaper editor William Duane in March 1811, two years after his retirement, Jefferson anxiously surveyed "the situation of our country" and urged fractious Republicans in Pennsylvania to make peace with one another. "During the bellum omnium in omnia of Europe," the former president counseled, the country's safety and survival required

> the union of all it's friends to resist it's enemies within & without. If we schismatise on either men or measures, if we do not act in phalanx, as when we rescued it from the satellites of monarchism, I will not say our party, the term is false and degrading, but our nation will be undone. For the republicans are the nation. Their opponents are but a <u>faction,</u> weak in numbers, but powerful & profuse in the command of money, & backed by a <u>nation,</u> powerful also & profuse, in the use of the same means.[64]

Republicans were not a "party": They were the nation. Their Federalist opponents, still dominant but on the defensive in New England, were a mere "faction," drawing strength from a hostile foreign "nation"—Britain, of course—still determined to reverse the Revolution's outcome. When the cold war turned hot in 1812, it came as no surprise to Jefferson that Federalist leaders in New England plotted to destroy the union and forge an alliance with the former mother country. Yet even in New England, he could take comfort in the growing number of Republican patriots who mobilized in defense of their continental country.

"Merciless Indian Savages"

The War of 1812 clarified loyalties in the Federalist heartland. Until they were forced to choose, New Englanders' ultimate commitments were ambiguous: Republicans had gained enough local support before the war to be competitive at the polls—and sometimes to win.[65] New Englanders had taken the lead in the Revolution and might come to their patriotic senses yet again. In the meantime it behooved Jeffersonians to avoid alienating potential allies as they sought to isolate and neutralize Federalist counterrevolutionaries. The opposite was true for Indigenous peoples and enslaved Blacks. In the wake of chronic warfare on the settlement frontier and given the long, brutal history of racial slavery—an institutionalized state of war—the enmity of these peoples was perfectly legible to revolutionaries. In practice there were exceptions to the racial rule: Some Indigenous nations, including some Oneidas and Stockbridge-Mohicans, had good reasons to ally with the patriots; the slave-owning American commander, George Washington, was eventually convinced to enlist some free Blacks in the Continental Army. But Jefferson eschewed nuance in the Declaration of Independence. In the midst of war it was natural to exaggerate threats on all fronts, to exploit the fears and prejudices of potential patriots—even at the risk of alienating potential friends across the color line. Mobilization was a numbers game. Building support within the mass of the Euro-American populace meant excluding and stigmatizing peoples of color.

For the modern reader one of the most striking, and disturbing, passages in the Declaration of Independence is Jefferson's reference to Native peoples. Among the crimes that he laid at George III's feet, Jefferson charged him with bringing "on the inhabitants of our frontiers, the merciless Indian Savages, whose known rule of warfare, is an undistinguished destruction of all ages, sexes and conditions."[66] What Jefferson had given with one hand, in proclaiming that "all men are created equal," he took away with the other: Native Americans—the continent's original, Indigenous proprietors—were excluded from the Declaration's assertion of universal equality; they were clearly not among those whose opinions deserved "decent respect." Although Jefferson's stereotypical characterization of Native peoples now seems unforgivably offensive, the context of its deployment is critical. The Declaration's purpose was to mobilize would-be citizens for war: Patriotic Americans needed to distinguish friends from foes.

Thomas Jefferson did not always strike such strident notes. In 1812 he wrote of Native Americans, "a people with whom, in a very early part of my life, I was very familiar, and acquired impressions of attachments & commiseration for them which have never been obliterated." Born in 1743 at Shadwell on the Rivanna River in Virginia—on land expropriated from the Monacan people that his father, Peter, a land surveyor, had acquired in 1735—Jefferson had become familiar with Native diplomats traveling to Williamsburg, the provincial capital. Among these visitors were delegations led by Outasettè, "the warrior and orator of the Cherokees," who, Jefferson wrote, "was always the guest of my father, on his journeys to and from Williamsburg." In 1762, when the Cherokee leader traveled to the colonial capital en route to London, Jefferson, then a student at William and Mary, heard Outasettè speak. "I was in his camp when he made his great farewell oration to his people, the evening before his departure for England. . . . His sounding voice, distinct articula-tion, animated action, and the solemn silence of his people at their several fires, filled me with awe & veneration, altho' I did not under-stand a word he uttered."[67]

Jefferson greatly admired Indigenous oratory. Two decades after he witnessed Outasettè's Williamsburg address, he observed that Native leadership was based on "eloquence in the council, bravery and address in war." He included an example of Native oratory in his *Notes on Virginia*. "Logan's Lament," he claimed, equaled the rhetorical efforts of Demosthenes and Cicero. The "Lament" was an impromptu speech by the Cayuga leader Tachnehdorus, known to British Americans as John Logan Shickellamy, who had allied with British American settlers during the Seven Years' War but whose family was murdered by Virginia militia in 1774. In the wake of this slaughter Logan explained why he took up arms against his former allies in a widely circulated talk that Jefferson included in his *Notes*.[68]

Jefferson's conception of Indigenous Americans was informed by the thinking of Scottish Enlightenment writers, who argued that soci-eties progressed through successive stages of civilization culminat-ing in the advanced commercial societies of western Europe—most notably (and unsurprisingly) Britain. The "stadial theory" shaped Jefferson's conjectures about the history of Native societies in North America. According to this grand schema, Euro-Americans encoun-tered Indigenous peoples in North America at a primitive stage of political and economic development similar to that of Europeans north of the Alps at the time of the Roman Empire. While not inher-ently inferior, Native Americans supposedly lagged far behind the European American settlers who displaced them (though the dif-ferences were not conspicuous to most contemporary observers). Given enough time and a change of environment, Jefferson believed, Natives could achieve the same level of civilization as colonizing set-tlers.[69] "We shall probably find they are formed in mind as well as in body, on the same module with the Homo sapiens Europæus," Jefferson wrote in *Notes on Virginia*. Late in life he assured a visitor to Monticello that Native Americans were "quite on a level, as respects intellectual character with the Whites."[70]

How do we reconcile Jefferson's professed sympathy for Native Americans and belief in their natural or potential equality with Europeans with his description of them as "merciless Indian savages"? As we have seen, the Declaration of Independence was radically reductive, mixing exalted principles with wartime propaganda in order to mobilize American colonists to sever their ties with Britain and wage war for their independence. The Revolutionary War confronted Indigenous Americans with an array of difficult choices: They could choose between the British or the American rebels, seek to play one side against the other, or remain neutral. While most Native nations would have preferred neutrality, the revolutionaries and their counterrevolutionary enemies sought to draw them into the conflict. Compelled to choose, many more nations opted to fight for the British, concluding that a rebel victory posed the greatest threat to their land and autonomy.[71] Fearing Indigenous–British alliances, Jefferson encouraged white American settlers to join the rebel cause, thus driving many unaligned Natives into the arms of the British.[72]

Jefferson followed the bellicose language in the Declaration with action during the Revolutionary War when he served as Virginia's governor from 1779 until 1781. In that capacity he was responsible for defending the state and its citizens, including the Kentucky District where settlers were engaged in bitter war with Native peoples and the British in the Ohio River Valley. On January 1, 1780, Jefferson wrote George Rogers Clark, commander of Virginia's forces in the transmontane West, asking him to choose between besieging the British at Detroit or attacking the Native peoples on the far side of the Ohio River who threatened Virginia settlers in Kentucky. "Against these Indians the end proposed should be their

extermination, or their removal beyond the lakes or Illinois river,"
Jefferson alleged. "The same world will scarcely do for them and
us."[73] The Declaration's rhetoric inspired Native American–hating
patriots to kill many innocent Native people during the war—and
long after it had ended. Jefferson understood this would happen and,
indeed, as governor of Virginia actively encouraged it.

Jefferson's genocidal language reflected Americans' vulnera-
bility in a vast western hinterland where they were incapable of
exercising jurisdiction.[74] In the absence of law, might made right.
No power could keep the peace, and all combatants were "merciless" in their savagery—including American settlers, as Jefferson
well knew. Revolutionary leaders did not hesitate to recruit "white
savages," and they also forged wartime alliances with their Native
counterparts whenever possible, thus blurring the clear racial
boundary Jefferson mapped in the Declaration. When he wrote
to Clark, he referred to "*these* Indians," that is, the Shawnees,
Mingoes, Munsees, and Wyandots north of the Ohio River who
were at war with Virginia settlers in Kentucky.[75] Jefferson thought
of Indigenous people who opposed American independence in similar terms to those loyalists who supported British rule, as enemies
who must be defeated.

What of those Native Americans who did not fight with the
British? President Jefferson outlined his policy for Native Americans
in 1803. "Our system is to live in perpetual peace with the Indians,"
he wrote, "to cultivate an affectionate attachment from them, by
every thing just & liberal which we can do for them within the
bounds of reason, and by giving them effectual protection against
wrongs from our own people." The oft-repeated offer of "perpetual
peace" was doubly misleading, for American negotiators assumed
that successive treaties would push territorial boundaries progressively deeper into "Indian country." The federal government lacked
the coercive capacity to protect Natives from encroachments by
their white neighbors, whatever they promised. Peace would only

be perpetual when Native peoples removed themselves—or were forcibly removed—from harm's way.

Recognizing that violent and lawless western settlers unjustly threatened Native peoples, Jefferson urged them to cede their lands, find new homes beyond the settlement frontier, and adopt white ways, thus progressing to the advanced stage of agricultural and commercial development supposedly modeled by civilized white settlers. Native people thus faced a stark choice: "They will in time either incorporate with us as citizens of the US or be removed beyond the Missisipi." Jefferson held out the possibility that Native people could become republican citizens but acknowledged that the obstacles—including the "savage," uncivilized whites who preceded civilized settlers into contested frontier regions—were daunting. He knew he was effectively asking Indigenous peoples to transform themselves into "Americans" by submitting to American jurisdiction and rule of law. When they were incorporated into a foreign body politic, they would sacrifice their tribal identities. This was the precise opposite of corporate self-preservation, the first law of nature and nations that Americans invoked in their own struggle for independence.

Jefferson was adamant that Indigenous people could only become citizens of the United States if they gave up their land and culture. "We presume that our strength & their weakness is now so highly visible that they must see we have only to shut our hand and crush them," he wrote, "& that all of liberalities to them proceed from motives of pure humanity only. Should any tribe be fool-hardy enough to take up the hatchet at any time, the seizing of the whole country of that tribe & driving them across the Missisipi, as the only condition of peace, would be an example to the others, and a further-ance of our final consolidation." Native Americans could not hope to emerge from the long war against a superior civilization—and its overwhelming firepower. Voluntary submission to the terms of trea-ties that expedited their movement through time and space "is cer-tainly the termination of their history most happy for themselves."[76]

Native people, Jefferson believed, must choose between assimila-tion or removal. They could not remain on their lands adjacent to, or within, the United States and negotiate diplomatic agreements to maintain peace between themselves and the new American repub-lic. For Jefferson, who tended to view political and moral choices in binary terms, such an outcome was impossible for two reasons. First, his vision of political economy was premised on the idea that most US citizens would live as independent farmers who owned their own land. Given the burgeoning population of the new republic, Americans' access to land would come at the expense of Native peo-ples.[77] Furthermore, Jefferson assumed, Indigenous nations did not have the capacity to establish effective jurisdiction that could keep the peace and protect property rights. They were, as Jefferson had told Madison in 1787, peoples "without government." They could not negotiate and enforce binding—or "perpetual"—agreements with other peoples, the defining attributes of modern, civilized "powers of the earth." Faced with the prospect of anarchy in the West, Jefferson thus concluded, Native people must either assimilate or move beyond the pale of civilization.[78]

Jefferson's totalizing, genocidal rhetoric testified to the threat that Native polities—however primitive and undeveloped he imag-ined them to be—presented to the collective security of a vulnerable federal union in an era of chronic warfare and geopolitical instability among imperial powers. Assessing threats on all fronts, he not sur-prisingly concluded that Indigenous *peoples* who opposed American independence or refused to assimilate into British American culture must be defeated, even driven off the continent. Yet he also held out the possibility that naturally gifted Indigenous *people* who—as individuals—did assimilate and accept the principles and practices on which the republic was founded could become citizens. This was consistent with his view that acceptance in the new American republic was contingent on political allegiance and a willingness to take up arms on behalf of the nation. Although Native people would

pay a higher price than other citizens, they could become a constitu-
ent part of the American people.

This was not a choice that Jefferson thought should be offered to
enslaved people who had been emancipated. If Natives were invited
to partake in the "gifts" of "civilization," to *demobilize* and give up
their corporate identity, enslaved people could not give up a corporate identity forged through generations of enslavement. Held in
check by slavery, freed people would mobilize against their former
enslavers and slaughter them. The only "peace" Jefferson could imagine between these two warring peoples, white and Black, would
result from the colonization and expatriation of freed people in a
country of their own, at some remote and distant location, with no
common boundary.

"A Distant People"

Over the entire course of his life Thomas Jefferson lived with and
depended on enslaved Black people. His earliest memory was of being
carried on a pillow by an enslaved servant on horseback.[79] As he lay
dying at Monticello on July 4, 1826, Jefferson asked another slave,
Burwell Colbert, to adjust his pillow: It was his final utterance.[80]

The brutal facts speak for themselves. Jefferson owned at least
607 enslaved men, women, and children in his lifetime. Most labored
in his fields; some served in the plantation house; and Sally Hemings,
an enslaved woman, bore five of his children, the unrecognized products of a protracted sexual relationship. Living on close terms with
the enslaver and his family, these people were hardly strangers or
"savages": As far as we know, none of them ever threatened him
(whatever thoughts they may have harbored). Yet despite his familiar, intimate, or biological relationships with many enslaved members
of his plantation household, Jefferson could not consider them collectively as part of his own family—or of the American people. They

belonged instead to a distinct and necessarily hostile nation or race, defined by their enslaved status and the color of their skin. Held in chains, they were by definition Jefferson's enemies, for slavery itself was an institutionalized state of war.[81]

Jefferson was not the only enslaver who recognized slavery's injustice while rallying to the patriot cause. But it was Jefferson who proclaimed that "all men are created equal," thus refuting the institution's fundamental premise—and provoking skeptical readers of the Declaration of Independence in his time and ours to wonder how he could justify his continuing ownership of so many of his fellow human beings. Jefferson insisted that his antislavery convictions never wavered, even as opposition to a general emancipation among his fellow planters intensified with the passing years.

Jefferson condemned slavery before he wrote the Declaration of Independence. As a young man newly elected to the House of Burgesses, he supported a bill to allow for the manumission of slaves in Virginia, as he recalled in a fragmentary autobiography drafted a few years before his death.[82] In his 1774 *Summary View of the Rights of British America*, he proclaimed that "the abolition of domestic slavery is the great object of desire of those colonies, where it was unhappily introduced in their infant state." Abolishing slavery immediately might not be possible, but the Chesapeake colonies had already signaled their eagerness to limit the supply of newly enslaved people by regulating the Atlantic slave trade. Anticipating his indictment of George III in the Declaration, Jefferson blamed the king for vetoing provincial legislation setting high, potentially prohibitory duties on slave imports.[83]

When Jefferson drafted *A Summary View*, he did not intend it for publication. The same cannot be said of the Declaration of Independence. Among the charges he leveled against the king in his original draft, the longest and most fully developed concerned the Atlantic slave trade. According to Jefferson, George III

has waged cruel war against human nature itself, violating
it's most sacred rights of life & liberty in the persons of a
distant people who never offended him, captivating & carrying them into slavery in another hemisphere, or to incur
miserable death in their transportation thither. This piratical warfare, the opprobrium of infidel powers, is the warfare
of the CHRISTIAN king of Great Britain. Determined to
keep open a market where MEN should be bought & sold, he
has prostituted his negative for suppressing every legislative
attempt to prohibit or to restrain this execrable commerce:
and that this assemblage of horrors might want no fact of
distinguished die, he is now exciting those very people to rise
in arms among us, and to purchase that liberty of which he
has deprived them, & murdering the people upon whom he
also obtruded them; thus paying off former crimes committed against the liberties of one people, with crimes which he
urges them to commit against the lives of another.[84]

In its collective wisdom Congress deleted this tendentious passage. Until the end of his life Jefferson insisted that Congress's dele-
tion of his slave-trade clause fatally compromised the integrity of the
Declaration it finally adopted.

Contemporary critics instead find the clause acutely embarrass-
ing: How could Jefferson possibly blame the king for imposing slavery
on innocent American slaveholders, including Jefferson himself? The
Declaration's author could not—and never did—deny his implication
in a radically unjust institution. As he drafted the nation-making
document, Jefferson instead identified the cause of revolutionary
Americans, facing the prospect of their own imminent enslavement,
with that of oppressed and enslaved peoples everywhere.

Jefferson recognized that Africans ensnared in the slave trade
could justly claim the same natural rights and liberties that American
patriots claimed for themselves. Natural rights were universal, the

rightful legacy of all humanity. Becoming conscious of themselves as a people and declaring their independence, Jefferson and his fellow Americans became conscious of the presence of another, *alien* people in their country, unjustly held in captivity, "a distant people" torn from their homeland. Identifying with enslaved Blacks as a captive nation, Jefferson recognized that their struggle for freedom would necessarily take the form of war against their owners, aided and abetted—as it in fact was—by King George's counterrevolutionary forces. This, Jefferson was convinced, was the king's greatest crime against America.[85]

Jefferson envisioned a comprehensive peace settlement that would ultimately lead to the emancipation of enslaved people. When he left Congress in 1776 and returned to Virginia, he proposed a plan for the gradual emancipation and removal of the commonwealth's enslaved population. Although his failed proposal left no trace in the legislative record, Jefferson later elaborated on its provisions in his *Notes on the State of Virginia*: All those enslaved before the act's adoption would remain in bondage, but their children would become free; after receiving appropriate training, these children would be required to leave the state. At different times Jefferson suggested sending former slaves to Africa, the trans-Mississippi West, or the Caribbean. Virginia would gradually become freer *and* whiter as enslaved people (and their descendants) were deported from the state, to be replaced by free, white, European migrants.[86] Removed to a safely distant location, freed people and their former enslavers would no longer struggle for control of the land whites owned and Blacks worked. Enemies could become friends.

Jefferson posed the obvious question: "Why not retain and incorporate the Blacks into the state, and thus save the expence of supplying, by importation of white settlers, the vacancies they will leave?" In answer he asserted that it would be impossible for whites and free Blacks to live alongside each other because of "physical and moral" differences between them and the memories that formerly enslaved people would have of the injustices and abuse visited upon them by their former enslavers. Racial differences marked a "natural" boundary that enlightened students of natural philosophy should acknowledge. If Jefferson had a "suspicion only, that the blacks, whether originally a distinct race, or made distinct by time and circumstances, are inferior to the whites in the endowments of both body and mind," he did not doubt that the *distinction* between Blacks and whites—a racial boundary inscribed in nature—was real.[87]

While Jefferson knew slavery was an unjust institution and believed it should be abolished, he could not conceive of a post-emancipation society in which Blacks and whites could live together in harmony. Emancipation without expatriation would lead to the extermination of the weaker race—presumably formerly enslaved Blacks—in a genocidal race war. In his passage excoriating George III for the slave trade, he acknowledged the rights and liberties of Africans while describing them as "a distant people." They were not part of Jefferson's conception of the American people. Unlike Native Americans, whom he could conceive as citizens, he did not believe there ever could be a place for the formerly enslaved in the new republic. In his imagined war against the unjustly enslaved, he could not envision a lasting peace. Slavery afflicted the enslaved with a common identity, as members of a captive nation, that they could never escape. Their continuing presence was a stark reminder to white Virginians of their implication in a fundamentally unjust institution that compromised *their* character.

Citizenship, in Jefferson's view, was predicated on the willingness of citizens to mobilize in defense of the republic. Slavery was a form of war—a battlefront—that endangered America's experiment with republican government. In the deleted slave-trade clause of the Declaration of Independence, Jefferson described George III's complicity in the slave trade as "cruel war against human nature itself." When he imagined what would become of his beloved commonwealth if enslaved people gained their freedom but remained in place, he conjured up horrific images of death and destruction. "Deep rooted prejudices entertained by the whites," he wrote, "ten thousand recollections by the blacks, of the injuries they have sustained; new provocations; the real distinctions which nature has made; and many other circumstances will divide us into parties, and produce convulsions which will probably never end but in the extermination of one or the other race." This descent into a savage and brutal state of nature—the war of all against all—would jeopardize everything patriotic Americans fought for and hoped to achieve in their Revolution. Saving the republic thus took precedence for Jefferson over the moral questions raised by slavery. Yet it was nonetheless true that Americans must in due course rectify slavery's radical injustice or face disastrous consequences. "Indeed," he concluded, "I tremble for my country when I reflect that God is just: that his justice cannot sleep forever."[88]

In November 1824 the Marquis de Lafayette, who was then touring the United States, visited Jefferson at Monticello for twelve days. Israel Gillette, a young enslaved man, remembered driving the two old revolutionaries around the plantation. One day Lafayette raised the subject of slavery with Jefferson. According to Gillette, "Lafayette remarked that he thought that the slaves ought to be free; that no man could rightfully hold ownership in his brother man; that he gave his best services to and spent his money in behalf of the Americans freely because he felt that they were fighting for a great and noble principle—the freedom of mankind; that instead of all being free a portion were held in bondage, (which seemed to grieve his noble heart); that it would be unusually beneficial to masters and slaves if the latter were educated, and so on." The enslaved coachman also recorded his master's response: "Mr. Jefferson replied that he thought the time would come when the slaves would be free, but did not indicate when or in what manner they would get their freedom. He seemed to think that the time had not then arrived."[89]

We can dismiss Jefferson's conversation with Lafayette as

rhetorical posturing. When confronted by criticism over slavery, especially from Europeans, Jefferson would declare that the time for abolition had not yet arrived, as he did to Lafayette in 1824. What is interesting about this exchange is how we know about it. Almost fifty years after the conversation, Israel Gillette recalled the exchange between Lafayette and Jefferson in a newspaper interview in 1873: "The conversation turned upon the condition of the colored people—the slaves. Lafayette spoke English indifferently; sometimes I could scarcely understand him. But on this occasion my ears were eagerly taking in every sound that proceeded from the venerable patriot's mouth." Gillette appreciated the significance of the conversation for himself and for all of the enslaved people at Monticello and beyond. "This conversation was very gratifying to me," he recalled, "and I treasured it up in my heart."

After he had purchased his freedom, Israel Gillette adopted the surname "Jefferson" at the suggestion of the county clerk who issued his freedom papers, observing "that it should be Jefferson, because I was born at Monticello and had been a good and faithful servant to Thomas Jefferson. Besides, he said, it would give me more dignity to be called after so eminent a man. So I consented to adopt the surname Jefferson, and have been known by it ever since." Israel Gillette, enslaved by Thomas Jefferson, acknowledged his connection to Jefferson and Monticello despite Jefferson's failure to secure the freedom and well-being of his "people." As he demonstrated during that carriage ride with Jefferson and Lafayette, he understood the importance of their antislavery views, however limited they might be. In this Gillette was, as the historian Hannah Spahn has shown, like many Black thinkers in nineteenth-century America who embraced and expanded on Jefferson's conception of freedom and equality and made the principles of the Declaration of Independence truly universal. They fulfilled Jefferson's faith in the ability of future generations to build on his legacy, even if his pessimistic assessment of their abilities was constrained by his own prejudice.[90]

"Remember the Ladies"

On January 22, 1801, after a deadlock in the Electoral College between Jefferson and Aaron Burr signaled the end of John Adams's presidency, Vice President Jefferson had dinner with President Adams and his wife, Abigail, as well as numerous members of Congress. The outgoing, Federalist-dominated House of Representatives would soon have to choose between Jefferson and Burr. It took thirty-six ballots before Jefferson prevailed over his fellow Republican on February 17.

But on January 22, Jefferson was seated next to Abigail Adams, his longtime friend. Once very close, Jefferson and the wife of his presidential rival were now coolly cordial at best. Abigail believed that Jefferson and his followers had traduced her husband and betrayed their friendship, particularly in the run-up to the 1800 election. She and Jefferson had what she described to her son, Thomas Boylston Adams, as a "curious conversation" about politics. When Abigail Adams asked Jefferson if he ever went to watch debates in the House of Representatives, he replied, "I cannot. I am sure there are persons there [who] would take a pleasure in saying something, purposely to affront me." Adams said she avoided the House for the same reason, lamenting, "Party spirit is much alike on both sides." But when Jefferson tried to turn the conversation to the ongoing election controversy, the president's wife demurred: "That is a subject which I do not chuse to converse upon." She instead related an apposite anecdote about a clergyman who, addressing "some difficulty amongst his people," chose "these words—'and they knew not what to do'" as his text. "'When a people were in such a Situation, that they do not know what to do,'" the clergymen concluded, "'they should take great care that they do not do—they know not what.'" Jefferson "laught out," Adams told her son, "and here ended the conversation."[91]

With the fate of his candidacy hanging in the balance, Jefferson sought to exploit his friendship with Adams for political advantage. Perhaps she could influence her Federalist friends to support him instead of Burr? If so, he failed to recognize that Adams did not share his comforting—and convenient—conception of the gendered distinction between private and public spheres. She may not have been qualified to vote, but as her husband's staunchest supporter and a fierce partisan, Adams had always taken a deep personal interest in politics. Though Jefferson might imagine that the friendship he had forged with the Adamses in France could survive the bitterly vituperative partisan polemics of the 1790s, Abigail Adams could not.

Jefferson embraced the patriarchal role of protector, defending dependent household members against the dangers of a conflict-ridden, male-dominated world at war. His idealized conception of home—the "domestic sphere"—was a refuge from the "torments" of politics, a microcosm of "society," the intimate and affectionate web of connections among families that made them a "people."[92] The early death of Jefferson's wife, Martha, in 1782 and his many protracted absences from Monticello thereafter undoubtedly reinforced his tendency to draw lines between his private and public worlds and make binary distinctions. For Abigail Adams, however, Jefferson's "gender frontier" was a contested borderland, as a now famous exchange with husband John in the weeks leading up to American independence in 1776 makes clear.[93]

While John was making history at the Continental Congress in Philadelphia, Abigail Adams remained at their home in Braintree, Massachusetts, tending to their children and managing their farm— that is, assuming the responsibilities of household head. The British had only recently evacuated Boston, a few miles away, after a siege by patriot forces unleashed disease in the neighborhood. With the movement toward independence in train, Abigail might well challenge John and his congressional colleagues to broach the broader social and legal implications of regime change. "I long to hear that you have declared an independancy," she wrote, "and by the way in the new Code of Laws which I suppose it will be necessary for you to make I desire you would Remember the Ladies, and be more generous and favourable to them than your ancestors." At the very least, she could question the common law doctrine of coverture, vesting the property wives brought to their marriages in their husbands' names. She did not hesitate to deploy the arguments of male patriots against them, enjoining John not to "put such unlimited power into the hands of the Husbands. Remember all Men would be tyrants if they could. If perticuliar care and attention is not paid to the Laidies we are determined to foment a Rebelion, and will not hold ourselves bound by any Laws in which we have no voice, or Representation."[94]

Abigail Adams did not intend to hijack the Revolution and mobilize the "ladies" against the tyrannical men who presumed to govern them. Congressman Adams responded in kind, railing against the "Despotism of the Peticoat" that Abigail playfully threatened. Yet John clearly got the message. The patriot cause could only succeed if women as well as men mobilized against the counterrevolutionary threat. The sacrifices women made to sustain the war effort and protect their homes and homeland—often, as in Abigail's case, in the absence of putatively protective males—were vitally, even decisively important.[95] Jefferson surely recognized women's contributions to the war effort as well, but nonetheless considered the transgression of customary gender roles as aberrational and unnatural, testifying eloquently to their loving, self-sacrificing devotion to their families at a time of existential crisis—not as evidence of their civic capacity or, worse yet, an unseemly ambition to participate in the sordid business of a man's world.

"Nature" was a key word for Jefferson. In making a highly conjectural case for republican government to James Madison, he compared Indigenous peoples (of too little law) to subjects of despotic monarchical polities in Europe (too much law) and citizens of the new American republics (just the right amount of law). In Notes on the State of Virginia, he assessed gender roles in similar fashion, again concluding that American republicans struck the proper balance. Among Native peoples, he claimed, "The women are submitted to unjust drudgery. This is I believe the case with every barbarous people." Here was the brutal state of nature, Thomas Hobbes's infamous war of all against all, and a leading justification for the progress of civilization. With the Americans' "barbarous neighbors," he asserted, "force is law. It is civilization alone which replaces women in the enjoyment of their natural equality."[96] Women could not *return* to nature to gain "equality" but must instead embrace a civilized legal regime that secured their natural roles within the household as wives and mothers. Civilizing Indigenous peoples meant protecting their women and disarming their men, making them all dependent on their civilized American neighbors.

Native peoples could only be protected if they were first pacified and then subjected to the rule of law. In the context of a nation-making revolution and subsequent conflicts in vulnerable frontier regions, this was the enlightened *casus belli* for supposedly defensive wars against "merciless savages." Jefferson could not imagine that his normatively "natural" gender boundary would ever be the site of conflict, much less the kind of war or "rebellion" Abigail Adams teasingly evoked. Would homemakers by nature ever make war against their own homes, presumably in alliance or under the pernicious influence of their husbands' avowed (or secret) enemies? The very idea threatened a fundamental premise of Jefferson's republican faith. George III had withdrawn *his* protection from his American subjects, leaving them to protect their own families and the republic they established, the all-inclusive, generational family of families.

History taught revolutionary Americans that societies characterized by moral and political degeneracy could not long survive as republics. For a republic to endure, Jefferson believed, its citizens must be virtuous, and women, as wives and mothers, should inculcate private and public virtue in their children while ensuring that their husbands were morally sound. There was no space for women to participate in politics or public life without compromising their disinterested patriotic commitments.[97] As Jefferson wrote to Anne Willing Bingham, another elite American woman, from Paris in 1787, "The society of your husband, the fond cares for the children, the arrangements of the house, the improvements of the grounds, fill every moment with a healthy and . . . useful activity. Every exertion is encouraging, because to present amusement, it joins the promise of some future good."[98] By sacrificing themselves and modeling virtue, republican wives earned the protection and inspired the patriotism of the citizen-soldiers who would sacrifice all in their defense. This was the virtuous circle that would redeem and renew the republic, an antidote to the classical progress of corruption, degradation, and despotism in ancient and modern worlds alike.

A year later, on the eve of the French Revolution, Jefferson again wrote to Bingham. He described the situation in Paris: "All the world is run politically mad. Men, women, children talk nothing else; and you know that naturally they talk much, loud and warm. Society is spoilt by it." Women's political engagement outside of the home was pathological, undermining everything valuable, lovable, and worth defending in society. Noting that Bingham herself had been politicized, Jefferson assured her that the mass of American women were in good health in their happy homes. "You too have had your political fever. But our good ladies, I trust, have been too wise to wrinkle their foreheads with politics. They are contented to soothe and calm the minds of their husbands returning ruffled from political debate. They have the good sense to value domestic happiness above all other, and the art to cultivate it beyond all others." While elite women might discuss politics with elite men like Jefferson, their most important role, and the role of free women generally, was to promote domestic happiness. "There is no part of the earth where so much of this is enjoyed as in America," Jefferson concluded.[99]

For Jefferson, women and men had different, complementary roles to play in society. Men should participate in politics and, when called to do so, take up arms to defend the republic. Men were expected to serve the public and protect society. The civic-political domain was thus gendered male. Women, by contrast, were civilizers and social arbiters. They held sway in the home, setting the moral tone and sustaining the social attachments that bound families together. Women should maintain households and educate their children, inculcating republican values. This would require what Jefferson described as "a solid education, which might enable them, when [they] become mothers to educate their own daughters, and even direct the course for sons, should their fathers be lost, or incapable, or inattentive." Most importantly, women should train their daughters in what Jefferson termed "household economy." "We all know its value," he wrote, "and that diligence and dexterity in all its processes are inestimable treasures. The order and economy of a house are as honorable to the mistress as those of the farm to the master, and if either is neglected, ruin follows, and children destitute of the means of living."[100]

Jefferson's thinking about the appropriate role for women in society was not at odds with his belief that mobilization for war (or politics) was the common bond that defined Americans as a people. While he believed that men and women should play different roles in the common cause, he held that those roles—defending the republic on the battlefield or ballot box for men, maintaining the home and promoting republican values for women—were complementary. Men had a sacred obligation to defend the country because in so doing they defended their homes. The household was the fundamental unit of the republic and the nation, coming before the town or ward, the county, the state, or, indeed, the federal republic. The nation itself was the aggregate of an increasing number of households. Organizing society and politics around the household transcended time as well as space. Jefferson conceived of a generation as the family writ large, a family of families. It was the means by which they perpetuated the nation. Citizens of the United States were a people because they shared deep, quasi-familial social attachments. These attachments bound men and women, as well as households and generations, together.

Legacy

We have shown that Jefferson sought to mobilize Americans for war with the Declaration of Independence. In so doing he helped to define them as a people. Although they were a people born of war, Jefferson's hope was that revolutionary mobilization would bind Americans together in a way that would ultimately allow them to live in peace.

On March 4, 1801, Jefferson walked from his boardinghouse in Washington, DC, to the unfinished Capitol building to swear the presidential oath and deliver his inaugural address. Almost a thousand people crammed into the Senate chamber; most missed Jefferson's barely audible address. His words, widely printed in the newspapers, were aimed at the American people in the aftermath of the recent bit-ter and contested election. Jefferson called for unity between politi-cal adversaries. "During the contest of opinion through which we have past," he said, "the animation of discusions and of exertions has sometimes worn an aspect which might impose on strangers unused to think freely, and to speak and to write what they think; but this being now decided by the voice of the nation, announced according to the rules of the constitution all will of course arrange themselves under the will of the law, and unite in common efforts for the com-mon good." He reminded his auditors (and readers) that while the will of the majority must prevail in a republic, the views of the minority must be respected and protected by law. He continued, "Let us then, fellow citizens, unite with one heart and one mind, let us restore to social intercourse that harmony and affection without which lib-erty, and even life itself, are but dreary things." Drawing a contrast between the religious violence and tumult that beset the despotic kingdoms of the Old World and the relatively peaceful environs of the United States, he warned his fellow Americans, "We have yet gained little if we countenance a political intolerance, as despotic, as wicked, and capable of as bitter and bloody persecutions." In the most famous passage in his address, Jefferson reminded his countrymen that "every difference of opinion is not a difference of principle. We have called by different names brethren of the same principle. We are all republicans: we are all federalists."

The new president sought to reassure his fellow citizens that their republic would endure. "I know indeed that some honest men fear that a republican government cannot be strong; that this government is not strong enough," he said. "But would the honest patriot, in the full tide of successful experiment, abandon a government which has so far kept us free and firm, on the theoretic and visionary fear, that this government, the world's best hope, may, by possibility, want energy to preserve itself?" he asked. Answering his own question, he continued, "I believe this, on the contrary, the strongest government on earth. I believe it is the only one, where every man, at the call of the law, would fly to the standard of the law, and would meet invasions of the public order as his own personal concern." Just as in 1776, Americans, members of the same extended social and political family—a family that transcended partisanship— would in a crisis mobilize in defense of their homes and their homeland and follow "the road which alone leads to peace, liberty and safety."[101]

Jefferson could not include Native peoples and enslaved Africans in this vision for the American people not because he was, as we might now conclude, a racist. They were instead excluded because he believed that they were not yet, in the case of Native Americans, or never could be, in the case of enslaved Africans and African Americans, a single people bound together in mutual affection with those European Americans who banded together to fight for their liberty and independence. Not all European Americans were included either, as we have seen. The American people first emerged when a broad and inclusive alliance of patriots, native-born and immigrant, mobilized in an ongoing conflict with a wide and inclusive array of enemies, foreign and domestic. Not everyone drawn into the war fit into the neat, predetermined cast of characters featured in Jefferson's Declaration of Independence: Patriots and loyalists affirmed or betrayed their allegiance, enslaved Blacks gained their freedom by fighting for one side or the other, Indigenous peoples calculated their chances under rapidly changing circumstances. Peace came, war resumed, and slavery tightened its hold over an expanding domain. Women made their own choices, some following husbands into exile. The boundaries of American nationhood were always fluid, incorporating former enemies and accommodating to changing times. *Nobody*, including even Jefferson, could possibly know who *we* would become.

This brings us back to the naturalization ceremony held each year at Monticello, a ceremony that powerfully demonstrates that the racial and gendered limits of Jefferson's conception of the people have been overcome. Women and men of all backgrounds and from around the world stand on the portico of Jefferson's home and pledge their loyalty to the United States. When they do so, they are incorporated into the people, a single people committed to a set of republican principles and to each other. This is Jefferson's greatest legacy.

◼◣◢◣◢◣◤◼

JEFFERSON WRITES

"T homas Jefferson survives," John Adams supposedly
exclaimed on his deathbed on July 4, 1826.[1] Adams was mistaken, if that is what he actually said: Jefferson had already
died. But it is true that both patriots passed away on that day, exactly
a half century after they signed the Declaration of Independence.
After Adams died, only one signer, Maryland's Charles Carroll of
Carrollton, was still alive (until 1832). These now old men doubtless
knew in 1776 that if the republican experiment failed, their signatures would make them conspicuous targets of royal retribution, perhaps cutting their lives short. But Americans vindicated their claim
to independence in the Revolution and yet again in the War of 1812,
and signers could know, as they lay dying, that "the union survives."
As long as it did, they would enjoy a kind of immortality, living on
in the historical memory of a grateful people.[2]

Jefferson's conception of generational sovereignty simultaneously expressed exalted hopes for and profound anxieties about the
future. How could he be sure that successive generations would rise
to the challenges of their times? Jefferson acknowledged that future

generations, facing their own distinctive challenges, would necessarily be different—and, he prayed, progressively more enlightened—
not mere replicas of their predecessors. Yet his experience as a
patriotic participant and engaged observer in the new nation's
unfolding history challenged his faith in progress. At the time of
his death, Virginia still lacked a proper constitution. Deepening partisan and sectional conflicts, most notably over the future of slavery, threatened to rend an increasingly fragile union. For better (and
perhaps for worse), past generations, including Jefferson's, could not
control the future. The earth instead belongs to the "living generation," until it too fades into the past.

Every generation, Jefferson believed, is responsible for the peaceful succession to the next, bloodlessly and benignly reenacting the
nation-making Revolution. But every generation is also free to squander its inheritance and betray its responsibilities. Even as he delivered his inaugural address asking his fellow Americans to envision
their future as a single, united people, with a domain vast enough
to accommodate thousands of generations, Jefferson also evoked a
capacious framework for future failure, drawing our attention to the
fractures and divisions that jeopardize the union and threaten the
nation's survival.

Our goal in this short book has been to encourage readers to
hear what Thomas Jefferson had to say about the new American
nation's uncertain prospects in a dangerous world. Jefferson can only
matter to us in a meaningful way if we situate him in his own time
and place, recognizing his presence in our increasingly distant past,
a lost world and "foreign country." He speaks to us—in the present tense—when we restore him to that past. Acutely aware of his
own mortality, Jefferson was aware he could not know us. He could
only pray that patriotic Americans would renew the patriotic commitment to self-government and self-determination from generation
to generation. Americans, he hoped, would recognize each other in
the history they made and shared, honoring the principles of equal

rights and civic responsibility, mobilizing to defend and secure their country—the great national estate—for their successors.

We have focused on a few key texts in the Jeffersonian archive to illuminate the broader contours of his world and the challenges he and his contemporaries faced. In the context we have reconstructed, he writes—and we can begin to hear him—in the present tense. Arranged chronologically, these texts constitute a brief outline of Jefferson's public career and political philosophy, tracking his ongoing engagement with the existential challenges of regime change and nation-making in a world at war. Our crises are not his, but they bear, and will continue to bear, a strong family resemblance—as long as we situate ourselves in a shared national narrative, looking to history to understand who we are now and who we might become as a people.

1774: Imperial Crisis

Thomas Jefferson's first great contribution to the patriot cause was originally drafted for consideration by the extraconstitutional Virginia convention that met in Williamsburg in August 1774, as instructions for its delegates to the forthcoming meeting of the First Continental Congress the following month in Philadelphia.[3] Although illness prevented Jefferson from attending the convention and arguing for adoption of his controversial draft, like-minded radicals gave the essay its title and arranged for its anonymous publication. A *Summary View of the Rights of British America* staked out a radical position on the imperial crisis, asserting the independence of colonial legislatures and their exclusive authority over taxation and calling on George III to uphold "the balance of a great, if a well poised empire." A *Summary View* also offered a compelling account of colonial history that expressed and promoted the emerging continental consciousness that set the stage for the break with Britain.

Jefferson's authorship was no secret and his fame (and notoriety) as a patriot penman paved the way for his service in the Second Continental Congress. The anonymity he assumed in his pamphlet was rhetorically appropriate, for his ultimate goal was to speak for a broad British American public that resistance to imperial policies was bringing into existence. Jefferson's rhetorical stance, speaking for the "people," was just as important as the claims he made on the people's behalf, anticipating his later achievement in the Declaration of Independence. Jefferson wrote himself into history by identifying with the people, giving them a voice, and fashioning himself their "servant"—the role he asked George III to play and that he would later assume as the new nation's third president.

July 1774

DRAFT OF INSTRUCTIONS TO THE VIRGINIA DELEGATES IN THE CONTINENTAL CONGRESS: MANUSCRIPT TEXT OF *A SUMMARY VIEW OF THE RIGHTS OF BRITISH AMERICA* (EXCERPTS)[4]

Resolved that it be an instruction to the said deputies when assembled in General Congress with the deputies from the other states of British America to propose to the said Congress that an humble and dutiful address be presented to his majesty begging leave to lay before him as chief magistrate of the British empire the united complaints of his majesty's subjects in America; complaints which are excited by many unwarrantable incroachments and usurpations, attempted to be made by the legislature of one part of the empire, upon those rights which god and the laws have given equally and independently to all. To represent to his majesty that these his states have often individually made humble application to his imperial throne, to obtain thro' it's intervention some redress of their injured rights; to none of which was ever even an answer condescended. Humbly to hope that this their joint address, penned in the language of truth, and divested of those expressions of servility which would persuade his majesty that we are asking favors and not rights, shall obtain from his majesty a more respectful acceptance. And this his majesty will think we have reason to expect when he reflects that he is no more than the chief officer of the people, appointed by the laws, and circumscribed with definite powers, to assist in working the great machine of government erected for their use, and consequently subject to their superintendance. And in order that these our rights, as well as the invasions of them, may be laid more fully before his majesty, to take a view of them from the origin and first settlement of these countries.

To remind him that our ancestors, before their emigration to America, were the free inhabitants of the British dominions in Europe, and possessed a right, which nature has given to all men, of departing from the country in which chance, not choice has placed them, of going in quest of new habitations, and of there establishing new societies, under such laws and regulations as to them shall seem most likely to promote public happiness. That their Saxon ancestors had under this universal law, in like manner, left their native wilds and woods in the North of Europe, had possessed themselves of the island of Britain then less charged with inhabitants, and had established there that system of laws which has so long been the glory and protection of that country. Nor was ever any claim of superiority or dependance asserted over them by that mother country from which they had migrated: and were such a claim made it is beleived his majesty's subjects in Great Britain have too firm a feeling of the rights derived to them from their ancestors to bow down the sovereignty of their state before such visionary pretensions. And it is thought that no circumstance has occurred to distinguish materially

the British from the Saxon emigration. America was conquered, and her settlements made and firmly established,
at the expence of individuals, and not of the British public.
Their own blood was spilt in acquiring lands for their settlement, their own fortunes expended in making that settlement
effectual. For themselves they fought, for themselves they
conquered, and for themselves alone they have right to hold.
No shilling was ever issued from the public treasures of his
majesty or his ancestors for their assistance, till of very late
times, after the colonies had become established on a firm and
permanent footing. That then indeed, having become valuable to Great Britain for her commercial purposes, his parliament was pleased to lend them assistance against an enemy
who would fain have drawn to herself the benefits of their
commerce to the great aggrandisement of herself and danger
of Great Britain. Such assistance, and in such circumstances,
they had often before given to Portugal and other allied states,
with whom they carry on a commercial intercourse. Yet these
states never supposed that, by calling in her aid, they thereby
submitted themselves to her sovereignty. Had such terms
been proposed, they would have rejected them with disdain,
and trusted for better to the moderation of their enemies, or
to a vigorous exertion of their own force. We do not however mean to underrate those aids, which to us were doubtless valuable, on whatever principles granted: but we would
shew that they cannot give a title to that authority which the
British parliament would arrogate over us; and that they may
amply be repaid, by our giving to the inhabitants of Great
Britain such exclusive privileges in trade as may be advanta-
geous to them, and at the same time not too restrictive to
ourselves. That settlements having been thus effected in the
wilds of America, the emigrants thought proper to adopt that
system of laws under which they had hitherto lived in the

mother country, and to continue their union with her by submitting themselves to the same common sovereign, who was
thereby made the central link connecting the several parts of
the empire thus newly multiplied. . . .

That the exercise of a free trade with all parts of the world,
possessed by the American colonists as of natural right, and
which no law of their own had taken away or abridged, was
next the object of unjust incroachment. Some of the colonies
having thought proper to continue the administration of their
government in the name and under the authority of his majesty king Charles the first, whom notwithstanding his late
deposition by the Common-wealth of England, they continued in the sovereignty of their state, the Parliament for the
Common-wealth took the same in high offence, and assumed
upon themselves the power of prohibiting their trade with
all other parts of the world except the island of Great Britain.
This arbitrary act however they soon recalled, and by solemn
treaty entered into on the 12th. day of March 1651, between
the said Commonwealth by their Commissioners and the colony of Virginia by their house of Burgesses, it was expressly
stipulated by the 8th. article of the said treaty that they
should have "free trade as the people of England do enjoy to
all places and with all nations according to the laws of that
Commonwealth." But that, upon the restoration of his majesty King Charles the second, their rights of free commerce
fell once more a victim to arbitrary power: and by several acts
of his reign as well as of some of his successors the trade of the
colonies was laid under such restrictions as shew what hopes
they might form from the justice of a British parliament were
its uncontrouled power admitted over these states. History
has informed us that bodies of men as well as individuals are
susceptible of the spirit of tyranny. A view of these acts of
parliament for regulation, as it has been affectedly called,

of the American trade, if all other evidence were removed out of the case, would undeniably evince the truth of this observation. . . .

Single acts of tyranny may be ascribed to the accidental opinion of a day; but a series of oppressions, begun at a distinguished period, and pursued unalterably thro' every change of ministers, too plainly prove a deliberate, systematical plan of reducing us to slavery. . . . Not only the principles of common sense, but the common feelings of human nature must be surrendered up, before his majesty's subjects here can be persuaded to beleive that they hold their political existence at the will of a British parliament. Shall these governments be dissolved, their property annihilated, and their people reduced to a state of nature, at the imperious breath of a body of men whom they never saw, in whom they never confided, and over whom they have no powers of punishment or removal, let their crimes against the American public be ever so great? Can any one reason be assigned why 160,000 electors in the island of Great Britain should give law to four millions in the states of America, every individual of whom is equal to every individual of them in virtue, in understanding, and in bodily strength? Were this to be admitted, instead of being a free people, as we have hitherto supposed, and mean to continue, ourselves, we should suddenly be found the slaves, not of one, but of 160,000 tyrants, distinguished too from all others by this singular circumstance that they are removed from the reach of fear, the only restraining motive which may hold the hand of a tyrant.

That by "an act to discontinue in such manner and for such time as are therein mentioned the landing and discharging lading or shipping of goods wares and merchandize at the town and within the harbor of Boston in the province of Massachusett's bay in North America" which was passed at the last session of British parliament, a large and populous town, whose trade was their sole subsistence, was deprived of that trade, and involved in utter ruin. Let us for a while suppose the question of right suspended, in order to examine this act on principles of justice. An act of parliament had been passed imposing duties on teas to be paid in America, against which act the Americans had protested as inauthoritative. The East India company, who till that time had never sent a pound of tea to America on their own account, step forth on that occasion the asserters of parliamentary right, and send hither many ship loads of that obnoxious commodity. The masters of their several vessels however, on their arrival in America, wisely attended to admonition, and returned with their cargoes. In the province of New England alone the remonstrances of the people were disregarded, and a compli-ance, after being many days waited for, was flatly refused. Whether in this the master of the vessel was governed by his obstinacy or his instructions, let those who know, say. There are extraordinary situations which require extraordinary interposition. . . . Not the hundredth part of the inhabitants of that town had been concerned in the act complained of; many of them were in Great Britain and in other parts beyond sea; yet all were involved in one indiscriminate ruin, by a new executive power unheard of till then, that of a British parlia-ment. A property of the value of many millions of money was sacrifised to revenge, not repay, the loss of a few thousands. This is administering justice with a heavy hand indeed! And when is this tempest to be arrested in it's course?. . . . And we do earnestly intreat his majesty, as yet the only mediatory power between the several states of the British empire, to rec-ommend to his parliament of Great Britain the total revoca-tion of these acts, which however nugatory they be, may yet prove the cause of further discontents and jealousies among us.

That we next proceed to consider the conduct of his majesty, as holding the executive powers of the laws of these states, and mark out his deviations from the line of duty. By the constitution of Great Britain as well as of the several American states, his majesty possesses the power of refusing to pass into a law any bill which has already passed the other two branches of legislature. His majesty however and his ancestors, conscious of the impropriety of opposing their single opinion to the united wisdom of two houses of parliament, while their proceedings were unbiassed by interested principles, for several ages past have modestly declined the exercise of this power in that part of his empire called Great Britain. But by change of circumstances, other principles than those of justice simply have obtained an influence on their determinations. The addition of new states to the British empire has produced an addition of new, and sometimes opposite interests. It is now therefore the great office of his majesty to resume the exercise of his negative power, and to prevent the passage of laws by any one legislature of the empire which might bear injuriously on the rights and interests of another. Yet this will not excuse the wanton exercise of this power which we have seen his majesty practice on the laws of the American legislatures. For the most trifling reasons, and sometimes for no conceivable reason at all, his majesty has rejected laws of the most salutary tendency. The abolition of domestic slavery is the great object of desire in those colonies where it was unhappily introduced in their infant state. But previous to the infranchisement of the slaves we have, it is necessary to exclude all further importations from Africa. Yet our repeated attempts to effect this by prohibitions, and by imposing duties which might amount to a prohibition, have been hitherto defeated by his majesty's negative: thus preferring the immediate advantages of a few British corsairs to the lasting interests of the American states, and to the rights of human nature deeply wounded by this infamous practice. . . .

But in what terms reconcileable to majesty and at the same time to truth, shall we speak of a late instruction to his majesty's governor of the colony of Virginia, by which he is forbidden to assent to any law for the division of a county, unless the new county will consent to have no representative in assembly? That colony has as yet affixed no boundary to the Westward. Their Western counties therefore are of indef-inite extent. Some of them are actually seated many hundred miles from their Eastern limits. Is it possible then that his maj-esty can have bestowed a single thought on the situation of those people, who, in order to obtain justice for injuries how-ever great or small, must, by the laws of that colony, attend their county court at such a distance, with all their witnesses, monthly, till their litigation be determined? Or does his maj-esty seriously wish, and publish it to the world, that his sub-jects should give up the glorious right of representation, with all the benefits derived from that, and submit themselves the absolute slaves of his sovereign will? Or is it rather meant to confine the legislative body to their present numbers, that they may be the cheaper bargain whenever they shall become worth a purchase? . . .

When the representative body have lost the confidence of their constituents, when they have notoriously made sale of their most valuable rights, when they have assumed to them-selves powers which the people never put into their hands, then indeed their continuing in office becomes dangerous to the state, and calls for an exercise of the power of disso-lution. Such being the causes for which the representative body should and should not be dissolved, will it not appear strange to an unbiassed observer that that of Great Britain was not dissolved, while those of the colonies have repeatedly incurred that sentence?

But your majesty or your Governors have carried this power beyond every limit known or provided for by the laws. After dissolving one house of representatives, they have refused to call another, so that for a great length of time the legislature provided by the laws has been out of existence. From the nature of things, every society must at all times possess within itself the sovereign powers of legislation. The feelings of human nature revolt against the supposition of a state so situated as that it may not in any emergency provide against dangers which perhaps threaten immediate ruin. While those bodies are in existence to whom the people have delegated the powers of legislation, they alone possess and may exercise those powers. But when they are dissolved by the lopping off one or more of their branches, the power reverts to the people, who may use it to unlimited extent, either assembling together in person, sending deputies, or in any other way they may think proper. We forbear to trace consequences further; the dangers are conspicuous with which this practice is replete.

That we shall at this time also take notice of an error in the nature of our landholdings, which crept in at a very early period of our settlement. The introduction of the feudal tenures into the kingdom of England, though antient, is well enough understood to set this matter in a proper light. In the earlier ages of the Saxon settlement feudal holdings were certainly altogether unknown, and very few, if any, had been introduced at the time of the Norman Conquest. Our Saxon ancestors held their lands, as they did their personal property, in absolute dominion, disencumbered with any superior, answering nearly to the nature of those possessions which the Feudalists term Allodial: William the Norman first introduced that system generally. . . . A general principle indeed was introduced that "all lands in England were held either mediately or immediately of the crown": but this was borrowed from those holdings which were truly feudal, and only applied to others for the purposes of illustration. Feudal holdings were therefore but exceptions out of the Saxon laws of possession, under which all lands were held in absolute right. These therefore still form the basis or groundwork of the Common law, to prevail wheresoever the exceptions have not taken place. America was not conquered by William the Norman, nor it's lands surrendered to him or any of his successors. Possessions there are undoubtedly of the Allodial nature. Our ancestors however, who migrated hither, were laborers, not lawyers. The fictitious principle that all lands belong originally to the king, they were early persuaded to beleive real, and accordingly took grants of their own lands from the crown. And while the crown continued to grant for small sums and on reasonable rents, there was no inducement to arrest the error and lay it open to public view. But his majesty has lately taken on him to advance the terms of purchase and of holding to the double of what they were, by which means the acquisition of lands being rendered difficult, the population of our country is likely to be checked. It is time therefore for us to lay this matter before his majesty, and to declare that he has no right to grant lands of himself. From the nature and purpose of civil institutions, all the lands within the limits which any particular society has circumscribed around itself, are assumed by that society, and subject to their allotment only. This may be done by themselves assembled collectively, or by their legislature to whom they may have delegated sovereign authority: and, if they are allotted in neither of these ways, each individual of the society may appropriate to himself such lands as he finds vacant, and occupancy will give him title. . . .

But his majesty has no right to land a single armed man on our shores; and those whom he sends here are liable to our laws for the suppression and punishment of Riots, Routs, and unlawful assemblies, or are hostile bodies invading us in defiance of law. . . . He possesses indeed the executive power of the laws in every state; but they are the laws of the particular state which he is to administer within that state, and not those of any one within the limits of another. Every state must judge for itself the number of armed men which they may safely trust among them, of whom they are to consist, and under what restrictions they are to be laid. To render these proceedings still more criminal against our laws, instead of subjecting the military to the civil power, his majesty has expressly made the civil subordinate to the military. But can his majesty thus put down all law under his feet? Can he erect a power superior to that which erected himself? He has done it indeed by force; but let him remember that force cannot give right.

That these are our grievances which we have thus laid before his majesty with that freedom of language and sentiment which becomes a free people, claiming their rights as derived from the laws of nature, and not as the gift of their chief magistrate. Let those flatter, who fear: it is not an American art. To give praise where it is not due, might be well from the venal, but would ill beseem those who are asserting the rights of human nature. They know, and will therefore say, that kings are the servants, not the proprietors of the people. Open your breast Sire, to liberal and expanded thought. Let not the name of George the third be a blot in the page of history. You are surrounded by British counsellors, but remember that they are parties. You have no ministers for American affairs, because you have none taken from among us, nor amenable to the laws on which they are to give you advice. It behoves you therefore to think and to act for your-self and your people. The great principles of right and wrong are legible to every reader: to pursue them requires not the aid of many counsellors. The whole art of government consists in the art of being honest. Only aim to do your duty, and man-kind will give you credit where you fail. No longer persevere in sacrificing the rights of one part of the empire to the inor-dinate desires of another: but deal out to all equal and impar-tial right. Let no act be passed by any one legislature which may infringe on the rights and liberties of another. This is the important post in which fortune has placed you, holding the balance of a great, if a well poised empire. This, Sire, is the advice of your great American council, on the observance of which may perhaps depend your felicity and future fame, and the preservation of that harmony which alone can continue both to Great Britain and America the reciprocal advantages of their connection. It is neither our wish nor our interest to separate from her. We are willing on our part to sacrifice every thing which reason can ask to the restoration of that tranquility for which all must wish. On their part let them be ready to establish union on a generous plan. Let them name their terms, but let them be just. Accept of every commercial preference it is in our power to give for such things as we can raise for their use, or they make for ours. But let them not think to exclude us from going to other markets, to dispose of those commodities which they cannot use, nor to supply those wants which they cannot supply. Still less let it be proposed that our properties within our own territories shall be taxed or regulated by any power on earth but our own. The god who gave us life, gave us liberty at the same time: the hand of force may destroy, but cannot disjoin them. This, Sire, is our last, our determined resolution: and that you will be pleased to interpose with that efficacy which your earnest endeavors

> may insure to procure redress of these our great grievances, to quiet the minds of your subjects in British America against any apprehensions of future incroachment, to establish frater- nal love and harmony thro' the whole empire, and that that may continue to the latest ages of time, is the fervent prayer of all British America.

1776: Independence

Thomas Jefferson may have claimed "authorship" of the Declaration of Independence on his tombstone, but the only such claim he could make when the document was drafted—and heavily edited by fel- low committeemen and Congress as a whole—was as one of its many signers, acting in their official capacity as representatives of the "peoples" of their respective provinces.[5] Jefferson famously chafed at his colleagues' editorial changes. The scholarly consensus is that the congressionally approved Declaration was a significant improvement over Jefferson's "Rough draft" and that his unhappiness with the revisions was the predictable response of a thin-skinned author— with whom we scholars can so easily identify. Yet we might more generously grant that Jefferson sublimated his authorial ego in his self-consciously *public* voice as he strove to articulate the (emerg- ing) common sense of the people. Approaching the end of his life, he may have resented changes that he thought compromised and mis- represented the people's principled commitments in 1776, when *they* declared independence. In any case, Jefferson swallowed his misgiv- ings and joined fellow signers in *collectively* owning authorship at that time, proudly affirming his identity with the nation-founding generation. Significantly, it was only when Republican opposition- ists claimed to represent and speak for the people in the partisan war- fare of the 1790s that Jefferson's key role in drafting the Declaration became widely known.[6] Jefferson did not claim that role for himself.

It was instead the "living generation" that now honored him for giving such eloquent voice to its revolutionary predecessors.

Jefferson incorporated successive drafts of the Declaration and
his notes on congressional debates in a brief and uncompleted autobiography he composed in 1821 when the ongoing controversy over
Missouri statehood threatened the survival of the union. Juxtaposing
his original draft with the one Congress adopted and (tendentiously)
explaining why misguided and short-sighted colleagues made them,
Jefferson called into question the solidarity of the American people—
or at least of their patriot leaders—in 1776, even as he charged the
present-day parricidal generation with destroying the union.[7] When
the Missouri controversy subsided, Jefferson's faith was restored.
Coming to its senses, the living generation acknowledged its indebtedness to its predecessors and its responsibilities to succeeding generations. Sorely tried, the generational chain remained unbroken.
Jefferson would be remembered, his tombstone a reminder of why
he mattered.

June–July 1776

JEFFERSON'S "ORIGINAL ROUGH DRAUGHT" OF THE DECLARATION OF INDEPENDENCE[8]

Portions of Jefferson's text excised in subsequent revisions are
enclosed parenthetically and *italicized*.

Additions and substitutions to the draft that was adopted
and published by Congress are in **bold**.

(*A Declaration of the Representatives of the UNITED
STATES OF AMERICA, in General Congress assembled.*)

IN CONGRESS, JULY 4, 1776.

THE UNANIMOUS DECLARATION OF THE
THIRTEEN UNITED STATES OF AMERICA,

When in the Course of human events, it becomes necessary for (*a*) **one** people **to dissolve the political bands which have connected them with another, and** (*advance from that subordination in which they have hitherto remained, &*) to assume among the powers of the earth the equal (*& independant*) station to which the Laws of Nature **and** (*&*) of Nature's God entitle them, a decent respect to the opinions of mankind requires that they should declare the causes which impel them to the **separation** (*change*).

We hold these truths to be **self-evident,** (*sacred & undeniable;*) that all men are created equal (*& independant*), **that they are endowed by their Creator with certain unalienable Rights,** (*that from that equal creation they derive rights inherent & inalienable,*) **that** among **these are Life, Liberty and the pursuit of Happiness.** (*which are the preservation of life, & liberty, & the pursuit of happiness;*) That to secure these **rights** (*ends*), Governments are instituted among Men, deriving their just powers from the consent of the governed, (*;*) That whenever any Form of Government **becomes** (*shall become*) destructive of these ends, it is the Right of the People to alter or to abolish it, **and** (*&*) to institute new Government, laying **its** (*it's*) foundation on such principles **and organizing its** (*& organising it's*) powers in such form, as to them shall seem most likely to effect their Safety **and** (*&*) Happiness. Prudence, indeed, will dictate that Governments long established should not be changed for light **and** (*&*) transient causes; (*:*) and accordingly all experience hath shewn, that mankind are more disposed to suffer, while evils are sufferable, than to right themselves by abolishing the forms to which they are accustomed. But when a long train of abuses **and** (&) usurpations, (*begun at a distinguished period,* &) pursuing invariably the same Object (,) evinces a design to **reduce** (*subject*) them **under absolute Despotism** (*to arbitrary power*), it is their right, it is their duty, to throw off such Government, **and** (&) to provide new Guards for their future security. Such has been the patient sufferance of these Colonies; **and** (&) such is now the necessity which constrains them to **alter** (*expunge*) their former Systems of Government. The history of **the present King of Great Britain** (*his present majesty,*) is a history of **repeated** (*unremitting*) injuries and usurpations, (*among which no one fact stands single or solitary to contradict the uniform tenor of the rest, all of which have*) **all having** in direct object the establishment of an absolute Tyranny over these States. To prove this, let Facts be submitted to a candid world. (, *for the truth of which we pledge a faith yet unsullied by falsehood.*)

He has refused his Assent to Laws, the most wholesome and necessary for the public good. (:)

He has forbidden his Governors to pass Laws of immediate **and** (&) pressing importance, unless suspended in their operation till his Assent should be obtained; and when so suspended, he has neglected utterly to attend to them. (:)

He has refused to pass (*other*) Laws for the accommodation of large districts of people, unless those people would relinquish the right of Representation **in the Legislature**, a right inestimable to them **and** (, &) formidable to tyrants **only**. (*alone:*)

He has called together legislative bodies at places unusual, uncomfortable, and distant from the depository of their public Records, for the sole purpose of fatiguing them into compliance with his measures.

He has dissolved Representative Houses Repeatedly (& *continually*), for opposing with manly firmness his invasions on the rights of the people. (:)

He has refused for a long (*space of*) time, **after such dissolutions,** to cause others to be elected; (,) whereby the Legislative powers, incapable of Annihilation, have returned to the People at large for their exercise; (,) the State remaining in the mean time exposed to all the dangers of invasion from without, **and** (&) convulsions within. (:)

He has endeavoured to prevent the population of these States; for that purpose obstructing the Laws for Naturalization of Foreigners; refusing to pass others to encourage their migrations hither, (; &) raising the Conditions of new Appropriations of Lands. (:)

He has **obstructed** (*suffered*) the Administration of Justice (*totally to cease in some of these colonies*), **by** refusing his Assent to Laws for establishing Judiciary powers. (:)

He has made (*our*) Judges dependent on his Will alone, for the tenure of their offices, and amount **and payment** of their salaries. (:)

He has erected a multitude of New Offices, (*by a self-assumed power,* &) **and** sent hither swarms of Officers to harrass our people, **and** (&) eat out their substance. (:)

He has kept among us, in times of peace, standing Armies **without the Consent of our legislatures.** (& *ships of war:*)

He has affected to render the Military (,) independent of **and** (&) superior to the Civil power. (:)

He has combined with others to subject us to a jurisdiction foreign to our constitution(s), and unacknowledged by our laws; giving his Assent to their (*pretended*) Acts **of pretended** Legislation: (,)

For Quartering large bodies of armed troops among us: (;)

For protecting them, by a mock (-) Trial, from punishment for any Murders they should commit on the Inhabitants of these States: (;)

For cutting off our Trade with all parts of the world: (;)

For imposing Taxes on us without our Consent: (;)

For depriving us in many cases of the benefits of Trial by Jury: (;)

For transporting us beyond Seas to be tried for pre-tended offences:

For abolishing the free System of English Laws in a neighbouring Province, establishing therein an Arbitrary government, and enlarging its Boundaries so as to render it at once an example and fit instrument for introducing the same absolute rule into these Colonies:

For taking away our Charters, abolishing our most valuable Laws, and (&) altering fundamentally the Forms of our Governments: (;)

For suspending our own Legislatures, and (&) declaring themselves invested with power to legislate for us in all cases whatsoever. (;)

He has abdicated government here, by declaring us out of his Protection and waging War against us. (withdrawing his governors, & declaring us out of his allegiance & protection:)

He has plundered our seas, ravaged our Coasts, burnt our towns, and (&) destroyed the Lives of our people. (:)

He is at this time transporting large Armies of foreign Mercenaries to compleat the works of death, desolation and (&) tyranny, already begun with circumstances of Cruelty & perfidy scarcely paralleled in the most barbarous ages, and totally unworthy the head of a civilized nation. (:)

He has constrained our fellow Citizens taken Captive on the high Seas to bear Arms against their Country, to become the executioners of their friends and Brethren, or to fall themselves by their Hands.

He has excited domestic insurrections amongst us, and endeavoured to bring on the inhabitants of our frontiers, the merciless Indian Savages, whose known rule of warfare, is an undistinguished destruction of all ages, sexes **and** (, &) conditions. (*of existence:*

he has incited treasonable insurrections in our fellow-subjects, with the allurements of forfeiture & confiscation of our property:

he has waged cruel war against human nature itself, violating it's most sacred rights of life & liberty in the persons of a distant people who never offended him, captivating & carrying them into slavery in another hemisphere, or to incur miserable death in their transportation thither. this piratical warfare, the opprobrium of infidel *powers, is the warfare of the* CHRISTIAN *king of Great Britain. determined to keep open a market where* MEN *should be bought & sold, he has prostituted his negative for suppressing every legislative attempt to prohibit or to restrain this execrable commerce: and that this assemblage of horrors might want no fact of distinguished die, he is now exciting those very people to rise in arms among us, and to purchase that liberty of which he has deprived them, by murdering the people upon whom he also obtruded them; thus paying off former crimes committed against the liberties of one people, with crimes which he urges them to commit against the lives of another.*)

In every stage of these Oppressions **We** have Petitioned for Redress in the most humble terms: (;) Our repeated Petitions have been answered **only** by repeated injury. A Prince, whose character is thus marked by every act which may define a Tyrant, is unfit to be the ruler of a **free** people. (*who mean to be free. future ages will scarce believe that the hardiness of one man, adventured within the short compass of 12 years only, on so many acts of tyranny without a mask, over a people fostered & fixed in principles of liberty.*)

Nor have **We** been wanting in attentions to our Brittish

brethren. We have warned them from time to time of attempts by their legislature to extend an **unwarrantable** jurisdiction over **us**. (*these our states.*) We have reminded them of the circumstances of our emigration **and** (*&*) settlement here. (, *no one of which could warrant so strange a pretension: that these were effected at the expence of our own blood & treasure, unassisted by the wealth or the strength of Great Britain: that in constituting indeed our several forms of government, we had adopted one common king, thereby laying a foundation for perpetual league & amity with them: but that submission to their parliament was no part of our constitution, nor ever in idea, if history may be credited: and*) **We have** appealed to their native justice **and** (*&*) magnanimity, **and we have conjured them by** (*as well as to*) the ties of our common kindred to disavow these usurpations, which, **would inevitably** (*were likely to*) interrupt our **connections and** correspondence. (*& connection.*) They too have been deaf to the voice of justice **and** (*&*) of consanguinity. (, *& when occasions have been given them, by the regular course of their laws, of removing from their councils the disturbers of our harmony, they have by their free election re-established them in power. at this very time too they are permitting their chief magistrate to send over not only soldiers of our common blood, but Scotch & foreign mercenaries to invade & deluge us in blood. these facts have given the last stab to agonizing affection, and manly spirit bids us to renounce for ever these unfeeling brethren.*) **We must, therefore, acquiesce in the necessity, which denounces our Separation, and** (*endeavor to forget our former love for them, and to*) **hold them, as we hold the rest of mankind, Enemies in War, in Peace Friends.** (*we might have been a free & a great people together; but a communication of grandeur & of freedom it seems is below their dignity. be it so, since they will have it: the road to glory & happiness is open to us too; we will climb it in a*

separate state, and acquiesce in the necessity which pronounces
our everlasting Adieu!)

We, therefore, the representatives of the united States of America, in General Congress, Assembled, **appealing to the Supreme Judge of the world for the rectitude of our intentions**, do, in the Name, **and** (*&*) by Authority of the good People of these **Colonies** (*states, reject and renounce all alle-giance & subjection to the kings of Great Britain & all others who may claim by, through, or under them; we utterly dissolve & break off all political connection which may have heretofore subsisted between us & the people or parliament of Great Britain; and finally we do assert and declare these colonies*) **solemnly publish and declare, That these United Colonies are, and of Right ought** to be Free and Independent States; **that they are Absolved from all Allegiance to the British Crown, and that all political connection between them and the State of Great Britain, is and ought to be totally dissolved;** and that as Free **and** (*&*) Independent States, they (*shall hereafter*) have **full** Power to levy War, conclude Peace, contract Alliances, establish Commerce, **and** (*&*) to do all other Acts and Things which Independent States may of right do. And for the support of this Declaration, **with a firm reliance on the protection of divine Providence,** we mutually pledge to each other our Lives, our Fortunes (, *&*) **and** our sacred honour.

1789: Generational Sovereignty

"*The earth belongs in usufruct to the living,*" Jefferson wrote his friend and ally James Madison from Paris during the opening phase of a revolution in France that promised to extend the blessings of republican self-government to the monarchical regimes of the Old World. The American minister's speculative essay on generational sovereignty reflected his intensive engagement with French friends as they envisioned a republican future for their country.[9] At the same time, Jefferson's distance from home offered him a detached perspective on recent developments in America. While Madison and fellow authors of the new federal Constitution sought to consolidate republican rule and bring the American Revolution to a peaceful conclusion, Jefferson looked toward a dangerous and unpredictable future. The obstacles that the French would have to overcome to *become* a "people"—the deeply entrenched hierarchical social and political order of the *ancien régime*—represented the future Jefferson feared for complacent Americans, *if* they should fail to sustain their revolutionary spirit from generation to generation.

Displaced from his own country, thinking about how revolutions begin and end, Jefferson assumed the prophetic voice of a philosophical historian. Applying what he took to be universal principles to particular cases, Jefferson in his conjectures focused the attention of citizens on the future crises they might face and the preemptive, defensive measures they should take to preserve their liberties. A vigilant people could make its own history, avoiding the unrelenting cycle of liberty and tyranny—life and death—that historically afflicted human communities as well as individual humans. Civic consciousness, Jefferson concluded, was historical consciousness, the collective awareness of a free, self-governing people that they *could* shape their own future. Monarchies failed in succession crises. So, too, republics would be doomed to fail if they did not adequately secure the peaceful succession of generations.

At first Madison did not know what to make of Jefferson's essayistic letter.[10] Perhaps, as the editors of the Jefferson Papers surmise, it was not really meant for his younger friend.[11] But the principles Jefferson articulated here would prove critically important for both men and a widening circle of political "friends" and allies in the very near future. However much we now venerate the federal Constitution and hold it as the enduring bulwark of our liberties,

Madison soon came to recognize, with Jefferson, that the union could all too easily be torn asunder, the Constitution become a dead letter, and the American people cease to exist.

September 6, 1789, Paris

THOMAS JEFFERSON TO JAMES MADISON
(EXCERPTS)[12]

I sit down to write to you without knowing by what occa-sion I shall send my letter. I do it because a subject comes into my head which I would wish to develope a little more than is practicable in the hurry of the moment of making up general dispatches.

The question Whether one generation of men has a right to bind another, seems never to have been started either on this or our side of the water. Yet it is a question of such consequences as not only to merit decision, but place also, among the fundamental principles of every government. The course of reflection in which we are immersed here on the elementary principles of society has presented this question to my mind; and that no such obligation can be so transmit-ted I think very capable of proof.—I set out on this ground, which I suppose to be self evident, "*that the earth belongs in usufruct to the living*": that the dead have neither powers nor rights over it. The portion occupied by any individual ceases to be his when himself ceases to be, and reverts to the society. If the society has formed no rules for the appropriation of it's lands in severality, it will be taken by the first occupants. These will generally be the wife and children of the decedent. If they have formed rules of appropriation, those rules may give it to the wife and children, or to some one of them, or to the legatee of the deceased. So they may give it to his creditor.

But the child, the legatee, or creditor takes it, not by any natural right, but by a law of the society of which they are members, and to which they are subject. Then no man can, by *natural right*, oblige the lands he occupied, or the persons who succeed him in that occupation, to the paiment of debts contracted by him. For if he could, he might, during his own life, eat up the usufruct of the lands for several generations to come, and then the lands would belong to the dead, and not to the living, which would be the reverse of our principle.

What is true of every member of the society individually, is true of them all collectively, since the rights of the whole can be no more than the sum of the rights of the individuals.—To keep our ideas clear when applying them to a multitude, let us suppose a whole generation of men to be born on the same day, to attain mature age on the same day, and to die on the same day, leaving a succeeding generation in the moment of attaining their mature age all together. Let the ripe age be supposed of 21. years, and their period of life 34. years more, that being the average term given by the bills of mortality to persons who have already attained 21. years of age. Each successive generation would, in this way, come on, and go off the stage at a fixed moment, as individuals do now. Then I say the earth belongs to each of these generations, during it's course, fully, and in their own right. The 2d. generation receives it clear of the debts and incumberances of the 1st. the 3d of the 2d. and so on. For if the 1st. could charge it with a debt, then the earth would belong to the dead and not the living generation. Then no generation can contract debts greater than may be paid during the course of it's own existence. At 21. years of age they may bind themselves and their lands for 34. years to come: at 22. for 33: at 23. for 32. and at 54. for one year only; because these are the terms of life which remain to them at those respective epochs.—But a material difference must be noted between the succession of an individual, and that of a whole generation. Individuals are parts only of a society, subject to the laws of the whole. These laws may appropriate the portion of and occupied by a decedent to his creditor rather than to any other, or to his child on condition he satisfies the creditor. But when a whole generation, that is, the whole society dies, as in the case we have supposed, and another generation or society succeeds, this forms a whole, and there is no superior who can give their territory to a third society, who may have lent money to their predecessors beyond their faculties of paying.

What is true of a generation all arriving to self-government on the same day, and dying all on the same day, is true of those in a constant course of decay and renewal, with this only difference. A generation coming in and going out entire, as in the first case, would have a right in the 1st. year of their self-dominion to contract a debt for 33. years, in the 10th. for 24. in the 20th. for 14. in the 30th. for 4. whereas genera-tions, changing daily by daily deaths and births, have one con-stant term, beginning at the date of their contract, and ending when a majority of those of full age at that date shall be dead. The length of that term may be estimated from the tables of mortality, corrected by the circumstances of climate, occupa-tion &c. peculiar to the country of the contractors. Take, for instance, the table of M. de Buffon wherein he states 23,994 deaths, and the ages at which they happened. Suppose a soci-ety in which 23,994 persons are born every year, and live to the ages stated in this table. The conditions of that society will be as follows. 1st. It will consist constantly of 617,703. persons of all ages. 2ly. Of those living at any one instant of time, one half will be dead in 24. years 8. months. 3dly. 10,675 will arrive every year at the age of 21. years complete. 4ly. It will constantly have 348,417 persons of all ages above 21.

years. 5ly. And the half of those of 21. years and upwards living at any one instant of time will be dead in 18. years 8. months, or say 19. years as the nearest integral number. Then 19. years is the term beyond which neither the representa- tives of a nation, nor even the whole nation itself assembled, can validly extend a debt. . . .

I suppose that the recieved opinion, that the public debts of one generation devolve on the next, has been suggested by our seeing habitually in private life that he who succeeds to lands is required to pay the debts of his ancestor or testator: without considering that this requisition is municipal only, not moral; flowing from the will of the society, which has found it convenient to appropriate lands, become vacant by the death of their occupant, on the condition of a paiment of his debts: but that between society and society, or generation and generation, there is no municipal obligation, no umpire but the law of nature. We seem not to have percieved that, by the law of nature, one generation is to another as one indepen- dant nation to another.

The interest of the national debt of France being in fact but a two thousandth part of it's rent roll, the paiment of it is practicable enough: and so becomes a question merely of honor, or of expediency. But with respect to future debts, would it not be wise and just for that nation to declare, in the constitution they are forming, that neither the legislature, nor the nation itself, can validly contract more debt than they may pay within their own age, or within the term of 19. years? And that all future contracts will be deemed void as to what shall remain unpaid at the end of 19. years from their date? This would put the lenders, and the borrowers also, on their guard. By reducing too the faculty of borrowing within it's natural limits, it would bridle the spirit of war, to which too free a course has been procured by the inattention

of money-lenders to this law of nature, that succeeding generations are not responsible for the preceding.

On similar ground it may be proved that no society can
make a perpetual constitution, or even a perpetual law. The
earth belongs always to the living generation. They may manage it then, and what proceeds from it, as they please, during
their usufruct. They are masters too of their own persons,
and consequently may govern them as they please. But persons and property make the sum of the objects of government. The constitution and the laws of their predecessors
extinguished then in their natural course with those who
gave them being. This could preserve that being till it ceased
to be itself, and no longer. Every constitution then, and every
law, naturally expires at the end of 19 years. If it be enforced
longer, it is an act of force, and not of right.—It may be said
that the succeeding generation exercising in fact the power
of repeal, this leaves them as free as if the constitution or
law had been expressly limited to 19 years only. In the first
place, this objection admits the right, in proposing an equivalent. But the power of repeal is not an equivalent. It might
be indeed if every form of government were so perfectly con-
trived that the will of the majority could always be obtained
fairly and without impediment. But this is true of no form.
The people cannot assemble themselves. Their representation
is unequal and vicious. Various checks are opposed to every
legislative proposition. Factions get possession of the public
councils. Bribery corrupts them. Personal interests lead them
astray from the general interests of their constituents: and
other impediments arise so as to prove to every practical man
that a law of limited duration is much more manageable than
one which needs a repeal.

This principle that the earth belongs to the living, and not
to the dead, is of very extensive application and consequences,

in every country, and most especially in France. It enters into the resolution of the questions Whether the nation may change the descent of lands holden in tail? Whether they may change the appropriation of lands given antiently to the church, to hospitals, colleges, orders of chivalry, and other-wise in perpetuity? Whether they may abolish the charges and privileges attached on lands, including the whole cata-logue ecclesiastical and feudal? It goes to hereditary offices, authorities and jurisdictions; to hereditary orders, distinc-tions and appellations; to perpetual monopolies in commerce, the arts and sciences; with a long train of et ceteras: and it renders the question of reimbursement a question of generos-ity and not of right. In all these cases, the legislature of the day could authorize such appropriations and establishments for their own time, but no longer; and the present holders, even where they, or their ancestors, have purchased, are in the case of bonâ fide purchasers of what the seller had no right to convey.

Turn this subject in your mind, my dear Sir, and particu-larly as to the power of contracting debts; and develope it with that perspicuity and cogent logic so peculiarly yours. Your station in the councils of our country gives you an opportunity of producing it to public consideration, of forc-ing it into discussion. At first blush it may be rallied, as a theoretical speculation: but examination will prove it to be solid and salutary. It would furnish matter for a fine preamble to our first law for appropriating the public revenue; and it will exclude at the threshold of our new government the con-tagious and ruinous errors of this quarter of the globe, which have armed despots with means, not sanctioned by nature, for binding in chains their fellow men. We have already given in example one effectual check to the Dog of war by transfer-ring the power of letting him loose from the Executive to the

Legislative body, from those who are to spend to those who are to pay. I should be pleased to see this second obstacle held out by us also in the first instance. No nation can make a declaration against the validity of long-contracted debts so disinterestedly as we, since we do not owe a shilling which may not be paid with ease, principal and interest, within the time of our own lives.—Establish the principle also in the new law to be passed for protecting copyrights and new inventions, by securing the exclusive right for 19. instead of 14. years. Besides familiarising us to this term, it will be an instance the more of our taking reason for our guide, instead of English precedent, the habit of which fetters us with all the political heresies of a nation equally remarkeable for it's early excitement from some errors, and long slumbering under others.

1801: Envisioning the Future

In his first inaugural address Thomas Jefferson speaks to, rather than for, the American people at a particular moment—March 4, 1801—that he believed marked the beginning of another chapter in the unfolding national story, which he later titled the "Revolution of 1800."[13] The people had survived another nearly fatal crisis of union, mobilizing in the recent presidential elections and in the deadlocked votes in the Electoral College and Congress that threatened to defy and suppress the voice of the people. Jefferson's seemingly absurd efforts to calculate the length of a generation in his 1789 letter— mocked by generations of scholars—proved remarkably accurate; if we join Jefferson in considering the Missouri Crisis of 1819–1821 as yet again threatening the nation's existence, the generational chronology seems to carry through his lifetime and beyond, culminating in the union's denouement in the American Civil War.

That Americans, including Jefferson, feared the worst in the 1800–1801 presidential succession crisis is clear, and it is this fear that animates his inaugural address. Jefferson urges his auditors and readers to look forward to the new nation's boundless prospects, "with room enough for our descendants to the thousandth and thousandth generation," as they seek to escape the all too predict-able fate of other peoples. Ever mindful of their always precarious position, patriotic Americans should project their energies and ambi-tions across time and space. Preserving the republic is the predicate of progress.

Jefferson's rhetorical challenge was to convince his countrymen that he would not exploit the power he could now wield to advance personal or partisan interests. Reminding them of a generational identity based on shared values, common interests, and their obliga-tion to future generations, he assumes the modest persona of a public servant that he had demanded of George III in A Summary View. He would follow the lead of George Washington, whose "pre-eminent services" secured American independence. But Jefferson does not presume to liken himself to "our first and greatest revolutionary character." Washington led the new nation through the hazards of war; the assignment for Jefferson and his successors is to keep the peace from generation to generation, sustaining a civic and historical consciousness that would enable the people to mobilize effectively against future threats. The United States would then demonstrate that a self-governing people possesses "the strongest government on earth."[14] It is "the world's best hope," a model and inspiration to other peoples as they sought to govern themselves and write their own histories.

March 4, 1801

FIRST INAUGURAL ADDRESS[15]

Called upon to undertake the duties of the first Executive office of our country, I avail myself of the presence of that portion of my fellow citizens which is here assembled to express my grateful thanks for the favor with which they have been pleased to look towards me, to declare a sincere consciousness that the task is above my talents, and that I approach it with those anxious and awful presentiments which the greatness of the charge, and the weakness of my powers so justly inspire. A rising nation, spread over a wide and fruitful land, traversing all the seas with the rich productions of their industry, engaged in commerce with nations who feel power and forget right, advancing rapidly to destinies beyond the reach of mortal eye; when I contemplate these transcendent objects, and see the honour, the happiness, and the hopes of this beloved country committed to the issue and the auspices of this day, I shrink from the contemplation & humble myself before the magnitude of the undertaking. Utterly indeed should I despair, did not the presence of many, whom I here see, remind me, that, in the other high authorities provided by our constitution, I shall find resources of wisdom, of virtue, and of zeal, on which to rely under all difficulties. To you, then, gentlemen, who are charged with the sovereign functions of legislation, and to those associated with you, I look with encouragement for that guidance and support which may enable us to steer with safety the vessel in which we are all embarked, amidst the conflicting elements of a troubled world.

During the contest of opinion through which we have past, the animation of discusions and of exertions has sometimes worn an aspect which might impose on strangers unused to think freely, and to speak and to write what they think; but this being now decided by the voice of the nation, announced according to the rules of the constitution all will of course arrange themselves under the will of the law, and unite in common efforts for the common good. All too will bear in mind this sacred principle, that though the will of the majority is in all cases to prevail, that will, to be rightful, must be reasonable; that the minority possess their equal rights, which equal laws must protect, and to violate would be oppression. Let us then, fellow citizens, unite with one heart and one mind, let us restore to social intercourse that harmony and affection without which liberty, and even life itself, are but dreary things. And let us reflect that having banished from our land that religious intolerance under which mankind so long bled and suffered, we have yet gained little if we countenance a political intolerance, as despotic, as wicked, and capable of as bitter and bloody persecutions. During the throes and convulsions of the ancient world, during the agonising spasms of infuriated man, seeking through blood and slaughter his long lost liberty, it was not wonderful that the agitation of the billows should reach even this distant and peaceful shore; that this should be more felt and feared by some and less by others; and should divide opinions as to measures of safety; but every difference of opinion is not a difference of principle. We have called by different names brethren of the same principle. We are all republicans: we are all federalists. If there be any among us who would wish to dissolve this Union, or to change its republican form, let them stand undisturbed as monuments of the safety with which error of opinion may be tolerated, where reason is left free to combat it. I know indeed that some honest men fear that a republican government cannot be strong; that this government is not strong enough. But would the honest patriot, in the full tide of successful experiment, abandon a government which has so far kept us free and firm, on the theoretic and visionary fear, that this government, the world's best hope, may, by possibility, want energy to preserve itself? I trust not. I believe this, on the contrary, the strongest government on earth. I believe it the only one, where every man, at the call of the law, would fly to the standard of the law, and would meet invasions of the public order as his own personal concern.—Sometimes it is said that man cannot be trusted with the government of himself. Can he then be trusted with the government of others? Or have we found angels, in the form of kings, to govern him? Let history answer this question.

Let us then, with courage and confidence, pursue our own federal and republican principles; our attachment to union and representative government. Kindly separated by nature and a wide ocean from the exterminating havoc of one quarter of the globe; too high minded to endure the degradations of the others, possessing a chosen country, with room enough for our descendants to the thousandth and thousandth generation, entertaining a due sense of our equal right to the use of our own faculties, to the acquisitions of our own industry, to honor and confidence from our fellow citizens, resulting not from birth, but from our actions and their sense of them, enlightened by a benign religion, professed indeed and practised in various forms, yet all of them inculcating honesty, truth, temperance, gratitude and the love of man, acknowledging and adoring an overruling providence, which by all its dispensations proves that it delights in the happiness of man here, and his greater happiness hereafter; with all these blessings, what more is necessary to make us a happy and a prosperous people? Still one thing more, fellow citizens, a wise and frugal government, which shall restrain men from injuring one another, shall leave them otherwise free to regulate their own pursuits of industry and improvement, and shall not take from the mouth of labor the bread it has earned. This is the sum of good government; and this is necessary to close the circle of our felicities.

About to enter, fellow citizens, on the exercise of duties

which comprehend every thing dear and valuable to you, it
is proper you should understand what I deem the essential
principles of our government, and consequently those which
ought to shape its administration. I will compress them
within the narrowest compass they will bear, stating the general principle, but not all its limitations.—Equal and exact
justice to all men, of whatever state or persuasion, religious or
political:—peace, commerce, and honest friendship with all
nations, entangling alliances with none:—the support of the
state governments in all their rights, as the most competent
administrations for our domestic concerns, and the surest bulwarks against anti-republican tendencies:—the preservation
of the General government in its whole constitutional vigor,
as the sheet anchor of our peace at home, and safety abroad: a
jealous care of the right of election by the people, a mild and
safe corrective of abuses which are lopped by the sword of
revolution where peaceable remedies are unprovided:—absolute acquiescence in the decisions of the majority, the vital
principle of republics, from which is no appeal but to force,
the vital principle and immediate parent of the despotism:—
a well disciplined militia, our best reliance in peace, and for
the first moments of war, till regulars may relieve them:—the
supremacy of the civil over the military authority:—economy
in the public expence, that labor may be lightly burthened:—
the honest payment of our debts and sacred preservation of
the public faith:—encouragement of agriculture, and of commerce as its handmaid:—the diffusion of information, and
arraignment of all abuses at the bar of the public reason:—
freedom of religion; freedom of the press; and freedom of person, under the protection of the Habeas Corpus:—and trial by
juries impartially selected. These principles form the bright
constellation, which has gone before us and guided our steps
through an age of revolution and reformation. The wisdom of

our sages, and blood of our heroes have been devoted to their attainment:—they should be the creed of our political faith; the text of civic instruction, the touchstone by which to try the services of those we trust; and should we wander from them in moments of error or of alarm, let us hasten to retrace our steps, and to regain the road which alone leads to peace, liberty and safety.

I repair then, fellow citizens, to the post you have assigned me. With experience enough in subordinate offices to have seen the difficulties of this the greatest of all, I have learnt to expect that it will rarely fall to the lot of imperfect man to retire from this station with the reputation, and the favor, which bring him into it. Without pretensions to that high confidence you reposed in our first and greatest revolutionary character, whose pre-eminent services had entitled him to the first place in his country's love, and destined for him the fairest page in the volume of faithful history, I ask so much confidence only as may give firmness and effect to the legal administration of your affairs. I shall often go wrong through defect of judgment. When right, I shall often be thought wrong by those whose positions will not command a view of the whole ground. I ask your indulgence for my own errors, which will never be intentional; and your support against the errors of others, who may condemn what they would not if seen in all its parts. The approbation implied by your suffrage, is a great consolation to me for the past; and my future solicitude will be, to retain the good opinion of those who have bestowed it in advance, to conciliate that of others by doing them all the good in my power, and to be instrumental to the happiness and freedom of all.

Relying then on the patronage of your good will, I advance with obedience to the work, ready to retire from it whenever you become sensible how much better choices it is in your

power to make. And may that infinite power, which rules the
destinies of the universe, lead our councils to what is best,
and give them a favorable issue for your peace and prosperity.

1816: Divide to Unite

In this 1816 letter to constitutional reformer "Henry Tompkinson"
(pseudonym of Samuel Kercheval, a lawyer from Frederick County,
Virginia), Thomas Jefferson returned to the generational sovereignty
theme that he first broached with James Madison in 1789. Jefferson
also looked homeward, focusing on Virginia's failure to replace an ill-
conceived, hastily written revolutionary constitution that the people of the commonwealth had not ratified. Among the many defects
of the 1776 charter, Jefferson and Kercheval agreed, was the conspicuously unequal representation of Frederick and other western
counties. Jefferson was also particularly distressed by the absence of
local self-government and institutions, notably schools, that would
cultivate civic capacity and patriotic sentiments.[16]

As he developed his mature understanding of federalism in yet
another frustrated campaign for constitutional reform, the former
president's anxieties about the new nation's future came to the fore.
In his inaugural address President Jefferson resolutely faced forward,
evoking a boundless continental domain for countless future generations. In 1816 he feared that Virginians would not meet the generational challenge of reconstituting their commonwealth and fulfilling
the republican Revolution's original promise. The national future
he envisioned depended on more perfect unions within and among
states, old and new, and across generations. The ultimate challenge
was constitutional, for republicanism could only flourish where self-
governing citizens could recognize and identify with each other
across the generational and geographical lines that divided them in an
expanding and enduring union. "Who can limit the extent to which
the federative principle may operate effectively?" Jefferson asked his

fellow Americans in his second inaugural address on March 4, 1805.[17] The temporal and spatial divisions that secured the rights and fostered the civic capacity of republican citizens would enable them to become a single, great, self-governing people. But all of those lines of division were also potential fracture lines, as the Missouri Crisis would soon confirm.

Jefferson enjoined "Hopkinson" not to make his confidential sentiments known to anyone else: "Keep them to yourself as the effusions of withered age and useless time." This was a characteristic stance for the obsessively private Jefferson, although he probably and quite rightly feared that his sentiments would be controversial and countersuggestive, providing critical readers with a road map to disunion. His self-deprecating posture also reflected a characteristically exaggerated modesty, reinforced by his sense of generational identity: if, as it turned out, he still had another decade of life before him, he was no longer part of the politically active, public-facing, "living" generation. Yet he clearly felt he had something important to say—and that it would be better said by someone like the younger (forty-nine-year-old) Kercheval.

By the time the letter was later published, after Jefferson's death, it would have the posthumous authenticity of a heartfelt and timeless testament of his fundamental beliefs.[18] We speculate that Jefferson might want it to be read someday as if he were offering advice in the present tense, assuming its relevance and resonance in another generation's real time.

July 12, 1816, Monticello

THOMAS JEFFERSON TO "HENRY TOMPKINSON" (SAMUEL KERCHEVAL) (EXCERPTS)[19]

I duly recieved your favor of June 13. with a copy of the letters on the calling a Convention, on which you are pleased

to ask my opinion. I have not been in the habit of mysteri-
ous reserve on any subject, nor of buttoning up my opinions
within my own doublet. On the contrary, while in public
service especially, I have thought the public entitled to frank-
ness, and intimately to know whom they employed. But I am
now retired: I resign myself, as a passenger, with confidence
to those at the present helm, and ask but for rest, peace and
good will. The question you propose, on equal representation, has become a party one, in which I wish to take no public share. Yet, if it be asked for your own satisfaction only,
and not to be quoted before the public, I have no motive to
withold it, & the less from you, as it coincides with your
own. At the birth of our republic, I committed that opinion
to the world, draught of a Constitution annexed to the Notes
on Virginia, in which a provision was inserted for a representation permanently equal. The infancy of the subject at
that moment, and our inexperience of self-government occa-
sioned gross departures, in that draught, from genuine republican canons. In truth, the abuses of monarchy had so much
filled all the space of political contemplation that we imagined
every thing republican which was not monarchy. We had not
yet penetrated to the mother-principle that "governments
are republican only in proportion as they embody the will of
their people, and execute it." Hence, our first constitutions
had really no leading principle in them. But experience &
reflection have but more & more confirmed me in the particular importance of the equal representation then proposed. . . .

But, inequality of representation, in both houses of our
legislature is not the only republican heresy in this first essay
of our revolutionary patriots at forming a constitution. For let
it be agreed that a government is republican in proportion as
every member composing it has his equal voice in the direction of it's concerns, (not indeed in person, which would be

impracticable beyond the limits of a city, or small township, but) by representatives chosen by himself, & responsible to him at short periods, and let us bring to the test of this Canon every branch of our constitution.

In the legislature, the House of Representatives is chosen by less than half the people, and not at all in proportion to those who do chuse. The Senate are still more disproportion- ate, and for long terms of irresponsibility.—In the Executive, the Governor is entirely independant of the choice of the peo- ple, & of their controul; his Council equally so, and at best but a fifth wheel to a waggon.—In the Judiciary, the judges of the highest courts are dependant on none but themselves. In England, where judges were named, & removable at the will of an hereditary Executive, from which branch most mis- rule was feared, and has flowed, it was a great point gained, by fixing them for life, to make them independant of that Executive. But in a government founded on the public will this principle operates in an opposite direction, & against that will. There too they were still removable on a concurrence of the Executive and legislative branches. But we have made them independant of the nation itself. They are irremovable but by their own body for any depravities of conduct, and even by their own body for the imbecilities of dotage.—The justices of the inferior courts are self-chosen, are for life, and perpetuate their own body in succession forever, so that a fac- tion once possessing itself of the bench of a county can never be broken up, but hold their county in chains, forever indis- soluble. Yet these justices are the real Executive, as well as judiciary in all our minor and most ordinary concerns. They tax us at will; fill the office of sheriff, the most important of all the executive officers of the county, name nearly all our military leaders, which leaders, once named, are removable but by themselves.—The Juries, our judges of all fact, and of law when they chuse it, are not selected by the people, nor amenable to them. They are chosen by an officer named by the Court and Executive. Chosen, did I say? Picked up by the Sheriff from the loungings of the court yard, after every thing respectable has retired from it.—Where then is our republicanism to be found? Not in our constitution certainly, but merely in the spirit of our people. That would oblige even a despot to govern us republicanly. Owing to this spirit, and to nothing in the form of our constitution, all things have gone well. But this fact, so triumphantly misquoted by the enemies of reformation, is not the fruit of our constitution, but has prevailed in spite of it. Our functionaries have done well, because generally honest men. If any were not so, they feared to shew it.

But it will be said it is easier to find faults than to amend them. I do not think their amendment so difficult as is pretended. Only lay down true principles, and adhere to them inflexibly. Do not be frightened into their surrender by the alarms of the timid, or the croakings of wealth against the ascendancy of the people. If experience be called for, appeal to that of our 15. or 20. governments for 40. years, and shew me where the people have done half the mischief in these 40. years, that a single despot would have done in a single year; or shew half the riots and rebellions, the crimes & the punishments which have taken place in any single nation, under kingly government, during the same period. The true foundation of republican government is the equal right of every citizen in his person, & property, & in their management. Try by this, as a tally, every provision of our constitution, and see if it hangs directly on the will of the people. Reduce your legislature to a convenient number for full, but orderly discussion. Let every man who fights or pays exercise his just and equal right in their election. Submit them to approbation or rejection at short intervals.—Let the Executive be chosen in the same way, & for the same term, by those whose agent he is to be; and leave no screen of a council, behind which to skulk from responsibility.—It has been thought that the people are not competent electors of judges *learned in the law*. But I do not know that this is true, and, if doubtful, we should follow principle. In this, as in many other elec' tions, they would be guided by reputation, which would not err oftener perhaps than the present mode of appoint' ment. . . . The organisation of our county administrations may be thought more difficult. But follow principle, & the knot unties itself. Divide the counties into Wards of such size as that every citizen can attend when called on, and act in per' son. Ascribe to them the government of their wards in all things relating to themselves exclusively. A justice chosen by themselves, in each, a constable a military company, a patrole, a school, the care of their own poor, their own portion of the public roads, the choice of one or more jurors to serve in some court, & the delivery, within their own wards, of their own votes for all elective officers of higher sphere will relieve the county administration of nearly all it's business, will have it better done, and by making every citizen an acting member of the government, & in the offices nearest & most interesting to him, will attach him by his strongest feelings to the inde' pendance of his country, and it's republican constitution. The justices thus chosen by every ward, would constitute the county court, would do it's judiciary business, direct roads and bridges, levy county and poor-rates, and administer all the matters of common interest to the whole county. These Wards, called townships, in New England, are the vital prin' ciple of their governments, and have proved themselves the wisest invention ever devised by the wit of man for the per' fect exercise of self-government, and for it's preservation. We should thus marshal our government into 1. the General federal republic, for all concerns foreign & federal; 2. that of the State for what relates to our own citizens exclusively. 3. the County republics for the duties & concerns of the county, and 4. the Ward-republics, for the small, and yet numerous & interesting concerns of the neighborhood: and in government, as well as in every other business of life, it is by division and subdivision of duties alone, that all matters, great & small, can be managed to perfection. And the whole is cemented by giving to every citizen personally a part in the administration of the public affairs.

The sum of these amendments is 1. general suffrage. 2. equal representation in the legislature. 3. an Executive chosen by the people. 4. judges elective or amovable. 5. justices jurors, and sheriffs elective. 6. Ward-divisions. & 7. periodical amendment of the Constitution.

I have thrown out these, as loose heads of amendment, for consideration & correction: and their object is to secure self-government by the republicanism of our constitution, as well as by the spirit of the people; and it is to nourish and perpetuate that spirit. I am not among those who fear the people. They and not the rich, are our dependance for continued freedom. And, to preserve their independance, we must not let our rulers load us with perpetual debt. We must make our election between *economy & liberty*, or *profusion and servitude*. If we run into such debts as that we must be taxed in our meat and in our drink, in our necessaries & our comforts, in our labors & our amusements, for our callings and our creeds, as the people of England are, our people, like them, must come to labor 16. hours in the 24. give the earnings of 15. of these to the government for their debts and daily expences; and the 16th being insufficient to afford us bread, we must live, as they now do, on oatmeal & potatoes; have no time to think, no means of calling the mismanagers to account; but be glad to obtain subsistence by hiring ourselves to rivet their chains on the necks of our fellow sufferers. Our land hold-ers too, like theirs, retaining indeed the title and steward-ship of estates called theirs, but held really in trust for the treasury, must wander, like theirs, in foreign countries, and be contented with penury, obscurity, exile, and the glory of the nation. This example reads to us the salutary lesson that private fortunes are destroyed by public, as well as by private extravagance. And this is the tendency of all human govern-ments. A departure from principle in one instance becomes a precedent for a 2^d that 2^d for a 3^d and so on, till the bulk of the society is reduced to be mere automatons of misery, to have no sensibilities left but for sinning and suffering. Then begins indeed the bellum omnium in omnia, which some philoso-phers observing to be so general in this world, have mistaken it for the natural, instead of the abusive, state of man. And the forehorse of this frightful team is Public debt. Taxation follows that, and in it's train wretchedness and oppression.

Some men look at Constitutions with sanctimonious rever-ence, & deem them, like the ark of the covenant, too sacred to be touched. They ascribe to the men of the preceding age a wisdom more than human, and suppose what they did to be beyond amendment. I knew that age well: I belonged to it, and labored with it. It deserved well of it's country. It was very like the present, but without the experience of the present: and 40. years of experience in government is worth a century of book-reading: and this they would say themselves, were they to rise from the dead. I am certainly not an advo-cate for frequent & untried changes in laws and constitutions. I think moderate imperfections had better be borne with; because when once known, we accomodate ourselves to them, and find practical means of correcting their ill effects. But

I know also that laws and institutions must go hand in hand
with the progress of the human mind. As that becomes more
developed, more enlightened, as new discoveries are made,
new truths disclosed, and manners and opinions change with
the change of circumstances, institutions must advance also,
and keep pace with the times. We might as well require a
man to wear still the coat which fitted him when a boy, as
civilised society to remain ever under the regimen of their
barbarous ancestors. It is this preposterous idea which has
lately deluged Europe in blood. Their monarchs, instead of
wisely yielding to the gradual changes of circumstances, of
favoring progressive accomodation to progressive improvement, have clung to old abuses, intrenched themselves behind
steady habits, and obliged their subjects to seek, thro' blood
& violence, rash & ruinous innovations, which, had they
been referred to the peaceful deliberations, & collected wisdom of the nation, would have been put into acceptable and
salutary forms. . . . And lastly, let us provide in our constitution for it's revision at stated periods. What these periods
should be Nature herself indicates. By the European tables of
mortality, of the Adults living at any one moment of time, a
majority will be dead in about 19. years. At the end of that
period then a new majority is come into place; or in other
words a new generation. Each generation is as independant of
the one preceding, as that was of all which had gone before.
It has then, like them, a right to chuse for itself the form of
government it believes most promotive of it's own happiness:
consequently to accomodate to the circumstances in which
it finds itself that recieved from it's predecessors; and it is
for the peace and good of mankind that a solemn opportunity of doing this every 19. or 20. years should be provided
by the constitution; so that it may be handed on, with periodical repairs, from generation to generation to the end of

time, if any thing human can so long endure. It is now 40. years since the constitution of Virginia was formed. The same tables inform us that, within that period, two thirds of the Adults then living are now dead. Have then the remaining third, even if they had the wish, the right to hold in obedience to their will, and to laws heretofore made by them, the other two thirds who, with themselves compose the present mass of Adults? If they have not, who has? the dead? But the dead have no rights. They are nothing; and nothing cannot own something. Where there is no substance, there can be no accident. This corporeal globe, and every thing upon it, belongs to it's present corporeal inhabitants, during their generation. They alone have a right to direct what is the concern of themselves alone, and to declare the law of that direction: and this declaration can only be made by their majority. That majority then has a right to depute representatives to a Convention, and to make the Constitution what they think will be best for themselves.

1826: Jefferson's Prayer

Thomas Jefferson would be heard once more while he still lived. Invited to attend a celebration of the new nation's fiftieth anniversary in Washington, DC, he wrote organizer Roger Chew Weightman that he was too ill to attend. Regretting that he would miss the opportunity to meet the Declaration's surviving signers, "the remnant of that host of worthies" who would represent his revolutionary generation, Jefferson seized the moment to speak to the posterity he would soon join.

If Jefferson's horizons had shrunk in recent years as he worried about Virginia's constitution and feared for the union's survival (interpreting the Missouri Crisis as the parricidal repudiation of his generation's legacy), he now embraces a more capacious perspective.

It is a "consolatory fact" for him that the union had survived for half a century and that Americans apparently "continue to approve the choice we made." But even if they should *not* continue to do so—and there were very good reasons to think they might not—the Declaration of Independence would inspire peoples elsewhere. "May it be to the world what I believe it will be (to some parts sooner, to others later, but finally to all) the Signal of arousing men to burst the chains" of despotism "and to assume the blessings & security of self government." He cannot know if this would be true, but it is what he needs to believe: it is the enduring core of his republican faith, his prayer for the future.

June 24, 1826, Monticello

THOMAS JEFFERSON TO ROGER CHEW WEIGHTMAN[20]

The kind invitation I recieve from you on the part of the citizens of the city of Washington, to be present with them at their celebration of the 50th anniversary of American indepindance; as one of the surviving signers of an instrument, pregnant with our own, and the fate of the world, is most flattering to myself, and heightened by the honorable accompaniment proposal for the comfort of such a journey. It adds sensibly to the sufferings of sickness, to be deprived by it of a personal participation in the rejoicings of that day. But acquiescence is a duty, under circumstances not placed among those we are permitted to controul. I should indeed, with peculiar delight, have met and exchanged there, congratulations personally, with the small band, the remnant of that host of worthies, who joined with us, on that day, in the bold and doubtful election we were to make, for our country, between submission, or the sword; and to have enjoyed with them the consolatory fact that our fellow citizens, after half a century of experience and prosperity, continue to approve the choice we made. May it be to the world what I believe it will be, (to some parts sooner, to others later, but finally to all.) the Signal of arousing men to burst the chains, under which Monkish ignorance and superstition had persuaded them to bind themselves, and to assume the blessings & security of self government. The form which we have substituted restores the free right to the unbounded exercise of reason and freedom of opinion. All eyes are opened, or opening to the rights of man. The general spread of the light of science has already laid open to every view the palpable truth that the mass of mankind has not been born, with saddles on their backs, nor a favored few booted and spurred, ready to ride them legitimately, by the grace of god. These are grounds of hope for others. For ourselves let the annual return of this day, for ever refresh our recollections of these rights and an undiminished devotion to them.

I will ask permission here to address the pleasure with which I should have met my ancient neighbors of the City of Washington and of it's vicinities, with whom I passed so many years of a pleasing social intercourse; an intercourse which so much relieved the anxieties of the public cares, and left impressions so deeply engraved in my affections, as never to be forgotten. With my regret that ill health forbids me the gratification of an acceptance, be pleased to recieve for yourself and those for whom you write the assurance of my highest respect and friendly attachments.

ACKNOWLEDGMENTS

In many respects this book took twenty-five years to write. We've been discussing Jefferson and his legacy since having lunch together at the Omohundro Institute for Early American History and Culture annual conference held in Glasgow in 2001. (Thanks to our friends Simon Newman and Marina Moskowitz for organizing that conference!) For many years we offered a summer seminar, "The Age of Jefferson," for schoolteachers from around the United States under the auspices of the Gilder Lehrman Institute for American History. This book reflects the discussions we had during those seminars and seeks to capture their spirit and flavor. We're grateful to the hundreds of teachers we met while conducting those seminars whose questions and ideas helped shape our understanding of Jefferson. We're especially grateful to the master teachers we worked with, especially Gloria Sesso and Ron Nash.

We have benefited enormously from the wisdom and scholarship of many friends, including Chris Bates, Christa Dierksheide, Eliga Gould, Jack P. Greene, Kevin R. C. Gutzman, Nicholas Guyatt, Jim Hrdlicka, Nancy Isenberg, Brendan McConville, Robert Parkinson, John Ragosta, Richard Samuelson, Hannah Spahn, Maurizio Valsania, Gordon S. Wood, and Nadine Zimmerli. The late and much missed Jan Lewis and Herb Sloan were wonderful scholars and dear friends.

We began writing this book in early 2024. Andrew Burstein, Joanne Freeman, Annette Gordon-Reed, Patrick Griffin, and George Van Cleve read the manuscript in part or entirely, and they improved it through their responses (and criticism). We broke the rules of publishing and sent the entire manuscript to Bob Weil at Liveright. Bob saw potential in the project and shared it with senior editor Haley Bracken. Haley went above and beyond to improve the manuscript. She began as a friend to the project and became a friend to us. We owe a huge debt of gratitude to Bob, Haley, and everyone at Liveright.

This is a book about generations. We have dedicated it to our posterity, but we want to thank our own generation who have supported us for so long. We must begin with Kristin Onuf and Mimi Cogliano. To their number we must add Beth Cogliano, David Cogliano, Lisa Cogliano, John Giangrande, Sally Giangrande, Andrea Katter, Chuck Katter, Sandy Keowen, Chris (Uncle Bro) Onuf, Claire Onuf, and Nick Onuf.

NOTES

INTRODUCTION

1. Margaret P. Battin, "July 4, 1826: Explaining the Same-Day Deaths of John Adams and Thomas Jefferson," *Historically Speaking* 6 (2005): 266–74; Andrew Burstein, *America's Jubilee: How in 1826 a Generation Remembered Fifty Years of Independence* (Alfred A. Knopf, 2001), ch. 11.
2. James Parton, *Life of Thomas Jefferson: Third President of the United States* (Boston: James R. Osgood & Co., 1874), preface, iii.
3. Jan Lewis and Peter S. Onuf, "American Synecdoche: Thomas Jefferson as Image, Icon, Character, and Self," *American Historical Review* 103 (1998): 125–36. The foundational study of Jefferson's reputation remains Merrill D. Peterson, *The Jefferson Image in the American Mind* (Oxford University Press, 1960; repr. University of Virginia Press, 1997). Also see Francis D. Cogliano, *Thomas Jefferson: Reputation and Legacy* (University of Virginia Press, 2006); and Andrew Burstein, *Democracy's Muse: How Thomas Jefferson Became an FDR Liberal, a Reagan Republican, and a Tea Party Fanatic, All the While Being Dead* (University of Virginia Press, 2015).
4. "President Roosevelt's Independence Day Address at Monticello," July 4, 1936, monticello.org; "President Points to 'Spirit of Youth' as Aid to Freedom," *New York Times*, July 5, 1936; Roosevelt's 1943 address at the dedication on the Jefferson Memorial, quoted in Cogliano, *Thomas Jefferson*, 5. For Roosevelt's admiration of Jefferson see Burstein, *Democracy's Muse*, ch. 1.
5. The best history of the commemoration of July 4 is Michael D.

Hattem, *The Memory of '76: The Revolution in American History* (Yale
University Press, 2024), 239–79.

6. Consider *The 1619 Project*, an initiative by the journalist Nikole
   Hannah-Jones launched by the *New York Times* in August 2019 to
   mark the four-hundredth anniversary of the first documented arrival
   of enslaved Africans in British America. Hannah-Jones sought to center the African experience in American history, arguing that the true
   founding date of the country should be 1619, not 1776. She offered a
   critical view of Jefferson as he wrote the Declaration of Independence
   in Philadelphia in June 1776 while served by the enslaved half-brother
   of his wife, Robert Hemings. Despite the perfervid response of some
   of its critics, the *1619 Project* did not cause a backlash against Jefferson
   and his fellow founders. Indeed, criticism of Jefferson had been building for nearly two decades before its appearance.

7. Ashley Southall, "Jefferson-Jackson Dinner Will Be Renamed," *New
   York Times*, August 8, 2015; Steve Almasy, "Dems in Jefferson's
   Home State Change Name of Jefferson-Jackson Dinner," CNN,
   March 3, 2018; Jeffery C. Mays and Zachary Small, "Jefferson Statue
   to Be Removed from NYC Council Chambers," *New York Times*,
   October 18, 2021.

8. Jennifer Schuessler, "Historians Question Trump's Comments on
   Confederate Statues," *New York Times*, August 15, 2017.

9. "Governor Ron DeSantis Unveils Thomas Jefferson Statue in Jefferson
   County as Part of Florida's America250 Celebration," July 2, 2025,
   flgov.com.

10. "Remarks by President Trump at South Dakota's 2020 Mount
    Rushmore Fireworks Celebration," July 4, 2020, National Archives.
    On January 29, 2025, President Trump issued an executive order reviv-
    ing the 1776 Commission he had created at the end of his first adminis-
    tration (which President Joe Biden had abolished). "The purpose of the
    1776 Commission is to promote patriotic education," Trump declared,
    "as well as to advise and promote the work of the White House Task
    Force on Celebrating America's 250th Birthday ('Task Force 250') and
    the United States Semiquincentennial Commission in their efforts
    to provide a grand celebration worthy of the momentous occasion of
    the 250th anniversary of American Independence on July 4, 2026."
    Donald J. Trump, "Ending Radical Indoctrination in K-12 Schooling,"
    Executive Order, January 29, 2025, whitehouse.gov.

11. See Pauline Maier, *American Scripture: Making the Declaration of
    Independence* (Alfred A. Knopf, 1997), for broad popular participation

in declaring independence in a multiplicity of "other declarations." For a close focus on the text of the Declaration that seeks to demonstrate its continuing—transhistorical—relevance, see Danielle Allen, *Our Declaration: A Reading of the Declaration of Independence in Defense of Equality* (Liveright, 2014).

12. Robert G. Parkinson, *Tyrants and Rogues: Understanding the Declaration of Independence* (W. W. Norton, 2026).

13. Thomas Jefferson (hereafter TJ) to John Adams, August 1, 1816, in *The Papers of Thomas Jefferson: Digital Edition*, ed. James P. McClure and J. Jefferson Looney (University of Virginia Press, Rotunda, 2008–2026) (hereafter *PTJDE*).

14. "President Roosevelt's Independence Day Address at Monticello," July 4, 1936, monticello.org; "President Points to 'Spirit of Youth' as Aid to Freedom," *New York Times*, July 5, 1936. The view of the West Portico of Monticello became familiar to generations of Americans after it was engraved on the reverse of the five-cent coin in 1938 at Roosevelt's behest. Since Roosevelt gave his address at Monticello, other world leaders have spoken there, including Gerald Ford in 1976 and Mikhail Gorbachev in 1993. Thousands of new Americans have taken their citizenship oaths on that spot at a ceremony held each year on the Fourth of July.

15. TJ to James Madison, September 6, 1789, *PTJDE*. We are indebted to Herbert E. Sloan's definitive scholarship on this letter and the significance of the themes it develops for TJ's thought. See Sloan, "The Earth Belongs in Usufruct to the Living," in *Jeffersonian Legacies*, ed. Peter S. Onuf (University of Virginia Press, 1993), 281–315; and Sloan, *Principle and Interest: Thomas Jefferson and the Problem of Debt* (Oxford University Press, 1995).

16. "essay, n.s.," in Samuel Johnson, *A Dictionary of the English Language*, 1755. "Essay" is derived from the French "essai" and owes much to Montaigne, who developed the modern form. For Montaigne, essays were short writings that attempted to redefine knowledge. We use "essay" in that spirit, but we hope to avoid Dr. Johnson's second definition: "a loose sally of the mind; an irregular indigested piece; not a regular and orderly composition."

17. We are not the only historians seeking to understand the meaning of TJ's legacy. All studies of Jefferson's legacy begin with Merrill D. Peterson's *The Jefferson Image in the American Mind*. We acknowledge the fine scholarship of Andrew Burstein, *Democracy's Muse*; Robert M. S. McDonald, *Confounding Father: Thomas Jefferson's Image in His*

Time (University of Virginia Press, 2016); Robert G. Parkinson, *The Common Cause: Creating Race and Nation in the American Nation* (University of North Carolina Press for the Omohundro Institute of Early American History and Culture, 2016); and Hannah Spahn, *Black Reason, White Feeling: The Jeffersonian Enlightenment in the African American Tradition* (University of Virginia Press, 2024). Revising our understanding of the history *within* the Declaration of Independence are Hans L. Eicholz, *Harmonizing Sentiments: The Declaration of Independence and the Jeffersonian Idea of Self-Government*, 2nd ed. (Peter Lang, 2024); Parkinson, *Tyrants and Rogues*; and Steven Sarson, *The Course of Human Events: The Declaration of Independence and the Historical Origins of the United States* (University of Virginia Press, 2025). Each of these scholars has shared their work and their wisdom with us over many years.

18. TJ, First Inaugural Address, March 4, 1801, *PTJDE*.

19. See Peter S. Onuf, *Jefferson's Empire: The Language of American Nationhood* (University of Virginia Press, 2000), esp. ch. 4; and Francis D. Cogliano, *Emperor of Liberty: Thomas Jefferson's Foreign Policy* (Yale University Press, 2014).

20. The Declaration of Independence as Adopted by Congress, July 4, 1776, *PTJDE*.

21. Parkinson, *Common Cause*.

22. James H. Kettner, *The Development of American Citizenship, 1608–1870* (University of North Carolina Press, 1978).

I. GENERATIONS

1. Jeffery C. Mays and Zachary Small, "Jefferson Statue Will Be Removed from N.Y.C. Council Chambers," *New York Times*, October 18, 2021.

2. Benjamin Park, "Thomas Jefferson, Sally Hemings, and Conroe ISD," *Houston Chronicle*, May 31, 2024; Mays and Small, "Jefferson Statue Will Be Removed."

3. L. P. Hartley, *The Go-Between* (1953; New York Review Press, 2002), 17.

4. For TJ's interest in the study of history see Francis D. Cogliano, *Thomas Jefferson: Reputation and Legacy* (University of Virginia Press, 2006), ch. 1; for figures on the number of history books Jefferson owned, see p. 20.

5. TJ to William Duane, April 4, 1813, *PTJDE*.

6. TJ, *Notes on the State of Virginia*, in Merrill D. Peterson, ed., *Thomas*

Jefferson: Writings (Library of America, 1984) (hereafter *TJW*), 123–325, Query XIV ("Laws"), 274. Jefferson proposed the plan to the Virginia Assembly without success in 1779. "Bill for the More General Diffusion of Knowledge," in "The Revisal of the Laws, 1776–1786," *PTJDE* [Bill no. 79].

7. For the Whig interpretation of history see H. Trevor Colbourn, *The Lamp of Experience: Whig History and the Intellectual Origins of the American Revolution* (University of North Carolina Press, 1965); and Bernard Bailyn, *The Ideological Origins of the American Revolution* (Harvard University Press, 1967). See Paul de Rapin-Thoyras, *Histoire d'Angleterre*, 10 vols. (La Haye: Alexandre de Rogissart, 1727); cited in E. Millicent Sowerby, ed., *Catalogue of the Library of Thomas Jefferson*, 5 vols. (Library of Congress, 1952–59), 1:156. For Jefferson's praise of Rapin see Francis Calley Gray, *Jefferson in 1814: Being an Account of a Visit to Monticello, Virginia* (Club of Odd Volumes, 1924), 72.

8. For the classic study of the great conflict between "power" and "liberty," see Bailyn, *Ideological Origins*.

9. Jack P. Greene, *Peripheries and Center: Constitutional Development in the Extended Polities of the British Empire and the United States, 1607-1788* (University of Georgia Press, 1986); Greene, *Constitutional Origins of the American Revolution* (Cambridge University Press, 2011); and Greene, *Evaluating Empire and Confronting Colonialism in Eighteenth-Century Britain* (Cambridge University Press, 2013).

10. "Notes on Early Career" (the so-called "Autobiography"), January 6–July 29, 1821, *PTJDE*.

11. Draft Instructions to the Virginia Delegates in the Continental Congress (ms. text of *A Summary View of the Rights of British America*) [July 1774], *PTJDE*. See the illuminating discussion in Brian Steele, *Thomas Jefferson and American Nationhood* (Cambridge University Press, 2012), 11–52.

12. "Notes on Early Career," *PTJDE*.

13. The Declaration as Adopted by Congress [July 6, 1775], *PTJDE*. For the complicated history of the evolution of the text with all of the various drafts by Jefferson and Dickinson, see "Declaration of the Causes and Necessity for Taking Up Arms" [June 26 to July 6, 1775], editorial note, *PTJDE*. On the Dickinson–Jefferson collaboration see Jane E. Calvert, *Penman of the Founding: A Biography of John Dickinson* (Oxford University Press, 2024), 275–76.

14. For antecedents to TJ's conception of the colonies as autonomous,

effectively independent polities, see Richard Bland, *An Inquiry into the Rights of the British Colonies* (Williamsburg, 1766); on British expectations that Americans would one day seek independence, see J. M. Bumsted, "'Things in the Womb of Time': Ideas of American Independence, 1633 to 1763," *William and Mary Quarterly* 31 (1974): 534–64; and Greene, *Evaluating Empire*, 86–91.

15. "His Majesty's most gracious speech to both houses of Parliament, on Friday, October 27, 1775" (New York, 1775). The speech was published throughout the colonies, appearing in Purdie's *Virginia Gazette* on January 19, 1776.

16. Richard Hakluyt, *The Principal Navigations, Voiages, Traffiques and Discoveries of the English Nation*, 3 vols. (London: George Bishop, Ralph Newberie and Robert Barker, 1598/99–1600).

17. "Refutation of the Argument that the Colonies were Established at the Expense of the British Nation" [after January 19, 1776], *PTJDE*.

18. Eric Foner, *Tom Paine and Revolutionary America* (Oxford University Press, 1976); W. A. Speck, *A Political Biography of Thomas Paine* (Pickering and Chatto, 2013); John Keane, *Tom Paine: A Political Life* (Bloomsbury, 1995); and Simon P. Newman and Peter S. Onuf, eds., *Paine and Jefferson in the Age of Revolutions* (University of Virginia Press, 2013). For *Common Sense* see Sophia Rosenfeld, *Common Sense: A Political History* (Harvard University Press, 2011). On Benjamin Rush's role in encouraging Paine to write *Common Sense*, see George W. Corner, ed., *The Autobiography of Benjamin Rush* (Princeton University Press, 1948), 113–14.

19. Thomas Paine, *Common Sense*, in *The Writings of Thomas Paine*, ed. Moncure Conway, 4 vols. (New York: G. P. Putnam's Sons, 1894–96), 67–120, quote on 112.

20. Paine, *Common Sense*, 83.

21. Paine, *Common Sense*, 86.

22. Thomas Nelson to TJ, February 4, 1776, *PTJDE*.

23. When settlers recognized the need for government, "some convenient tree will afford them a State House, under the branches of which the whole Colony may assemble to deliberate on public matters." Paine, *Common Sense*, 70.

24. Francis D. Cogliano, "'The Whole Object of the Present Controversy': The Early Constitutionalism of Paine and Jefferson," in *Paine and Jefferson in the Age of Revolutions*, ed. Simon P. Newman and Peter S. Onuf (University of Virginia Press, 2013), 26–48.

25. TJ to Joseph Priestley, March 21, 1801, *PTJDE*.

26. We are indebted here to Hannah Spahn, *Thomas Jefferson, Time, and History* (University of Virginia Press, 2011); and Sarson, *Course of Human Events*.

27. On the importance of war-related grievances see Parkinson, *Tyrants and Rogues*.

28. Benedict Anderson, *Imagined Communities: Reflections on the Origin and Spread of Nationalism*, rev. ed. (Verso, 2006).

29. Declaration of Independence as Adopted by Congress, July 4, 1776, *PTJDE*.

30. George Washington to Henry Lee Jr., September 22, 1788, *The Papers of George Washington: Digital Edition* (University of Virginia Press, Rotunda, 2008).

31. Daniel Hulsebosch, "Independence and Union: Imperfect Unions in Revolutionary British-America," in Eliga Gould, Paul Mapp, and Carla Gardina Pestan, eds., *Cambridge History of America and the World: Volume I, 1500-1820* (Cambridge University Press, 2021), 487–509.

32. See Jan Lewis, "The Republican Wife: Virtue and Seduction in the Early Republic," in *Family, Slavery, and Love in the Early American Republic: The Essays of Jan Ellen Lewis*, ed. Barry Bienstock et al. (University of North Carolina Press, for the Omohundro Institute of Early American History and Culture, 2021), 20–57.

33. Parkinson, *Common Cause*; Parkinson, *Thirteen Clocks: How Race United the Colonies and Made the Declaration of Independence* (University of North Carolina Press, for the Omohundro Institute of Early American History and Culture, 2021).

34. Eliga H. Gould, *Among the Powers of the Earth: The American Revolution and the Making of a New World Empire* (Harvard University Press, 2012); Gould, *Peace and Independence: The Turbulent History of the United States' Founding Treaty* (Oxford University Press, forthcoming).

35. TJ to "Henry Tompkinson" (Samuel Kercheval), July 12, 1816, *PTJDE*.

36. On the framers as "demigods," see TJ to John Adams, August 30, 1787, *PTJDE*.

37. Jonathan Gienapp, *The Second Creation: Fixing the American Constitution in the Founding Era* (Harvard University Press, 2018).

38. TJ to Kercheval, July 12, 1816, *PTJDE*.

39. Michael Warner, *The Letters of the Republic: Publication and the Public Sphere in Eighteenth-Century America* (Harvard University Press, 1990); on newspapers see Parkinson, *Thirteen Clocks*.

40. TJ to Henry Lee, May 8, 1825, *TJW*, 1501.

41. John Locke, *Second Treatise of Government: An Essay Concerning the True Original, Extent and End of Civil Government*, ed. Richard H. Cox (Harlan Davidson, 1982), ch. 2 ("Of the State of Nature"), para. 225, p. 138.

42. TJ to James Madison, September 6, 1789, in *PTJDE*. For authoritative discussion of this letter see Sloan, "Earth Belongs in Usufruct"; and Sloan, *Principle and Interest*.

43. At least until Madison politely dismissed his friend's argument in a February 4, 1790, letter, *PTJDE*. For further discussion see Andrew Burstein and Nancy Isenberg, *Madison and Jefferson* (Random House, 2010), 204–207; and Peter S. Onuf, *Jefferson and the Virginians: Democracy, Constitutions, and Empire* (Louisiana University Press, 2018), 104–109.

44. Richard K. Matthews, *The Radical Politics of Thomas Jefferson: A Revisionist View* (University Press of Kansas, 1984).

45. TJ, First Draft of Inaugural Address; First Inaugural Address, March 4, 1801, *PTJDE*, our emphases.

46. Kettner, *Development of American Citizenship, 1608-1870*.

47. Annette Gordon-Reed and Peter S. Onuf, "*Most Blessed of the Patriarchs*": *Thomas Jefferson and the Empire of the Imagination* (Liveright, 2016), 182–85.

48. Gordon-Reed and Onuf, "*Most Blessed of the Patriarchs*," 140–42.

49. Gienapp, *Second Creation*; Larry Kramer, *The People Themselves: Popular Constitutionalism and Judicial Review* (Oxford University Press, 2004).

50. TJ to Kercheval, July 12, 1816, *PTJDE*.

51. David C. Hendrickson, *Peace Pact: The Lost World of the American Founding* (University of Kansas Press, 2003).

52. TJ to James Madison, September 6, 1789, *PTJDE*.

53. On the parallel efforts of Madison and his fellow constitutionalists to "fix" the "original intentions" of the federal Constitution's authors, see Gienapp, *Second Creation*.

54. TJ to Henry Lee, May 8, 1825, *TJW*, 1501.

55. "Notes on Early Career," *PTJDE*. This is the definitive version of Jefferson's autobiography, and the accompanying editorial note traces the complicated history of its evolution.

56. Notes of Proceedings in the Continental Congress [June 7–August 1, 1776], *PTJDE*.

57. TJ's "original Rough draught," and the Declaration of Independence as Adopted by Congress, June 11–July 4, 1776, *PTJDE*.

58. Robert M. S. McDonald, "Thomas Jefferson's Changing Reputation as Author of the Declaration of Independence: The First Fifty Years," *Journal of the Early Republic* 19 (1999): 169–95; Cogliano, *Thomas Jefferson*, 138–41.

59. TJ to Henry Lee, May 8, 1825, *TJW*, 1501; Jay Fliegelman, *Declaring Independence: Jefferson, Natural Language and the Culture of Performance* (Stanford University Press, 1993).

60. TJ to James Madison, February 17, 1826, in J. C. A. Stagg, ed., *The Papers of James Madison, Digital Edition* (University of Virginia Press, 2010).

61. TJ to Madison, February 17, 1826, in Stagg, ed., *Papers of Madison*.

62. TJ's "original Rough draught" and the Declaration of Independence as Adopted by Congress, June 11–July 4, 1776, *PTJDE*.

63. TJ to James Madison, September 6, 1789, *PTJDE*, our emphasis.

64. TJ to Kercheval, July 12, 1816, *PTJDE*.

65. TJ, First Inaugural Address, March 4, 1801, *PTJDE*.

66. Declaration of Independence as Adopted by Congress, *PTJDE*.

67. TJ to Joseph Priestley, March 21, 1801, *PTJDE*.

II. MY COUNTRY

1. Sharon A. Brown, *Administrative History: Jefferson National Expansion Memorial National Historic Site, 1935–1980* (National Park Service, Washington, DC, 1984).

2. The classic source was Montesquieu (Charles Secondat), *The Spirit of the Laws* (Cambridge University Press, 1989), trans. and ed. Anne Cohler, Basia Carolyn Miller, and Harold Samuel Stone, Part I, ch. 9.

3. On the importance of space in British American political economy and subsequent political development, see Drew R. McCoy, *The Elusive Republic: Political Economy in Jeffersonian America* (University of North Carolina Press, for Institute of Early American History and Culture, 1980); and Major L. Wilson, *Space, Time, and Freedom: The Quest for Nationality and the Irrepressible Conflict, 1815–1861* (Greenwood Press, 1974).

4. James D. Drake, *The Nation's Nature: How Continental Presumptions Gave Rise to the United States of America* (University of Virginia Press, 2011).

5. TJ, "original Rough draught" of the Declaration of Independence, *PTJDE*, our emphasis.

6. Greene, *Peripheries and Center*; Greene, *Constitutional Origins of the American Revolution*.

7. *Massachusettensis, or a Series of Letters, Containing a Faithful State of Many Important and Striking Facts* . . . (London: J. Matthews, 1776; repr. Liberty Fund, 2010), preface.

8. John Phillip Reid, ed., *The Briefs of the American Revolution: Constitutional Arguments Between Thomas Hutchinson, Governor of Massachusetts Bay, and James Bowdoin for the Council and John Adams for the House of Representatives* (New York University Press, 1981).

9. *Nationalism* was coined in 1798. *Oxford English Dictionary*, s.v. "nationalism (n.)," December 2024. For *patriotism* see *Oxford English Dictionary*, s.v. "patriotism (n.)," July 2023. On the distinction between patriotism and nationalism, see John H. Schaar, "The Case for Patriotism," in Schaar, *Legitimacy in the Modern State* (Transaction Books, 1981), 285–311. For an insightful discussion of patriotism and identity formation in revolutionary New York, see Maurizio Valsania, *Laboring for Independence: Ann Eliza Bleecker and the American Quest for Identity* (Johns Hopkins University Press, forthcoming).

10. Christopher L. Tomlins, *Freedom Bound: Law, Labor, and Civic Identity in Colonizing English America, 1580-1865* (Cambridge University Press, 2010).

11. TJ, Minutes of the Board of Visitors, March 4, 1825, *TJW*, 479.

12. TJ to William Fleming, July 1, 1776, *PTJDE*.

13. TJ, Draft of Instructions to the Virginia Delegates in the Continental Congress (ms. text of *Summary View*), *PTJDE*.

14. Jerrilyn Greene Marston, *King and Congress: The Transfer of Political Legitimacy, 1774-1776* (Princeton University Press, 1987).

15. Mary Sarah Bilder, *The Transatlantic Constitution: Colonial Legal Culture and the Empire* (Harvard University Press, 2004).

16. Drake, *Nation's Nature*. See Samuel Williams, *A Discourse on the Love of Our Country: Delivered on a Day of Thanksgiving, December 15, 1774* (Salem, MA: Samuel and Ebenezer Hall, 1775), 23: "In that vast extent of country which reaches from Labrador to Florida, there is a climate adapted to health, vigour, industry, liberty, genius, and happiness."

17. TJ, Third Draft of Virginia Constitution (before June 13, 1776), *PTJDE*: "One or more territories shall be laid off Westward of the Alleghaney mountains for new colonies, which colonies shall be established on the same fundamental laws contained in this instrument, and shall be free and independant of this colony and of all the world."

18. Onuf, *Jefferson and the Virginians.*

19. TJ, *Summary View, TJW,* 106–107.

20. Calvert, *Penman of the Founding.*

21. The Declaration of Independence as Adopted by Congress, July 4, 1776, *PTJDE.*

22. James F. Hrdlicka, *Federal Empire: Constitution-Making in Revolutionary America* (University of Chicago Press, forthcoming).

23. John Adams, Plan of Treaties as Adopted (with Instructions), September 17, 1776, *The Adams Papers, Digital Edition,* ed. Sara Martin (University of Virginia Press, Rotunda, 2008–2024). For patriot treaty-making see Gould, *Peace and Independence.*

24. William Wirt, *Sketches of the Life and Character of Patrick Henry* (Philadelphia: James Webster, 1817), 12–23. The best discussion of the speech is in John Kukla, *Patrick Henry: Champion of Liberty* (Simon and Schuster, 2017), 165–72.

25. Charles Royster, *A Revolutionary People at War: The Continental Army and American Character, 1775-1783* (University of North Carolina Press for the Institute of Early American History and Culture, 1979).

26. TJ, Query XIX ("Manufactures"), *Notes on the State of Virginia, TJW,* 290, our emphasis.

27. TJ, Query XIX ("Manufactures"), *Notes on the State of Virginia, TJW,* 290.

28. TJ, Query XVIII ("Manners"), *Notes on the State of Virginia, TJW,* 288. For further discussion see Part III, "The People."

29. TJ, Query XIX ("Manufactures"), *Notes on the State of Virginia, TJW,* 291; Query XVIII ("Manners"), *Notes on the State of Virginia, TJW,* 289.

30. Robert G. Parkinson, *Heart of American Darkness: Bewilderment and Horror on the Early Frontier* (W. W. Norton, 2024), 237–38, passim.

31. TJ, First Inaugural Address, March 4, 1801, *PTJDE.*

32. TJ, First Inaugural Address, March 4, 1801, *PTJDE,* our emphases.

33. For Jeffersonian thinking on the merits and viability of larger republics, see McCoy, *Elusive Republic.* Also see Onuf, *Jefferson's Empire,* ch. 2 and 4; and Cogliano, *Emperor of Liberty,* ch. 6.

34. Ralph Lerner, "Commerce and Character: The British-American as New-Model Man," *William and Mary Quarterly,* 3rd ser., 36 (1979): 4–27; Peter S. Onuf, "Jefferson: Creole Nationalist and Commercial Republican," in Steven Frankel and John Ray, eds., *Commerce and Character: The Political Economy of the Enlightenment and the*

American Founding (University Press of Kansas, 2025), 136–61.

35. TJ, First Inaugural Address, March 4, 1801, *PTJDE*.

36. TJ to Joseph C. Cabell, February 2, 1816, *PTJDE*.

37. John William Ward, *Andrew Jackson: Symbol for an Age* (Oxford University Press, 1955).

38. TJ to Joseph Priestley, March 21, 1801, *PTJDE*.

39. Gregory Ablavsky, *Federal Ground: Governing Property and Violence in the First U.S. Territories* (Oxford University Press, 2021).

40. Hendrickson, *Peace Pact*.

41. Fred Anderson and Andrew Cayton, *The Dominion of War: Empire and Liberty in North America, 1500-2000* (Viking, 2005).

42. Peter S. Onuf, *Statehood and Union: A History of the Northwest Ordinance* (Indiana University Press, 1987). The best history of early American land policy is Michael A. Blaakman, *Speculation Nation: Land Mania in the Revolutionary American Republic* (University of Pennsylvania Press, 2023).

43. *Massachusettensis*, preface.

44. TJ to Joseph Priestley, March 21, 1801, *PTJDE*.

45. TJ, First Inaugural Address, March 4, 1801, *PTJDE*.

46. TJ to Joseph Cabell, January 31, 1814, *PTJDE*: "There are two sub-jects indeed which I shall claim a right to further as long as I breathe, the public education and the subdivision of the counties into wards. I consider the continuance of republican government as absolutely hang-ing on these two hooks." See William T. Hutchinson, "Unite to Divide; Divide to Unite: The Shaping of American Federalism," *Mississippi Valley Historical Review* 46 (1959): 3–18.

47. TJ to Joseph Cabell, February 2, 1816, *PTJDE*.

48. TJ to James Madison, January 30, 1787; TJ to Abigail Adams, February 22, 1787, *PTJDE*.

49. TJ to "Henry Tompkinson" (Samuel Kercheval), July 12, 1816, *PTJDE*.

50. Onuf, *Jefferson's Empire*.

51. TJ to Joseph C. Cabell, February 2, 1816, *PTJDE*, our emphasis.

52. TJ to Rev. James Madison, October 28, 1785, *PTJDE*: "The descent of property of every kind therefore to all the children, or to all the broth-ers and sisters, or other relations in equal degree is a politic measure, and a practicable one. Another means of silently lessening the inequal-ity of property is to exempt all from taxation below a certain point, and to tax the higher portions of property in geometrical progression as they rise." For further discussion see Matthews, *Radical Politics of Thomas Jefferson*.

53. TJ to "Henry Tompkinson" (Samuel Kercheval), July 12, 1816, *PTJDE*.

54. On this "release of energy," see James Willard Hurst, *Law and the Conditions of Freedom in the Nineteenth-Century United States* (University of Wisconsin Press, 1956).

55. TJ, First Inaugural Address, March 4, 1801, *PTJDE*.

56. TJ to William Ludlow, September 6, 1824, Founders Online, National Archives. TJ's account evokes the Scottish enlightenment conception of the stages of historical development. See Ronald L. Meek, *Social Science and the Ignoble Savage* (Cambridge University Press, 1976).

57. TJ, Query XI ("Aborigines"), *Notes on the State of Virginia*, *TJW*, 220; Onuf, *Jefferson's Empire*, 18–52.

58. Philip Kennicott, "50 Years Later, St. Louis's Gateway Arch Emerges with a New Name and a Skeptical View of Western Expansion," *Washington Post*, June 26, 2018.

59. Elizabeth Varon, *Disunion! The Coming of the American Civil War, 1789-1859* (University of North Carolina Press, 2008).

60. Peter B. Knupfer, *The Union as It Is: Constitutional Unionism and Sectional Compromise, 1787-1861* (University of North Carolina Press, 1992).

61. TJ to James Monroe, March 3, 1820, *PTJDE*; Onuf, *Jefferson's Empire*, 109–17.

62. TJ to John Holmes, April 22, 1820, *PTJDE*.

63. TJ to John Manners, June 12, 1817, *PTJDE*.

64. TJ to John Holmes, April 22, 1820, *PTJDE*.

65. TJ to John Holmes, April 22, 1820, *PTJDE*.

66. TJ to Spencer Roane, September 6, 1819, *PTJDE*.

67. TJ to Charles Pinckney, September 30, 1820, *PTJDE*.

68. TJ to Richard Rush, October 20, 1820, *PTJDE*. Rush avoided the Missouri controversy in his May 22, 1821, response; on October 9, 1822, he "sincerely rejoice[d] to find that the Missouri question is lulled," adding that "Europe has entered upon the work of constitution-making, and it will probably cost her ages of blood to learn as much as we know about it. How lamentable, should we throw away our experience."

69. On TJ's prejudices, see Spahn, *Black Reason, White Feeling*, 61–80.

70. James Heaton to TJ, April 20, 1826, Founders Online, National Archives. Heaton wrote, "Many of your devoted friends, and political deciples firmly believe, it would have a more certain, calm, permanent and irrisistible effect, than any, and all things, said, and written thereon since the existence of the american Government."

71. TJ to James Heaton, May 20, 1826, *TJW*, 1516.
72. TJ to Roger Chew Weightman, June 24, 1826, Founders Online, National Archives.

III. THE PEOPLE

1. "Naturalization Oath of Allegiance to the United States of America," United States Citizenship and Immigration Services, uscis.gov.
2. "Naturalization Oath of Allegiance."
3. Maier, *American Scripture*.
4. John Adams to Benjamin Kent, June 22, 1776, Martin, ed., *Adams Papers, Digital Edition*; Parkinson, *Thirteen Clocks*, 8.
5. Edmund Morgan, *Inventing the People: The Rise of Popular Sovereignty in England and America* (W. W. Norton, 1988).
6. The Declaration of Independence as Adopted by Congress, July 4, 1776, *PTJDE*.
7. TJ to Henry Lee, May 8, 1825, *TJW*, 1501.
8. Gould, *Peace and Independence*.
9. "2024 Independence Day Celebration and Naturalization Ceremony," monticello.org. See also Emily Hemphill, "'The Promise of America: Dozens Take Their Oath of Allegiance at Monticello," *Daily Progress* (Charlottesville, VA), July 4, 2024. In recent years former Virginia Supreme Court justice John Charles Thomas has read extracts from the Declaration before the new citizens take their oaths. Thomas does not read the entire Declaration. Undoubtedly this is owing to the pressure of time during the ceremony, but one might ask if the Thomas Jefferson Foundation does not feel that the full text of the Declaration of Independence is appropriate for the Fourth of July at Monticello, when and where should it be read in full?
10. TJ, First Inaugural Address, March 4, 1801, *PTJDE*.
11. The Declaration of Independence as Adopted by Congress, July 4, 1776, *PTJDE*, our emphasis.
12. On protection and allegiance see Onuf, *Jefferson's Empire*, 156–57; and Kettner, *Development of American Citizenship*, 165–72.
13. Emer de Vattel, *The Law of Nations, or, Principles of the Law of Nature, Applied to the Conduct and Affairs of Nations and Sovereigns*, ed. and intro. Bela Kapossy and Richard Whatmore, trans. Thomas Nugent (Liberty Press, 2008), Book I, ch. 2, paras. 13–19, 85–88. See Peter Onuf and Nicholas Onuf, *Federal Union, Modern World: The*

Law of Nations in an Age of Revolution, 1776-1814 (Madison House, 1993), 1-23.

14. Jefferson's "original Rough draught" of the Declaration of Independence, June 11-July 4, 1776, *PTJDE*.

15. Rick Atkinson, *The British Are Coming: The War for America, Lexington to Princeton, 1775-1777* (Henry Holt, 2019).

16. The Declaration of Independence as Adopted by Congress, July 4, 1776, *PTJDE*.

17. The Declaration of Independence as Adopted by Congress, July 4, 1776, *PTJDE*; *His Majesty's most gracious speech to both houses of Parliament, on Friday, October 27, 1775* (New York, 1775).

18. The Declaration of Independence as Adopted by Congress, July 4, 1776, *PTJDE*, our emphases.

19. Ira D. Gruber, *The Howe Brothers and the American Revolution* (University of North Carolina Press for Institute of Early American History and Culture, 1972).

20. Jack P. Greene, "The Case Against Parliamentary Sovereignty, 1765-1776," paper delivered at the Declaration of Independence at 250 Conference, Durham, NH, November 2023.

21. The Declaration of Independence as Adopted by Congress, July 4, 1776, *PTJDE*.

22. On the connection between the Revolution and constitutional development, see Hrdlicka, *Federal Empire*.

23. Hrdlicka, *Federal Empire*.

24. Onuf and Onuf, *Federal Union, Modern World*, 109-13; Hulsebosch, "Independence and Union," 487-509.

25. The Declaration of Independence as Adopted by Congress, July 4, 1776, *PTJDE*. For the definitive history of these themes see Parkinson, *Common Cause*.

26. Kettner, *Development of American Citizenship*; Rogers M. Smith, *Civic Ideals: Conflicting Visions of Citizenship in U.S. History* (Yale University Press, 1997).

27. On state constitutional development see Hrdlicka, *Federal Empire*; and Gordon S. Wood, *The Creation of the American Republic, 1776-1787* (University of North Carolina Press for Institute of Early American History and Culture, 1969).

28. For loyalism during the War of Independence see Jerry Bannister and Liam Riordan, eds., *The Loyal Atlantic: Remaking the British Atlantic in the Revolutionary Era* (University of Toronto Press, 2012); Ruma Chopra, *Unnatural Rebellion: Loyalists in New York City During the*

Revolution (University of Virginia Press, 2011); Maya Jasanoff, *Liberty's Exiles: American Loyalists in the Revolutionary World* (Alfred A. Knopf, 2011); Brad A. Jones, *Resisting Independence: Popular Loyalism in the Revolutionary British Atlantic* (Cornell University Press, 2021); and Judith Van Buskirk, *Generous Enemies: Patriots and Loyalists in Revolutionary New York* (University of Pennsylvania Press, 2002).

29. On Virginian cousinage see Francis D. Cogliano, *A Revolutionary Friendship: Washington, Jefferson, and the American Republic* (Harvard University Press, 2024), 9–12.

30. Agreement with John Randolph, April 11, 1771, *PTJDE*; TJ, Memorandum Books, entry for August 17, 1775, *PTJDE*.

31. TJ to John Randolph, August 25, 1775, *PTJDE*.

32. John Randolph to TJ, August 31, 1775, *PTJDE*.

33. Burak Kadercan, *Shifting Grounds: The Social Origins of Territorial Conflict* (Oxford University Press, 2023).

34. Jasanoff, *Liberty's Exiles*, 351–58; Mary Beth Norton, *The British-Americans: The Loyalist Exiles in England, 1774–1789* (Little, Brown, 1972).

35. "The summer soldier and sunshine patriot will, in this crisis, shrink from the service of their country." In Thomas Paine, *The Crisis*, no. I, in Conway, ed., *Writings of Thomas Paine*, 1:170.

36. Royster, *Revolutionary People at War*; John Shy, *A People Numerous and Armed: Reflections on the Military Struggle for American Independence* (Oxford University Press, 1976), esp. the classic essay, "The Military Conflict Considered as a Revolutionary War," 213–44; T. H. Breen, *The Will of the People: The Revolutionary Birth of America* (Harvard University Press, 2019).

37. Gould, *Among the Powers of the Earth*.

38. Douglas Bradburn, *The Citizenship Revolution: Politics and the Creation of the American Union, 1774–1804* (University of Virginia Press, 2009).

39. TJ to Thomas Lomax, March 12, 1776, *PTJDE*.

40. Michael Kammen, "The American Revolution as a *Crise de Conscience*," in Richard M. Jellison, ed., *Society, Freedom, and Conscience: The American Revolution in Virginia, Massachusetts, and New York* (W. W. Norton, 1976).

41. TJ, First Inaugural Address, March 4, 1801, *PTJDE*.

42. TJ to Maria Cosway, October 12, 1786, *PTJDE*.

43. TJ to James Madison, January 30, 1787, *PTJDE*.

44. TJ to James Madison, January 30, 1787, *PTJDE*.

45. TJ to Edward Carrington, January 16, 1787, *PTJDE*.

46. TJ to William Stephens Smith, November 13, 1787, *PTJDE*.

47. Conor Cruise O'Brien, *The Long Affair: Thomas Jefferson and the French Revolution* (University of Chicago Press, 1996).

48. TJ to William Stephens Smith, November 13, 1787, *PTJDE*; TJ to James Madison, September 6, 1789.

49. TJ to Thomas Lomax, March 12, 1799, *PTJDE*.

50. TJ to Joseph C. Cabell, February 2, 1816, *PTJDE*.

51. TJ to Joseph C. Cabell, February 2, 1816, *PTJDE*.

52. TJ, Query XIX ("Manufactures"), *Notes on the State of Virginia*, *TJW*, 290, our emphasis.

53. Carl von Clausewitz, *On War*, trans. J. J. Graham (1874; London, 1909), ii, emphasis in original.

54. TJ to Thomas Lomax, March 12, 1799, *PTJDE*.

55. TJ, First Inaugural Address, March 4, 1801, *PTJDE*.

56. On partisans (or "partizans") see *Oxford English Dictionary*, s.v. "partisan" (n.2 & adj). The term antedated the rise of modern political parties and referred to followers of military and political leaders and, in the early United States, to adherents to other countries. For "partisans of Britain," see TJ to Gouverneur Morris, April 28, 1792; and "partisans of France," TJ to William Branch Giles, December 31, 1795, both in *PTJDE*.

57. John R. Howe Jr., "Republican Thought and the Political Violence of the 1790s," *American Quarterly* 19 (1967): 147–65; Stanley Elkins and Eric McKitrick, *The Age of Federalism: The Early American Republic, 1788-1800* (Oxford University Press, 1993), ch. 7–8.

58. TJ, First Inaugural Address, March 4, 1801, *PTJDE*.

59. TJ to Roger Weightman, June 24, 1826, Founders Online, National Archives.

60. On British American relations and exceptionalism, see Peter S. Onuf, "American Exceptionalism and National Identity," *American Political Thought* 1 (2012): 77–100.

61. TJ to John Taylor, June 4, 1798, *PTJDE*.

62. TJ to George Washington, May 23, 1792, *PTJDE*.

63. On "Anglomen and monocrats" see TJ to Thomas Lomax, March 12, 1799, *PTJDE*. For other examples of Jefferson using similar language to criticize his opponents during the 1790s, see TJ to Thomas Mann Randolph Jr., November 2, 1792, and November 16, 1792; TJ to James Madison, December 28, 1794; TJ to Edward Rutledge, November 30, 1795; TJ to James Monroe, July 10, 1796, all in *PTJDE*. We are

indebted to the brilliant analysis of TJ's rhetoric in Andrew Burstein, *Being Thomas Jefferson: An Intimate History*, ch. 8 (Bloomsbury, 2026).

64. TJ to William Duane, March 28, 1811, *PTJDE*.

65. Richard Buel, *America on the Brink: How the Political Struggle over the War of 1812 Almost Destroyed the Young Republic* (Palgrave Macmillan, 2005).

66. The Declaration of Independence as Adopted by Congress, July 4, 1776, *PTJDE*.

67. TJ to John Adams, June 11, 1812, *PTJDE*.

68. *Notes on the State of Virginia*, *TJW*, 187–89; Parkinson, *Heart of American Darkness*.

69. For Jefferson's thinking on stadial theory and Native Americans, see Andrew Cayton, "Thomas Jefferson and Native Americans," in Francis D. Cogliano, ed., *A Companion to Thomas Jefferson* (Wiley-Blackwell, 2012), 237–52.

70. *Notes on the State of Virginia*, *TJW*, 187; Adam Hodgson's Account of a Visit to Monticello, [June 17, 1820], *PTJDE*.

71. Jeffrey Ostler, *Surviving Genocide: Native Nations and the United States from the American Revolution to Bleeding Kansas* (Yale University Press, 2019); Patrick Griffin, *American Leviathan: Empire, Nation, and Revolutionary Frontier* (Hill & Wang, 2007); Colin G. Calloway, *The Indian World of George Washington: The First President, the First Americans, and the Birth of a Nation* (Oxford University Press, 2018).

72. Parkinson, *Common Cause*, ch. 3.

73. TJ to George Rogers Clark, January 1, 1780, *PTJDE*.

74. Ablavsky, *Federal Ground*.

75. TJ to George Rogers Clark, January 1, 1780, *PTJDE*, our emphasis.

76. TJ to William Henry Harrison, February 27, 1803, *PTJDE*.

77. McCoy, *Elusive Republic*; Cogliano, *Emperor of Liberty*, ch. 6. Colin Calloway reminds us that for most of the eighteenth-century North America remained a "vast Indian continent." Calloway, *Indian World of George Washington*, 20.

78. TJ's doubts about Native state capacity were belied by the prolonged war that Indigenous nations in the Northwest waged against the new American government during the 1790s. Calloway, *Indian World of George Washington*, ch. 16.

79. Sarah N. Randolph, *The Domestic Life of Thomas Jefferson* (New York: Harper and Row, 1871), 23.

80. Henry S. Randall, *The Life of Thomas Jefferson*, 3 vols. (New York: Derby & Jackson, 1858), 3:545; Annette Gordon-Reed, *The Hemingses of Monticello: An American Family* (W. W. Norton, 2008), 650–51.

81. The best studies of the people that TJ enslaved and of his actions as an enslaver are Gordon-Reed, *Hemingses of Monticello*; and Lucia Stanton, *"Those Who Labor for My Happiness": Slavery at Thomas Jefferson's Monticello* (University of Virginia Press, 2012).

82. "Notes on Early Career," *PTJDE*; TJ to Edward Coles, August 25, 1814, *PTJDE*.

83. TJ, *Summary View*, *TJW*, 103–22, 115–16.

84. TJ, "original Rough draught," and the Declaration of Independence as Adopted by Congress, June 11–July 4, 1776, *PTJDE*. For a study of this clause and its meaning see Onuf, *Jefferson's Empire*, 147–88.

85. Peter Onuf, "Intentions, Context, and Principles: Thomas Jefferson's Slavery Problem," in *Understanding Jefferson: Slavery, Race, and the Declaration of Independence* (Liberty Matters Forum, Liberty Fund, July 2021).

86. *Notes on the State of Virginia*, *TJW*, 264; TJ to Rufus King, July 13, 1802, *PTJDE*; TJ to Albert Gallatin, December 26, 1820, *PTJDE*.

87. *Notes on the State of Virginia*, *TJW*, 270. For the passage on racial differences see pp. 264–70. TJ's views on race were not that unusual among enslavers in the British Atlantic world. Jamaican Edward Long argued for Black inferiority in terms similar to those TJ employed in *The History of Jamaica or, General Survey of the Antient and Modern State of That Island: With Reflections on Its Situation, Settlements, Inhabitants, Climate, Products, Commerce, Laws, and Government*, 3 vols. (London, 1774).

88. *Notes on the State of Virginia*, *TJW*, 264.

89. "Life among the Lowly, No. 3," *Pike County (Ohio) Republican*, December 25, 1873.

90. "Life among the Lowly, No. 3," *Pike County (Ohio) Republican*, December 25, 1873; Spahn, *Black Reason, White Feeling*.

91. Abigail Adams to Thomas Boylston Adams, January 25, 1801, in Martin, ed., *Adams Papers Digital Edition*.

92. Jan Ellen Lewis, "The Blessings of Domestic Society: Thomas Jefferson's Family and the Transformation of American Politics," in Bienstock et al., eds., *Family, Slavery, and Love in the Early American Republic*, 309–48.

93. Brian Steele, "Thomas Jefferson's Gender Frontier," *Journal of American History* 95 (2008): 17–42.

94. Abigail Adams to John Adams, March 31, 1776, in Martin, ed.,
    Adams Papers, Digital Edition.
95. John Adams to Abigail Adams, April 14, 1776, in Martin, ed., *Adams
    Papers, Digital Edition.*
96. *Notes on the State of Virginia, TJW,* 185–86.
97. Linda K. Kerber, "The Republican Mother: Women and the
    Enlightenment—An American Perspective," *American Quarterly*
    28 (1976): 187–205; Jan Lewis, "The Republican Wife: Virtue and
    Seduction in the Early Republic," *William and Mary Quarterly* 47
    (1987): 689–721; Rosemarie Zagarri, "Morals, Manners, and the
    Republican Mother," *American Quarterly* 44 (1992): 192–215.
98. TJ to Anne Willing Bingham, February 7, 1787, *PTJDE.*
99. TJ to Anne Willing Bingham, May 11, 1788, *PTJDE.*
100. TJ to Nathaniel Burwell, March 14, 1818, *PTJDE.*
101. TJ, First Inaugural Address, March 4, 1801, *PTJDE; National
    Intelligencer* (Washington, DC), March 4, 1801.

IV. JEFFERSON WRITES

1. Battin, "July 4, 1826."
2. Burstein, *America's Jubilee,* ch. 11.
3. For illuminating discussions of *A Summary View,* see Steele, *Thomas
   Jefferson and American Nationhood;* and Sarson, *Course of Human
   Events.*
4. *PTJDE.* Excised portions of the documents are indicated by ellipses.
5. The literature on the Declaration is vast, and we have learned much
   from the many sources cited throughout this book. We are particularly
   indebted to Fliegelman, *Declaring Independence;* Maier, *American
   Scripture;* and Sarson, *Course of Human Events.*
6. McDonald, *Confounding Father.*
7. "Notes on Early Career," editorial note and text, *PTJDE.* The two
   drafts are conveniently presented as a single, interlineated document in
   TJW, 19–24, with TJ's notes on congressional debates, 13–18.
8. The two drafts are taken from *PTJDE.*
9. For the classic analysis of this text see Sloan, *Principle and Interest.*
10. Burstein and Isenberg, *Madison and Jefferson,* 195–99; Lance Banning,
    *The Sacred Fire of Liberty: James Madison and the Founding of the
    Federal Republic* (Cornell University Press, 1995), 274–90; and Onuf,
    Jefferson and the Virginians, 79–116.
11. Editorial note, "The Earth Belongs in Usufruct to the Living," *PTJDE.*

12. *PTJDE.*
13. TJ to Spencer Roane, September 6, 1819, *PTJDE.* See the essays collected in James P. Horn, Jan Ellen Lewis, and Peter S. Onuf, eds., *The Revolution of 1800: Democracy, Race, and the New Republic* (University of Virginia Press, 2002).
14. On TJ's relationship with Washington and their posthumous "reconciliation," see Cogliano, *Revolutionary Friendship.*
15. *PTJDE.*
16. There is a rich literature on what TJ called "ward republics." The classic text is Matthews, *Radical Politics of Thomas Jefferson.*
17. TJ, Second Inaugural Address, March 4, 1805, *PTJDE.*
18. On this letter's publication history see "Proposals to Revise the Virginia Constitution," editorial note, *PTJDE.*
19. *PTJDE.*
20. Founders Online, National Archives.

INDEX

Page numbers after 208 refer to endnotes.